GUO WEI

THE POWER OF DATAFICATION

DISRUPTION, RECONSTRUCTION
AND THE RISE OF NEW BUSINESS ENGINES

ADVANCE PRAISE

"From digital civilization to digital economy, from data science to intelligent decision-making, from the digital transformation of enterprises to the new digital infrastructure of society, the author Mr. Guo Wei draws on his years of practical experience and deep contemplation in the technology field to present readers with the opportunities and challenges of the digital age. He also allows readers to fully experience the power of digitization."

Harry Heung-Yeung Shum, International Member of the
National Academy of Engineering, the United States,
Former Executive Vice President for Technology and Research,
Microsoft Corporation, and Council Chairman of the Hong Kong
University of Science and Technology (HKUST)

"With more than 30 years of experience, Mr. Guo Wei has continuously explored and contemplated the power of digitalization. Through the lens of enterprises, he has got valuable insights into the digital revolution, delving into practical applications and developing an array of fascinating ideas that have gradually formed a cohesive framework. This book represents his phased summary of years of practical experience and reflection. How do we recognize the value of data and unlock its potential? How do we decipher the hidden truths within vast amounts of data? How can we extract, summarize, and discover knowledge from diverse sources? And, equally important, how do we store, manage, and analyse big data while respecting ethical boundaries? These questions have become shared concerns for governments, academia, and industries alike. In this book, Mr. Guo Wei puts forwards suggestions on the concept, strategy, and path of enterprise digital transformation from a broad perspective, which are highly constructive."

Wenfei Fan, FRS, FREng, FRSE, FACM, ForMemCAS
Professor, School of Informatics, University of Edinburgh,
and Chief Scientist, Shenzhen Institute of Computing Sciences

"*Generative AI is an exciting technology, but we have focused too much on its value as an individual productivity tool. The real potential – for the business world as a whole – is how it will transform entire enterprises, by making available unstructured information and by helping individuals across companies to make better and more rapid decisions as a result. This is why Mr. Guo Wei's ideas about Data Cloud Integration are so important. Innovation happens across the entire digital value chain. It's fascinating to try to understand the latest generation of 'large language models' but, ultimately, there are only a few companies in the world with the expertise and deep pockets to create them. In reality, it is the deployment of these technologies, and the ways they create value for consumers and businesses, that really makes a difference. Mr. Guo Wei's insights are, therefore, particularly important as we start to imagine the way AI will actually change the business world. Some of the ideas he is proposing around Data Cloud Integration, middle platforms, and AI generated content are really important in this regard.*"

Julian Birkinshaw, Vice-Dean, Professor of Strategy
and Entrepreneurship, London Business School,
and Fellow of the British Academy, Strategic Management Society,
and the (American) Academy of Management

"The Power of Datafication *is an extremely broad book, which captures the current position of the IS revolution, how it got there, and where it is going. Embedded in deep historical context, using powerful examples, the author shows how today's technology allows a set of IT applications to be developed, which transforms the nature of enterprise. The book illustrates how data can be handled today in ways never before possible, which transforms a firm's operations. The book points a clear direction to the future. It is particularly significant that the book is written by a Chinese practitioner and is heavily informed by technology applications being developed both in China and the west. The only concern I have is there is likely to be much longer implementation time spans and more birthing problems than the author recognizes. At the core, however, the book is extremely well-written, captures a compelling version of where we have been and how it shapes where we are going. This is a book for both strategic planners and corporate CEOs.*"

F. Warren McFarlan, Albert H. Gordon Professor of Business
Administration Emeritus, Harvard Business School

Published by
LID Publishing
An imprint of LID Business Media Ltd.
LABS House, 15–19 Bloomsbury Way,
London, WC1A 2TH, UK

info@lidpublishing.com
www.lidpublishing.com

A member of:

businesspublishersroundtable.com

Printed by Gutenberg Press, Malta
ISBN: 978-1-915951-51-9
ISBN: 978-1-915951-52-6 (ebook)

Cover and page design: Caroline Li

GUO WEI

THE POWER OF DATAFICATION

DISRUPTION, RECONSTRUCTION
AND THE RISE OF NEW BUSINESS ENGINES

MADRID | MEXICO CITY | LONDON
BUENOS AIRES | BOGOTA | SHANGHAI

CONTENTS

FOREWORD

Mr. Guo Wei and I are of the same age and we have had many exchanges since my return to China. Although he runs a business and I am in academia, due to our similar educational backgrounds and shared expectations for the software industry, our conversations always spark inspiration and are deeply engaging. Whenever I listen to him passionately sharing his thoughts, I can feel the entrepreneur's deep thinking about the times we live in, his ambitions for the industry, and his relentless pursuit of technological advancements.

With more than 30 years of experience, Mr. Guo Wei has continuously explored and contemplated the power of digitalization. Through the lens of enterprises, he has got valuable insights into the digital revolution, delving into practical applications and developing an array of fascinating ideas that have gradually formed a cohesive framework. This book represents his phased summary of years of practical experience and reflection. While some of his views may be less familiar to me from academia, there are certain issues that resonate strongly with me.

In this era of digital civilization, data is growing explosively, revealing new patterns and knowledge that provide a more accurate understanding of the world. This presents an unprecedented opportunity to reshape our reality. However, it's important to recognize that the impact of digitalization can be viewed from both positive and negative perspectives. On the positive side, we see examples such as DeepMind, an AI company owned by Google, which has developed a tool for predicting protein structures, significantly speeding up the development of new medications. On the negative side, there are cases like the Cambridge Analytica scandal, where the firm obtained personal information from millions of Facebook users without their permission and employed this data to sway voter opinions during critical elections such as the 2016 US Presidential election. Whether positive or negative, these examples make people realize the power of data in understanding, predicting and self-evolving. This realization has prompted the world to place increasing importance on the value of data, leading to profound transformations in industries and social governance.

However, the vast amount of data also poses challenges. How do we recognize the value of data and unlock its potential? How do we decipher the hidden truths within vast amounts of data? How can we extract, summarize, and discover knowledge from diverse sources? And equally important, how do we store, manage, and analyse big data while respecting ethical boundaries? These questions have become shared concerns for governments, academia and industries alike. Data science has emerged as a new frontier in the field of computer science, an essential foundation for AI. This presents not just challenges but also opportunities.

In this book, Mr. Guo Wei puts forwards suggestions on the concept, strategy, and path of enterprise digital transformation from a broad perspective, which are highly constructive.

Wenfei Fan
FRS, FREng, FRSE, FACM, ForMemCAS, Professor, School of Informatics, University of Edinburgh, and Chief Scientist, Shenzhen Institute of Computing Sciences

FOREWORD

It is a pleasure to share my thoughts on Digital Transformation for Mr. Guo Wei's book, *The Power of Datafication*.

I met Mr. Guo Wei in August 2023 where he first explained his vision of the future of digital technology. We brainstormed a number of ideas – he shared some of the work he has done through Digital China, I shared my observations on leading edge practices in Europe and North America. I thought his insights would be fascinating to my students, so I embarked on writing a case study of Digital China, with a great deal of help from Mr. Guo Wei's advisor and graduate of London Business School's Sloan Fellowship, Dickie Liang-Hong Ke. We used the case study for the first time in May 2024. Digital China also decided to send a group of their most senior executives to London Business School for a customized training programme in May 2024.

Let me sketch out a couple of my own reflections on how digital technology is transforming the world.

First, Generative AI is an exciting technology, but we have focused too much on its value as an individual productivity tool. The real potential – for the business world as a whole – is how it will transform entire enterprises, by making available unstructured information and by helping individuals across companies to make better and more rapid decisions as a result. This is why Mr. Guo Wei's ideas about Data Cloud Integration are so important.

Second, the digital revolution is never over. We have lived through at least five eras of digital change in the business world – the mainframe era, the PC era, the networked era, the cloud computing era, and now the AI era. Each brings new tools and technologies, and it triggers a wave of further changes in how companies operate and how they create and capture value. The most successful companies are, therefore, the ones who are constantly on their toes, looking to rethink their approach to digital technology. And if you are saddled with legacy IT systems, you need to unburden yourself quickly, otherwise new competitors will run rings round you.

Third, innovation happens across the entire digital value chain. It's fascinating to try to understand the latest generation of "large language models" but, ultimately, there are only a few companies in the world with the expertise and deep pockets to create them. In reality, it is the deployment of these technologies, and the ways they create value for consumers and businesses, that really makes a difference. Mr. Guo Wei's insights are, therefore, particularly important as we start to imagine the way AI will actually change the business world. Some of the ideas he is proposing around data cloud integration, middle platforms, and AI generated content are really important in this regard.

Finally, don't lose the human touch. Some observers look at the inexorable rise of AI and picture a "brave new workplace" of automated and algorithm-driven decision making. My view is closer to Mr. Guo Wei's, who says that the purpose of digital intelligence is to "maximize human creativity and value." Business leaders today have a moral imperative to harness technology in a way that makes work more fulfilling. In the words of the original futurist, John Naisbitt: "Whenever a new technology is introduced into society, there must be a counterbalancing human response – that is, high touch – or the technology is rejected. We must learn to balance the material wonders of technology with the spiritual demands of our human nature."

Julian Birkinshaw
Vice-Dean, Professor of Strategy and Entrepreneurship,
London Business School, and Fellow of the British Academy,
Strategic Management Society, and the (American) Academy
of Management

PREFACE

Despite the impact of COVID-19 at the end of 2021, the stock prices of Apple, Microsoft, and other digital technology companies hit new highs, with their market caps exceeding $2.5 trillion and heading for $3 trillion. What has driven the share prices of digital technology companies to record highs over the past two decades and made these companies the locomotives of global economic dynamism? What has enabled these companies to maintain high growth rates against the very difficult global economy over the past two years? Is this signalling the onset of the third or the fourth industrial revolution, or the dawn of a new era?

This book traces back to the past, focuses on the present, and looks forwards to the future, discusses the nature of digitalization and the opportunities and challenges it brings to human development. Chapter 1 – "Surge of the New Wave in Digital Civilization" discusses digitalization from the perspective of human civilization evolution. Chapter 2 – "Reshaping Digital Thinking through Data Science" points out that human history is a process of continuous cognitive change, especially the evolution from mathematics to data science. Chapter 3 – "Digital Transformation Driven by Data Cloud Integration" explores how enterprises, as an important production unit of social wealth, could make use of digitalization and gain a deeper understanding of its characteristics and value. It also covers the core strategy of enterprises digital transformation, highlighting the Data Cloud Integration Strategy and the four feasible pathways. Chapter 4 – "Accelerating Digitalization with Cloud-Native Technology Paradigm" highlights the characteristics of technology paradigm for the digital age and its difference with the tools available for the more traditional information age. The technology paradigms are all different across the long history of humanity; for instance, the technology paradigm for the Stone Age is signified by stones. Chapter 5 – "Engine of Digital Economy Driven by Digital Infrastructure Construction," points out that the establishment of the infrastructure not only represents the characteristics of an age, but also portrays the progress of civilization. The new infrastructure construction in the digital age possesses new characteristics. I hope to explore the impact of the power of digitalization on us from the aspects of the disruption in cognition, the innovation in technological paradigm, the transformation in business models, the reconstruction of enterprise organization, industrial chain, and our society, and the new driving engine of civilization advancement as represented by the new infrastructure construction.

In the evolution of human civilization, the assumptions and definitions of the world have determined the direction of human civilization development. The ancient Greek philosophers put forwards the concept of "atoms" and defined the world as made up of atoms, which led to the continuous evolution of human cognition based on material science, thus created the great achievements of industrial civilization. Pythagoras believed that the world could be explained by numbers. Although human beings have, since Isaac Newton, taken mathematics as the foundation of science and the numerical expression of natural philosophy as the symbol of modern science, human beings have not fundamentally recognized the true meaning of "all is number." Isaac Newton believed that the world is composed of two parts: one is the objective world that human beings will never be able to fully understand, and the other is the world that human beings can define and coexist with. Over the past 400 years, human civilization has grown at an unprecedented rate, and the fundamental reason for this is the application of science and technology. Modern science and technology, based on mathematical methods, have allowed the power of the human will to flourish and kept human civilization moving forwards. The human civilization is completely built on the recognition of science and the invention of technologies, applying to all kinds of industries such as textile, transportations, manufacturing and all walks of life. Human cognition towards science has evolved from the generation of data in the laboratory to the interpretation of data. Today, the generation of data does not only rely on laboratories, but also from the process of commercial and social computing, where data on human behaviour, human interrelations, human-nature relations, and nature interrelations are generated in huge quantities all the time. Thus, how to collect (and produce), govern, analyse, apply, display the data, and ensure they are legally compliant and technologically secured, has become a global focus. The data relationships built up with digital technology will drastically disrupt our cognition, and the data assets generated based on this data will also create new conditions for us to reconfigure our business. We have seen the possibility through the metaverse that there is a digital virtual world parallel to the physical world, and the understanding and transforming towards this new world will take human civilization into a new era.

In this digital economy era, enterprises are going to be digitalized, proactively or reactively. The digitalization process of enterprises is also a process of reconfiguring and re-understanding. In this process of industrial civilization, we have become path-dependent due to the constraints of the original conditions, which led us to forget the original intention. Aristotle, who lived at the same time as Confucius, not only promoted the establishment of the Library of Alexandria that lit up the light of intelligence for human civilization, but also put forwards the significant First Principles theory: "Every system has its own first principle, which is the fundamental proposition or assumption that cannot be omitted or objected." Similarly, any enterprise has its own fundamental logic of existence, and digitalization of this fundamental logic forms the enterprise's data assets. The formation and accumulation of data assets help enterprises to set up agile business processes and provide products or services to their users, thus enhancing the competitiveness of the enterprise. Today's social networking technologies greatly support boundaryless growth of enterprises internally and externally, which in turn provides a solid foundation for the formation of more data assets. Enterprises that automate their decision-making processes with the support of intelligent computing power and artificial intelligence are similar to spinning flywheels, growing in power, speed, and competitiveness.

The digitalization process is also inseparable from the continuous evolution of technological paradigms. Cloud-native and digital-native technology paradigms are playing an increasingly important role in the digital age. To the average consumer, the "cloud" seems mysterious but, in fact, we've been living in the "cloud" since Apple invented its first smartphone. In Apple's App Store, each of the millions of apps is a "cloud." In the digital era, digital consumption has become an important part of people's consumption. In the past, we used to make phone calls on a time basis and were billed by the duration, whereas today, we use cellular networks to make calls and are billed by data usage, and data traffic consumption is digital consumption. The provision of cloud services and the change of the way of consumption start with the adoption of cloud-native and digital-native technologies. Today, the "cloud" has become the cornerstone of digital technologies. Those applications which were developed under the non-cloud architecture will be migrated to the cloud architecture. The cloud-native technology paradigm supports the multi-cloud integration technology framework to protect and recycle the existing IT investment, as well as the migration and sharing between multiple clouds. Although cloud-native may not be mature enough, the innovation of technological paradigm that it brings has created favourable conditions for the arrival of the digital age. It also created technical conditions for the digital-nativity realization of uncertain complex systems, the organic unification and evolution between systems, and the full circulation of data. More importantly, in the formation of the cloud-native technology paradigm, Chinese enterprises have been synchronizing with the world, and perhaps this is an opportunity for the Chinese enterprises to stand out from following and chasing to leading, provided they take a long-term approach and spirit.

Since ancient times, infrastructure has been both a symbol of civilization and a driving force in its evolution. The Library of Alexandria is a symbol of Mediterranean civilization, and its construction greatly promoted the progress of human civilization. The governance of the Yellow River not only accelerated the integration of the Chinese nation, but also created the conditions for agricultural civilization. Similarly, in the era of digital economy, new infrastructures based on virtual worlds are not only a symbol but also a new driving force for the digital civilization. Systems like the Global Positioning System (GPS) and the video conferencing systems are examples of new infrastructures in the new economy era. The infrastructure construction and operation based on cloud and big data is characterized by the fact that it is multi-layer, multiple market stakeholders, and mutually reliant. New technologies based on open-source and software-definition requires an open market environment and a reliable legal protection system. Challenges such as rural revitalization, financial risks resolution, and peak carbon dioxide emissions have not only determined the new direction of digitization, but also provided Chinese enterprises with the orientation and basis in building new infrastructures for coping with them.

Schumpeter defined innovation as the introduction of a new product, the adoption of a new mode of production, the opening of a new market, the procurement of a new supply source of raw materials or semi-manufactured goods, or the implementation of a new form of enterprise organization. According to this definition, digital economy is a disruptive innovation, which is not only reflected in products or raw materials, but also in new markets, new production relations, and organizational structures. Data has become the new factor of production. Unlike the traditional factors of production, which have their limitations, data is produced on a rolling basis in an exponential manner.

Nevertheless, we must recognize that digital evolution is developed upon the innovations of our predecessors. This is the result of continuous evolution of human civilization. Without the Edison effect, there would be no electronic tubes; without electronic tubes, there would be no electronics; without electronics, there would be no computers; without computers, there would be no large-scale integrated circuits; without the need for the highly specialized mode of operation as required by the large-scale integrated circuits manufacturing, there would be no cloud computing today. We should pay tribute to all scientists, engineers, and entrepreneurs. Without the accumulation of industrial civilization, there would be no digital civilization.

The future is here. Humanity has experienced agricultural and industrial civilizations, and is now embarking on a digital civilization. From mobile payment to digital currency in the consumption process, from value transfer to value sharing in the manufacturing process, from traditional spatial cognition and urban exploration to today's new geography and smart city based on digital space, from hierarchical bureaucratic system to the new development concept of "co-building, co-governing and sharing" based on data and cloud platforms, from "a smooth lake rises in the narrow gorges" to the construction of a human ecosystem and civilization community by using digital technologies, and from the commitment to the people of the world to traversing globally as a new generation of Chinese citizen ... Through digitalization, the intelligence of human beings is integrated with the physical world, creating an even more brilliant civilization at an unprecedented speed.

PREFACE TO THE REVISED EDITION

In 2022, *The Power of Digitalization* was published. This book encapsulates my reflections and practices from over thirty years in the industry, serving as a profound summary of my understanding of digitalization. Since this book's publication, I have engaged in frequent and extensive exchange with the business and academic communities. Through these exchanges, our thoughts and viewpoints have continually collided, generating sparks that often give me a sense of profound enlightenment. As a result, my understanding of digitalization has deepened. I have begun to scrutinize and ponder over past theoretical frameworks, and I am constantly incorporating new elements. Ultimately, after continuous deconstruction and reconstruction, a new strategic framework for enterprise digital transformation has emerged – the Data Cloud Integration Strategy.

Informatization primarily focuses on improving enterprise efficiency, while the fundamental purpose of digitalization is to continuously accumulate and form the enterprise's data assets, thereby creating a new growth flywheel for the company. Forming the enterprise's data assets will support the enterprise in pursuing business agility, rapid business iteration, and the business' second growth curve. Throughout the entire process of digital transformation, the first step for a company is the datafication of its business, followed by the second step of making business out of data. Completing this cycle leads the enterprise to enter the growth flywheel, which is the most crucial part of the Data Cloud Integration Strategy.

The term "Data Cloud Integration" refers to the integration of "Cloud" as the technological platform and tools supporting the entire data management process, and "Data" representing the data accumulated by the enterprise, including know-how, logic, customer profiles, and more. I refer to these as data assets. The management, application, and computation of this vast pool of data are carried out by the technological architecture of Data Cloud Integration.

This technological architecture is built on the foundation of cloud-native principles. I believe that the future of the entire business-to-business (B2B) landscape will be established on cloud architecture, making a paradigm shift in technology. Traditional information technology was driven by one server supporting one application, leading to fragmented sets of applications within the enterprises rather than forming a cohesive integrated system. In the early stages of informatization, companies had to artificially segment applications to enhance efficiency, posing a significant obstacle to digital transformation. Today, for enterprises to achieve digital transformation, a technological disruption is necessary, moving towards a new paradigm of being "conceived in the cloud, nurtured in the cloud." One reason for Steve Jobs' greatness is his ability to make us tangibly feel the presence of the cloud. Mobile apps exist in the cloud, and services like WeChat also reside in the cloud, backed by a complex architecture that brings user-centric convenience and agility in the application development. The disruptive nature of cloud-native technology is revolutionary, propelling humanity into the era of digital civilization. Under the traditional architectures, we could only achieve informatization, not digitalization. Cloud encompasses both public and private clouds, so in the future, all enterprises will engage in multi-cloud integration within the cloud-native architecture.

The underlying logic of the cloud is to use container technology to carry data, facilitating its rapid flow between multiple clouds. By connecting industries through the flow of data, it involves reconstructing and industrial re-engineering. The cloud has brought a rare opportunity to Chinese enterprises and entrepreneurs because traditional information technology is bound to be phased out, replaced by continually evolving digital technologies. Correspondingly, traditional infrastructure no longer meets the demands of the digital age, and it will be replaced by digital infrastructure. Digital infrastructure serves as the cornerstone of the entire Data Cloud Integration strategic architecture, providing essential support for the technological architecture and the core growth flywheel.

In the first half of 2023, over a period of four months, I conducted multiple visits to the United States, Australia and several European countries, engaging in in-depth discussions with numerous enterprises and academic institutions. During conversations with professors at INSEAD, they mentioned that they were also researching the impact of digitalization on philosophy, culture, and history, as well as its potential societal risks, influence on business innovation, and effects on individual lifestyles and work patterns. The content of *The Power of Datafication* aligns closely with their concerns and research directions and resonates deeply with their perspectives.

My exchanges with the INSEAD professors profoundly impacted my inner thoughts, and I keenly felt the universality of knowledge. This experience inspired me to consider revising *The Power of Digitalization*. I believe that I should share my latest thoughts and insights on digital transformation, along with the new strategic architecture of Data Cloud Integration. Using the book as a bridge, I aim to connect with the world. This is not only my responsibility as an entrepreneur but also the mission bestowed upon me by the times.

Simultaneously, I also hope that the Data Cloud Integration Strategy can provide assistance to businesses seeking digital transformation or those facing challenges in the process. I aim to help them find suitable paths for change, accelerate the accumulation of data assets, enter the growth flywheel, and seamlessly embrace the digital economy for a promising future.

CHAPTER 1

SURGE OF THE NEW WAVE IN DIGITAL CIVILIZATION

When Alvin Toffler published his seminal work *The Third Wave* in 1980, he depicted an illuminating blueprint of future society that astonished countless people. However, more than forty years later, we find ourselves in astonishment again: the future has arrived in the form of a digital civilization that is on the rise and delivering successive shocks to human society.

The emergence of digital civilization was not unprecedented. Ever since human society began, civilization has undergone an extensive and protracted evolutionary journey. From the agricultural to the industrial, and now to the digital age, the birth of every successive civilization has been established on the groundwork of its predecessor. Similarly, the industrial age laid the groundwork for the digital age. The advancement of computers has equipped humans with the necessary hardware for the emergence of the digital civilization, while the advent of the internet has spawned an entirely new virtual world, opening the doors to a digitalized realm for humanity.

Reflecting on the historical and contemporary developments within digital civilization reinforces our conviction in the inevitability of this new wave. Today, we stand at a crossroads of major transformation, adjustment, and differentiation. Our future is predetermined by the decisions we make. We must undoubtedly follow the path of embracing change, welcoming new technologies, and seizing the opportunities and challenges of the digital age.

THE FUTURE HAS ARRIVED

ALVIN TOFFLER'S PREDICTIONS

The classification of human societal civilization into three discrete waves – agricultural, industrial, and informational – was introduced by Alvin Toffler in his 1980 book *The Third Wave*, illustrated in Figure 1.1.

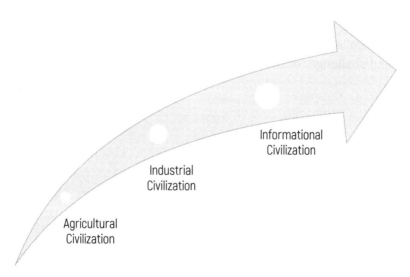

Informational
Civilization

Industrial
Civilization

Agricultural
Civilization

FIGURE 1.1
ALVIN TOFFLER'S THREE DIVISIONS OF THE HISTORY OF HUMAN DEVELOPMENT

Approximately 10,000 years ago, the agricultural civilization emerged as the first wave. In this phase, humanity transitioned from a primitive, barbaric society of foraging and hunting to being agriculturally oriented, a change that spanned several millennia.

In the late 17th century, the second wave emerged: the industrial revolution. It ravaged Europe and the globe at an unprecedented rate, displacing the antiquated agrarian systems and ushering in the industrial age.

The third wave, the information civilization, emerged during the latter half of the 20th century. Emerging as a formidable force, this new energy exerted its influence across multiple domains of human society, including economics, politics, and culture, while also permeating all facets of human existence and production. In the third wave, information technology predominates. According to Toffler, "Whoever captures information holds the network and commands the whole world."[1]

In his book, Toffler also made a significant prophecy: humanity shall enter the era of information civilization, wherein the advancement of contemporary technology shall fundamentally transform social structures and lifestyles.

During the early 1980s, when China was undergoing its process of reform and opening up, the awakening Chinese yearned to break free from ideological constraints to escape the shackles of a closed and rigid system. Toffler's *The Third Wave* appeared precisely at the right time. It evoked aspirations and longings for a future society and furnished Chinese readers with a fundamental understanding of the information society through the provision of a vivid blueprint of that society. Simultaneously, the book provided the younger generation with an intellectual shock that sparked an unprecedented degree of initiative and creativity.

During those passionate years, 'Toffler Fever' swept across China. Intellectuals and workers alike read the book with insatiable curiosity. I am one of those readers who was deeply influenced. Toffler travelled to China in 1983, carrying a documentary and his book pertaining to the third wave. Enthusiastic attendees flooded the stage following the screening.

Now, more than forty years have passed, and the future predicted by Toffler has transformed into the present. The "information civilization" that Toffler spoke of is now referred to as the "digital civilization," in which each of us is immersed, experiencing the disruptions and innovations brought by the new tide. Never before in human history has an era experienced such rapid technological advancements at the forefront, driving industries and commerce to maturity and bringing about immense changes in the lives of billions of people. Due to the immense magnitude and potency of this wave, every aspect of our lives is perpetually and swiftly undergoing a transformation; the only constant is change itself.

In the early 1980s, those who were passionately reading *The Third Wave* likely anticipated the advent of a new era. Yet, even those with the most romantic and audacious imaginations could hardly foresee how much our lives would be constructed within the digital realm. Constantly surpassing our comprehension, emerging technologies such as cloud computing, virtual reality (VR), digital twin, the digital-native movement, and AIGC (Artificial Intelligence Generated Content) are continuously surpassing our understanding, transforming and reshaping our lifestyles, consumption habits, production relationships, and business structures from the ground up. Toffler predicted this transformation to some extent when he stated, "The only certainty is that tomorrow will bring about astonishment for everyone."

The answer to the question that previously alarmed many Chinese citizens has now been answered. When I first started working thirty years ago, China was not in step with the most cutting-edge technologies in the world, nor was it fully integrated into the ebb and flow of the global capital market. Upon my entry into the rapidly expanding IT sector, I had a vague sense of the technological and business prospects that were proliferating in anticipation of the digital age. With rapid technological advancements, China had entered its most rapid decades of development ever. Today, China is a prominent global force in the realm of digital technology, exhibiting substantial prospects for further development. The flourishing digital technologies continue to reshape the established business landscape, restructure industry value chains, propel the development of a new Chinese economy that is more globally competitive, and generate more dynamic local enterprises.

Looking towards the future, even when considering the present, it remains difficult to predict the forthcoming digital age. The progression of technology and society is a monumental undertaking, and it is impossible to precisely forecast the countless innovations and creations that will occur throughout the world. Nevertheless, I am quite certain that the dawn of the digital age has only recently begun to break, and it will persistently transform the way we live our lives and conduct business, creating an ecological system which fosters sharing, inclusiveness and openness while generating substantial market and societal benefits.

STEVE JOBS: IGNITING THE TORCH OF DIGITAL CIVILIZATION

1980 was an unforgettable milestone year, not just because Alvin Toffler made his renowned predictions about the future, but also because of a significant event that profoundly impacted the evolution of digital civilization: the public listing of Apple Inc., founded by Steve Jobs.

In April 1976, Jobs, just 21 years old, along with his friend Stephen Wozniak, painstakingly raised $1,300 and established the Apple Computer in their garage. This garage-born venture transformed into a publicly listed company in just four years, eventually becoming one of the world's most valuable companies in the world. It heralded an era of innovation synonymous with Apple.

Throughout his entrepreneurial journey, Jobs remained at the forefront of technology. Under his leadership, Apple rolled out a series of groundbreaking high-tech products, each echoing Jobs' innovative spirit. Simplicity, sophistication, and distinctiveness defined Apple's offerings, reflecting Jobs' ultimate aspiration. In an era of prioritizing user experience, Apple seamlessly merged visual artistry with technological innovation, enabling consumers to relish in products and services that transcended the boundaries between technology and artistry. Despite this, Jobs persistently pursued optimal user experience, continually innovating and refining business models, thus beginning a revolution grounded in digital technology.

While Jobs undeniably made monumental contributions to humanity and society, his role in digital civilization still remains understated. Many recognize him merely as Apple's founder, an innovator, or a business magnate, but overlook his pivotal role as a pioneer of the digital economy and a vanguard of the digital age, igniting the torch of digital civilization.

On January 9, 2007, at Apple's Macworld conference, Jobs unveiled the iPhone, a groundbreaking fusion of an iPod, mobile phone, and internet communication device, heralding it as a "revolutionary mobile phone."

The iPhone redefined the smartphone landscape, challenging the prevailing notions dominated by brands like Nokia and Motorola. Jobs' creation – a sleek, keyboard-less, non-removable battery, and aesthetically captivating device – revolutionized perceptions of what a phone could be. With its multi-touch screen and robust iOS ecosystem, the iPhone realized Jobs' vision of transforming the world yet again. This seismic shift propelled phones, once mere communication tools, into the intelligent era, catalysing a revolutionary pivot in the digital economy.

The advent of the iPhone heralded the era of digital consumption. It spurred the rapid proliferation and widespread adoption of smartphones, amplifying their entertainment capabilities. As apps for reading, gaming, socializing, mobile work, and education burgeoned, smartphones transcended communication, becoming indispensable lifestyle, social, travel, entertainment, work, and educational tools. Consequently, digital content production and consumption became integral facets of modern life. Today, consumers not only exhibit a penchant for paying for digital content but also engage in diverse domain-specific and novel consumption scenarios via mobile devices, establishing a comprehensive consumption ecosystem that spans all age demographics.

Jobs' introduction of the cloud service model with the iPhone is another significant contribution to the digital economy. Apple pioneered consumer cloud services, from the iTunes cloud music service to the App Store, innovating consumption paradigms for big data. Cloud services, facilitating internet-based computation and storage, empowered users to seamlessly store and access music, photos, apps, calendars, documents, and more from anywhere, anytime, enhancing user experiences. As industries increasingly integrate with digital technology, cloud services have permeated various sectors, emerging as catalysts for driving digital transformation and upgrades.

More importantly, the iPhone showcased the value and allure of data, ushering in an era where people began recognizing data not only as something to consume but also as an asset. It emerged as a novel factor of production that could be repeatedly utilized, enabling individuals to harness big data and create superior value. As Viktor Mayer-Schönberger, a prominent big data researcher, said, "In the twentieth century, value shifted from physical infrastructure like land and factories to intangibles such as brands and intellectual property. That now is expanding to data, which is becoming a significant corporate asset, a vital economic input, and the foundation of new business models. It is the oil of the information economy. Though data is rarely recorded on corporate balance sheets, this is probably just a question of time."[2] Jobs pioneered a data supply chain, emphasizing data's flexibility and showcasing its potential to facilitate precise decision-making, empower businesses, and disrupt industries.

Significantly, Jobs himself stood as a forerunner in leveraging big data. Even while battling pancreatic cancer, Jobs waged an eight-year-long relentless fight, achieving a remarkable feat in the annals of combating this deadly ailment. Typically referred to as the 'king of cancers,' pancreatic cancer has a dire prognosis, with an average survival time of around nine months post-diagnosis and a five-year survival rate of less than 2%. One pivotal reason Jobs managed to defy these odds for eight years lay in his adept utilization of data.

Upon learning of his diagnosis, the ever-data-conscious Jobs opted for data-driven analysis to curate his treatment regimen, meticulously selecting interventions tailored to his specific molecular profile. He documented and monitored his bodily changes and medical metrics throughout his treatment, engaging in regular discussions and analyses with his healthcare providers based on this data. Jobs even sequenced his DNA, especially his tumour DNA – an unprecedented, pioneering act. Armed with these insights, his medical team could craft treatment strategies with precision, making timely adjustments as needed. While Jobs ultimately succumbed to the dissemination of cancer cells throughout his body, his journey stands as a case study exemplifying the application of big data in medical decision-making.

As an entrepreneur, Jobs transformed Toffler's futurist predictions into present-day realities through Apple's resounding successes. Many credit him with ushering in a new era, although his contributions extend far beyond that. Steve Jobs rightfully emerges as a foundational pillar of the digital economy era, leaving an indelible imprint on the sands of time.

1.2 THE GENESIS AND EVOLUTION OF DIGITAL CIVILIZATION

INDUSTRIAL CIVILIZATION SERVES AS THE CORNERSTONE OF THE DIGITAL CIVILIZATION

From Toffler's predictions to Jobs' practical implementations, we have witnessed the advent of an intricate, glorious, and unpredictable digital age.

How do we comprehend this new era?

Today, the notion that the Earth is round is universally acknowledged. Yet, when we gaze into the distant horizon from atop a tall building, the Earth appears flat. This illusion arises because, compared to the vastness of Earth, humans are minuscule. It's akin to the saying by Su Shi,[3] a great scholar of the Song Dynasty,[4] "Why can't I tell the true shape of Lushan? Because I myself am in the mountain." But astronauts observing Earth from space can instantly perceive its spherical nature. Such illusions are commonplace, both in nature and daily life, as our individual insignificance makes it challenging to accurately discern our surroundings, especially when these environments are continuously evolving.

If our vision of the era remains obscured, we can distance ourselves and, through a historical lens, look back to understand our current civilization.

Civilizational shifts, even leaps, do not occur overnight but evolve through incremental accumulations leading to qualitative changes and breakthroughs. Each epoch's development lays robust foundational bedrock for subsequent eras, preparing ideologically, technologically, and practically for civilization's evolution. To comprehend the trajectory of digital civilization, we must revisit the age of industrial civilization.

Historically, shifts in civilizations correlate closely with advancements in science and technology. To some extent, the narrative of human societal evolution is essentially a chronicle of technological progress. Each significant technological innovation not only liberated contemporary productivity, but also brought about transformative shifts in civilization.

After tens of thousands of years in hunter-and-gatherer civilization, and agricultural civilization which developed slowly spanning tens of hundreds of years, humanity transitioned into the industrial civilization, which vastly accelerated the pace of human development. The technological revolution originating from England in the 18th century marked a monumental shift, heralding an era where machines supplanted manual tools. This revolution began with the invention of the spinning machine. In 1733, a mechanic named John Kay developed the 'flying shuttle,' which significantly enhanced textile production speeds, leading to an insatiable demand for raw materials like cotton. By 1765, textile worker James Hargreaves introduced the 'spinning jenny,' which propelled the cotton textile industry to new heights. A plethora of inventions and innovations emerged, marking the onset of the Industrial Revolution: advanced machines like the spinning mule in textiles, and machine-driven production in sectors ranging from coal mining to metallurgy. As machine-driven production proliferated across industries, traditional power sources like animal, water, and wind energy proved insufficient to meet industrial demands.

In 1785, James Watt improved the steam engine. His new steam engine provided a more convenient power source for industrial production. As a result, it quickly gained popularity and further accelerated the proliferation and development of machinery at the start of the Industrial Revolution.

This technological innovation also triggered a fundamental social transformation. As machine production gradually replaced manual labour in industrial production, capitalists began constructing workshops, introducing machinery, and employing an increasing number of workers for centralized production. Thus, a previously unseen form of production organization – the factory – was born. Serving as the primary form of industrialized production, factories played an increasingly crucial role. The first Industrial Revolution brought about revolutionary changes that propelled humanity into the new era of steam, and transitioning society from traditional agrarian to modern industrial.

Throughout the 19th century, with the continued advancement of the industrial revolution, the scientific research and innovations also saw significant development, leading to the continuous emergence of new technologies and creations. In 1866, German inventor Ernst Werner von Siemens invented the direct current generator, marking the first conversion of mechanical energy into electrical energy. After continuous improvements, practical generators were introduced in the 1870s. In 1879, Siemens further invented the electric motor, converting electrical energy back into mechanical energy, achieving a close integration of science and technology. In the same year, on October 21, American inventor Thomas Alva Edison, after extensive experimentation, finally ignited the world's first practically useful incandescent light bulb. Three years later, Edison established the world's first thermal power plant in the United States, driving a DC generator with a steam engine, making electricity practical in everyday life. Since then, through substations and transmission lines, affordable electricity has continuously flowed into factories and households.

With the vigorous rise of the second industrial revolution, humanity transitioned from the steam age to the electrical age. The second industrial revolution further enhanced production capabilities, changed lifestyles, expanded activity ranges, and strengthened interpersonal communication.

The industrial civilization is dynamic and creative. Although the industrial age lasted only two to three hundred years, it transformed the world, bringing economic growth, institutional improvements, lifestyle enhancements, and advancements in science and technology. This transformation is unparalleled compared to all civilizations created throughout human history.

It laid a solid material and technological foundation for humanity's transition into the digital age. Without the acquired knowledge of the industrial age, the leap to the digital civilization would be unimaginable. From this perspective, industrial civilization serves as the cornerstone of the digital age. Reflecting on the development of industrial civilization deepens our understanding of digital civilization.

Just as a seed must go through rooting, sprouting, growth, blossoming, and pollination stages before bearing fruit, the progression of human civilization follows a similar path. Another significant contribution of industrial civilization to the digital age is the information technology revolution. It profoundly influences the digital age and began in the industrial age.

Looking back at this long history, we can see that human society has experienced five information technology revolutions, as illustrated in Figure 1.2.

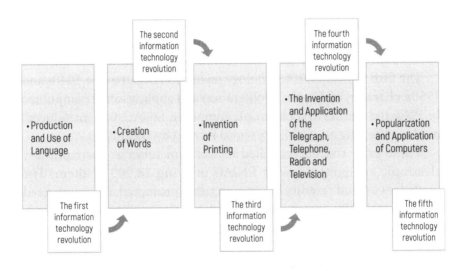

FIGURE 1.2

FIVE INFORMATION TECHNOLOGY REVOLUTIONS IN HUMAN HISTORY

The first major leap in information technology can be traced back to the natural development and use of spoken language.

It is the earliest and most significant information technology revolution in human history, marking a crucial milestone in human evolution and civilization's development. The advent of language enhanced human cognitive abilities, providing an effective tool for mutual communication and information dissemination.

The second information technology revolution was heralded by the invention of writing. Around 3500 BC, writing emerged as a medium for conveying information. This new form of information preservation allowed for knowledge and experiences to be stored long-term, breaking the constraints of time and space for information exchange.

The third information technology revolution was the invention of printing. It greatly facilitated information sharing, profoundly extending the dissemination of human culture. Among China's Four Great Inventions,[5] both papermaking and printing made huge contributions.

The fourth information technology revolution brought together the inventions and applications of telegraph, telephone, radio, and television. On May 24, 1844, Samuel Morse sent the first telegraph message in human history over an experimental line. Although the transmission distance was only 40 miles, it marked the onset of the fourth technological revolution. Subsequently, telecommunication witnessed rapid advancements. The widespread adoption of telephones, radios, and televisions revolutionized human economic and cultural life.

The fifth information technology revolution began in the 1940s and 1950s, characterized by the proliferation and application of computers. In 1946, the world's first electronic computer, ENIAC, was introduced, marking the advent of a binary world formed by '0's and '1's.

These early computers relied on vacuum tubes as their primary electronic components, with ENIAC utilizing 18,000 of them. The inefficiencies and fragility of vacuum tubes prompted a pressing need for more reliable, compact and affordable alternatives. In a ground-breaking moment on Christmas Eve 1947, researchers at Bell Labs, Shockley, Bardeen, and Brattain, demonstrated the amplification of weak electronic signals through a tiny component called a "transistor." This invention marked a monumental leap in electronics, and laid the groundwork for integrated circuits, microprocessors, and computer memory.

In 1955, William Shockley, known as the 'father of the semiconductor,' departed from Bell Labs and founded Shockley Semiconductor Laboratory in 1956. However, due to research setbacks and management issues, eight engineers left the lab in 1957, forming Fairchild Semiconductor. Their subsequent contributions played a pivotal role in the history of computing, paving the way for advancements in integrated circuits. The famous Moore's Law was also observed by Fairchild Semiconductor.

By 1967, despite Fairchild Semiconductor's significant commercial success, internal conflicts led to the departure of its founders. Some members, including Robert Noyce and Gordon Moore, founded Intel in August 1968, initiating another grand journey in computing. Other members, including Charles Sporck and Pierre Lamond, founded

National Semiconductor in 1967, while AMD was founded in 1968 by Jerry Sanders.

In 1969, Intel launched its first product: the 64K-bit static random-access memory (SRAM). By the 1970s, it dominated the memory chip market with 90% market share. However, by the 1980s, Japanese firms began overtaking Intel with dynamic random-access memory (DRAM) with higher product reliability, initiating fierce competition with prices always 10% below Intel, making Intel's market share drop significantly to 20%. At this point in time, six of the biggest ten semiconductor companies originated from Japan.

Amidst this competition, Intel pivoted to microprocessors, revitalising the U.S. semiconductor industry and laying favourable conditions for chip manufacturing. This not only made the US semiconductor companies be global leaders again, forming a new ecosystem, it also created a favourable environment for the rise and prosperity of the foundry industry.

In 1983, born in Ningbo, China, Morris Chang resigned from his senior vice president position at Texas Instruments in the U.S. and founded Taiwan Semiconductor Manufacturing Company (TSMC), pioneering the semiconductor foundry model. By 1988, TSMC secured orders from Intel, achieved international recognition and benchmarked production capabilities and international standards.

From the invention of the transistor in 1947 to advancements in semiconductors and integrated circuits, and from the upgrade from analogue circuits to digital circuits, every step in microelectronics hinted at a cloud-native and digital-native future, hurriedly ushering humanity into the digital age.

Intel propelled computers towards integration, high performance, and miniaturization, marking the era of mainframes and minicomputers. Meanwhile, IBM, known as the "Big Blue," dominated the computer world, initiating the age of commercial computing. However, computers remained bulky and expensive (IBM machines were sold at over one million dollars) and were only affordable for research institutes and large enterprises, until the advent of Apple's Apple 1 in 1976, the first general purpose personal computer available to businesses and households.

Apple's innovation catalysed products from IBM and Microsoft. By the 1980s, IBM introduced the IBM PC 5150, powered by Intel chips and Microsoft's DOS operating system, and combined to become the

"Wintel Empire,"[6] kickstarting the era of personal computers. The successive launch of Intel's 80286, 80383, and 80486 made personal computing prevalent, and "Wintel" became the dominating power during the transition from desktop computing to notebook computing. By the late 1990s, global PC penetration reached 7.06%, nearly tripling from 1990, with developed regions reaching 20%–45%.

The onset of the digital economy signalled the digitization of information. This binary language of "0–1" facilitated data processing and dissemination, and freed humans from repetitive cognitive tasks, paving the way for enhanced knowledge and innovation. The command language enabled by "0–1," with its nature of easy replicating, formatting, and other characteristics, is well-suited to data, and information handling and processing. Thus, humanity stood on the brink of the digital age.

THE VIRTUAL WORLD CREATED BY THE INTERNET

If the development of computers laid the hardware foundation for the digital civilization, the emergence of the internet ushered in an entirely new era. The internet seemed to offer a virtual "mapping" of human economic and social activities, projecting us from the real world into a virtual realm. This virtual world not only transformed the informational structure of our reality but also, through abundant software and information services, crafted diverse forms of expression like languages and graphics. This facilitated humanity's swift transition into the digital age.

At the end of the 20th century, as the internet gained momentum, no one foresaw its rapid expansion from military applications and elite institutions to the desktops of the general public within three decades. This expansion owes much to the standardization of TCP/IP for data transmission across networks. It propelled connections between network devices (switches, routers, etc.), various types of connection links, servers, and diverse computer terminals. Consequently, commercial internet users surpassed academic users in 1991. Innovations in retrieval methods and business models led to user-friendly web browsers and search engines in the 1990s. This era also witnessed an array of commercial software, making public information processing needs more evident, and internet information services more available. Thus, the digital world as connected by the internet via desktop computers was created. By 2000, global internet users reached 366 million, with an annual growth rate nearing 50%.

Entering the 21st century, propelled by the rapid advancements in mobile communication technologies and the proliferation of smart mobile devices, mobile internet achieved groundbreaking growth worldwide, far exceeding that of desktop internet. From laptops to smartphones, wearable devices, smart homes, and future autonomous vehicles, intelligent devices are experiencing exponential growth. Network operators, mobile device manufacturers, internet enterprises, and content providers are rolling out strategies to capitalize on the vast mobile internet market. The internet has transcended temporal and spatial boundaries, and is continuing to innovate information collection sources and methods, creating a new realm of mobile interconnectivity.

Parallel to this rapid evolution is the deepening understanding and appreciation of the digital economy. In the late 1990s, the U.S. spearheaded global research into the digital economy, prompting debates between economists and futurists on whether the digital economy disrupted the prevailing neoclassical economic framework. Concurrently, economic booms in countries like China, South Korea, and Singapore were reshaping the global internet landscape, involving more nations in the digital economic revolution.

As attention shifted towards the digital economy, the concept of 'big data' gained prominence. Initially overlooked by policy makers, even after a 2008 feature in *Nature* magazine, 'big data' soon became a global buzzword. Its impact on policy-making was neglected. Countries like the U.S., U.K., France, Germany, Japan, Australia, Canada, New Zealand, and Singapore unveiled national strategies for big data. China also established its national strategy, by issuing the Action Outline for Promoting the Development of Big Data, which was developed for the purpose of promoting the development and application of big data in China, and accelerating the construction of a powerful data nation.

Today, with the developments of emerging technologies like blockchain, artificial intelligence, 5G, privacy computing, digital twin, and digital-native, big data might seem outdated. Yet, as a pivotal component and foundation of the next-generation information technology industry, and the most indispensable part of digital transformation, its market continues to expand. According to IDC's 'China Big Data Platform Market Research Report 2020,' the global big data software market was valued at ¥481.36 billion RMB in 2020, with Microsoft, Oracle, and SAP contributing over 30% of the market share. Meanwhile, China's big data market reached ¥67.73 billion RMB in 2020, with software accounting for ¥9.22 billion RMB and hardware a staggering ¥58.51 billion RMB.

Big data is an inevitable outcome of digital technology's profound development, pointing directly to the core of the digital economy's new era: the value generated from massive and diverse data. If the internet crafted a virtual world, then big data, along with cloud computing, artificial intelligence, and numerous emerging technologies, has swung open the doors to the digital realm.

FROM DIGITAL TWIN TO DIGITAL-NATIVE

The continuous evolution of computers and the internet have further popularized the informatization of human society. Through the information revolution, people have been liberated from performing complex labour, allowing them to invest more energy in creative endeavours. Technology began to progress and accelerate at an unprecedented rate. Using various information technologies, humanity has been able to project parts of the physical world into virtual spaces, simulating the physical realm, leading to a deeper understanding, giving birth to the concept of digital twin.

The term 'digital twin' was introduced by Dr. Michael Grieves, a professor at the University of Michigan, in 2002. In an article, he mentioned digital twin when proposing that data from physical devices could construct a virtual entity and subsystem that represents the physical device within a virtual (informational) space.

To grasp the concept of digital twin, one might recall a scene from the movie *Iron Man*: the protagonist, Tony Stark, designs, repairs, and optimizes his Iron Man suit not through blueprints but by manipulating a digital virtual model. Through this digital representation, Tony Stark has an understanding of the suit's operations. This depiction showcases the film industry's visionary imagination of design scenarios, which today we refer to as digital twin.

NASA defines digital twin as the utilization of physical models, sensors, operational histories, and other data to integrate multi-disciplinary and multi-scale simulation processes. As a mirror of physical products in virtual space, it reflects the entire lifecycle of the corresponding physical entity. In essence, digital twin leverage digital technologies to map real-world objects, systems, and processes in real-time, creating a digital clone.

The pioneering application of digital twin was by NASA, when developing twin spacecraft for its Apollo program. The spacecraft left on Earth, termed as a "twin," reflected the status of the space-faring craft during missions.

On April 13, 1970, the Apollo 13 spacecraft encountered a malfunction, posing a serious threat to the safety of both the spacecraft and its astronauts. This was the first time this had happened in the history of human space exploration. Landing on the moon became impossible, and the focus of thousands of NASA ground support personnel shifted to ensuring the astronauts' survival and a safe return home.

To determine which systems were still operational and which were damaged, the astronauts continuously toggled various systems. The ground control centre synthesized information from various sources and rapidly diagnosed the root cause of the problem using a sophisticated ground simulation system. This comprehensive, high-level ground simulation system was originally designed as a simulator for astronaut training, encompassing all the mission operations astronauts might encounter in space and simulating how to handle various fault scenarios. Throughout the space program, the simulator represented the most technologically complex aspect, where the only real components were the crew, the capsule, and the mission control console – everything else was created by a multitude of computers, extensive formulas, and experienced technical personnel.

After evaluating the extent of spacecraft damage and considering factors like remaining electrical power, oxygen, and drinking water, NASA devised a bold plan to return to Earth. However, this plan far exceeded the spacecraft's design limits. Moreover, the plan had never been practiced before and its feasibility was uncertain. The cost of trial and error was exceptionally high, as any mistake would have left the astronauts with no chance of survival.

To ensure the plan's success, the ground control centre adjusted the simulator to match the current configuration of Apollo 13, reprogrammed the spacecraft's mainframe based on parameters such as mass, centre of gravity, and thrust, and collaborated with the lunar module manufacturer to determine a new landing process. Backup astronauts were then able to conduct operational rehearsals on the simulator, demonstrating the plan's feasibility and significantly boosting the confidence of ground control personnel and astronauts alike.

Ultimately, the astronauts escaped disaster and safely returned to Earth. The success of Apollo 13's rescue mission can be attributed in no small part to the simulator. In a way, these simulators represent a real-world application of the currently popular concept of digital twin. By recognizing the importance of 'twins,' NASA placed significant emphasis on the role of digital twin, pioneering their application in the field of aerospace.

The most crucial characteristic of digital twin is the mapping between the virtual and the real. This bidirectional mapping refers to the mutual representation of physical entities and digital models, achieved by constructing digital models of physical entities. Thanks to this feature, digital twin provides the foundation for the construction of Cyber-Physical Systems (CPS). The goal of CPS is to achieve the integration of the virtual and the real, connecting people, machines, and objects, seamlessly merging the physical and virtual worlds. Through big data analysis, cloud computing, artificial intelligence, and other digital technologies, CPS perform simulation analysis and predictions in the virtual world, driving operations in the physical world, using the most optimal results. Digital twin makes this a reality, enabling the replication of the operational framework and system of the real world in virtual space, creating a large-scale, collaborative, new system for human society. This opens up a new transformative path and driving force for industries such as manufacturing, smart education, intelligent transportation, and smart homes.

During the COVID-19 pandemic, the astonishingly rapid construction of the second Xiaotangshan Hospital in Wuhan, known as the Leishenshan Hospital, was made possible by leveraging digital twin technology.[7] Designed as an emergency infectious disease hospital, the Leishenshan Hospital adheres to the standards of infectious disease hospitals with its "three zones and two passages" layout. Given the complex processes and challenging design constraints, coupled with the urgent need for rapid construction due to the swift spread of the virus, how could they reconcile this high complexity with the pressing timeline? Entrusted with this critical task, the CSADI (Central-South Architectural Design Institute) utilized Building Information Modelling (BIM) technology to create a digital twin of the Leishenshan Hospital. By utilizing BIM technology to guide and validate the design according to project requirements, the efficiency of the design process was significantly enhanced.

Though originating in the field of engineering, digital twin technology has expanded into broader domains, such as urban planning and management. The emergence of digital twin cities has revolutionized people's visions of future urban landscapes.

From its initial planning stages, Xiong'an New Area emphasized the need to "persistently synchronize the planning and construction of the digital city with the physical city, proactively lay out intelligent infrastructure, promote real-time and controllable ubiquitous intelligent applications, establish a comprehensive big data asset management system, and construct a globally leading digital city with deep learning capabilities."[8]

If you were to visit Xiong'an New Area, you would undoubtedly be struck by the scenes of bustling machinery, vehicles weaving through, and round-the-clock construction. Yet, what might surprise you is the simultaneous development of a more astonishing 'Smart Xiong'an' – a digital intelligent city. The construction of a series of city-level intelligent platforms, including intelligent transportation infrastructure, big data platforms, intelligent computing cloud centres, autonomously controllable blockchain platforms, and City Information Modelling (CIM) platforms, continuously advances the development of Xiong'an New Area's digital twin city. For the first time in the history of urban development, digital cities and physical cities are being constructed synchronously.

Yang Baojun, the Director of the China Urban Planning and Design Research Institute, once summarized the value of Xiong'an New Area's digital twin city, stating, "Before implementing certain decisions, they can first be simulated in a virtual city. Based on the results, decisions can be made for construction or operation in the real city. Xiong'an will serve as a model for intelligent urban development."

The emergence of technologies integrating physical city and the virtual world redefines urban development paradigms, exemplified by the planning of Xiong'an New Area in China. This kind of pioneering efforts represents a primary development direction for the intelligence city realm in China.

Kevin Kelly, author of *Out of Control: The New Biology of Machines, Social Systems, and the Economic World*, highlighted the concept of the "mirror world" at the 2020 Digital Industry Expo. In Kelly's view, Mirror World is the third most revolutionary and disruptive technology platform in the history of internet. The first is the internet, which digitizes information. The second is social media, which digitizes humanity. The third is mirror world, which digitizes the whole world. He envisions the mirror world as a digital replica of our physical reality, suggesting that digital twin is instrumental in realizing this futuristic vision.

As we transition from a physical to a digital-centric worldview as led by digital twin, digital-native emerges as the next frontier, reflecting our evolving perspectives and aspirations in an increasingly digital-centric world.

TOWARDS DIGITAL-NATIVE

In any era, when we seek transformative insights and self-renewal, we must return to the fundamentals and see beyond the surface to understand the essence. To grasp the concept of being "digitally native," we need to revisit our initial intentions: what is the fundamental purpose of our pursuit of digitalization? In reality, everything we do aims to enhance people's lives, making them better and happier.

Have we achieved this goal? The answer is a resounding yes. Today, wherever you go, as long as you have a smartphone, you can effortlessly solve various problems. Mobile payments assist your purchases; platforms like Ctrip[9] help you book flights or train tickets; ride-hailing apps are at your service when you need transportation, and you can even find designated drivers. If you want to listen to music, Tencent Music[10] has you covered; for videos and news, an array of apps are available. Shopping? No need to visit a physical store; just pick and order through your phone. Today, all your activities are linked via the cloud, with services tailored to your behavioural data. If you enjoy classical music and listen to Beethoven's symphony, you'll receive recommendations from various conductors and orchestras, even suggestions from different eras of classical romantic composers. Our ability to lead such a convenient life stems from being digital-native.

Being "digitally native" implies that businesses' product services, operational processes, management methods, strategic decisions, business models, and marketing strategies are all designed based on digital technology. It signifies a shift from the physical world to the digital world. Cloud-native, AI-native, blockchain-native, IoT-native, and 5G-native are means to achieve this digital-native.

Subscription-based and on-demand services are vital manifestations of being digitally native. As a result, merely using a smartphone means you're living in the digital-native realm. The data generated from our consumption via smartphones is transformed into factors of production, continually refining our experiences in the background. This iterative process encapsulates the essence of being "digitally native."

Becoming digitally native is the ultimate goal of every company's digital transformation. Digital technology reshapes businesses, enabling them with cloud and intelligent architectures and capabilities. This transformation permeates every aspect of a company, from production and sales, business needs, organizational structures, human resource allocations, management culture, to strategic visions, all revolving around the digital world.

Digital-native giants like Apple and Amazon have the digital world as their foundation. They adeptly gather and store vast amounts of data and employ technologies like machine learning to analyse this data. This enables them to better understand user demands, continually enhance their digital innovation capabilities, and drive their robust growth.

Today, as we advance towards becoming digitally native, the physical and digital worlds will intertwine more closely, marking a transition in the digital economy from quantitative growth to qualitative transformation.

THE METAVERSE, VIRTUAL SPACE, AND THE FUTURE OF HUMANITY

In 1992, Neal Stephenson introduced the concept of the "metaverse" in his science fiction novel, *Snow Crash*. He described it as a space where individuals, equipped with headphones and goggles, could immerse themselves in a parallel virtual universe enabled by computer simulation, detached from the physical world. The protagonist, a delivery driver in reality living in a crowded small room, finds himself in a luxurious virtual mansion within this realm.

This depiction resonates with Steven Spielberg's film *Ready Player One*, where people escape their harsh realities by donning VR equipment, seeking a more thrilling existence in a virtual world. Here, they can be superheroes, effortlessly realizing their dreams and tasting success.

While these scenarios were once the realm of fiction, the digital age has been inching us closer to the concept of the metaverse.

What is the metaverse? Like some other cutting-edge technologies, the metaverse lacks a precise definition. It can be understood as a virtual world that is both reflective and independent of the real world, built on the foundation of the traditional cyberspace and the evolving internet, accompanied by the maturation of various digital technologies. The metaverse is characterized by connectivity, perception, and sharing, but it is not merely just a virtual space. It encompasses networks, hardware terminals, and users within a persistent, extensive virtual reality system. This system includes digitized replicas of the real world, as well as creations from the virtual world. The metaverse integrates the operational logic of the real world into the digital realm, enabling human interaction with the digital world through both primitive and higher-dimensional experiences.

During my visit to Xuzhou,[11] I was impressed by the urban planning conducted by architect and planner Wu Liangyong.[12] Professor Wu approached spatial design from a holistic perspective, weaving geography, infrastructure, and cultural elements to craft a captivating cityscape. His human-centric approach aimed to harmonize environmental factors with human emotions, aspiring to create aesthetically pleasing habitats. Yet, while geographical spaces can be meticulously designed, human emotions and spirits remain unpredictable. Perhaps the metaverse, which blurs the lines between reality and virtuality, holds the key to realizing Wu's vision of "organic renewal."

Fundamentally, the metaverse serves as a digital realm catering to human emotional needs, fostering a free-market digital world. Within this space, individuals forge new social and emotional connections, seeking sharing, recognition, and empathy. It's a world governed by economic principles, following rules and disciplines such as autonomous trading, clear property rights, and freedom of contract. This allows individuals to assume alternative identities, living divergent lives from their real-world counterparts.

Previously, the metaverse was deemed futuristic, remaining only in the imagination. However, the COVID-19 pandemic since 2020 accelerated the metaverse realization, gradually turning it into a reality. This means humanity is en route to a digital world.

As the COVID-19 pandemic continued to spread worldwide, people were limited in their mobility and interpersonal contacts in the physical world. As a result, many economic and social activities have since shifted to the virtual world. Technical ideas exchanges, graduation ceremonies, classroom teaching, and even concerts have moved online. The online-offline integration has brought the physical and virtual worlds closer, shaking up people's understanding of the world. The virtual world is not unreal or insignificant: in the digital age, it will become a novel living space for humanity.

While the pandemic confined people's physical movements, it ignited their enthusiasm for the metaverse. The wave of the metaverse is already rolling in.

The momentum behind the metaverse became evident in March 2021, Roblox, a tech company, went public on the New York Stock Exchange, marking the first metaverse-themed IPO.

Roblox's sandbox platform epitomizes the metaverse, establishing a dual-economic system centred on Robux[13] and introducing core principles such as:

1. Identity: each individual must have their own virtual identity in the metaverse.
2. Social Interactions/Friendship: the metaverse has social interaction capabilities, and each individual should have their own friends in the metaverse.
3. Immersion: individuals should have immersive experiences in the metaverse.
4. Low-Latency: everything in the metaverse should happen in real-time.

5. Diversity: content displayed in the metaverse should be diverse and exciting.
6. Accessible: the metaverse should be accessible from all hardware, at any time.
7. Self-sustaining Economy: the metaverse should have its own economy.
8. Civilization: the metaverse should have its own virtual civilization.

The technology industry's response has been overwhelming, bringing vitality and imagination to the long-dormant internet innovation and offered a glimpse of the bright future to many internet giants who subsequently swarmed into this new playing field. Companies like ByteDance[14] invested heavily in VR start-ups. They first acquired Pico and then invested ¥100 million RMB in the metaverse game developer Code Qiankun. Japanese giant GREE announced its foray into the metaverse business. Microsoft unveiled enterprise solutions for the metaverse at the Inspire Global Partner Conference, emphasizing its potential.

Notably, Facebook's rebranding as 'Meta' signalled its transformation from a social media entity to a metaverse powerhouse. On October 29, 2021, at Facebook's Connect developer conference, CEO Mark Zuckerberg announced a replacement of the company's 17-year-old name Facebook with the new name Meta, derived from "metaverse." This marked a transformation from a social media company to a "metaverse company" bringing together the real world and the virtual world.

In his open letter, Zuckerberg outlined his prospects for the metaverse: "In the future, you will be able to teleport to the office or a concert with friends in holographic form without commuting. You can spend more time on things that matter to you, and reduce commuting time and carbon footprint. Think about how many of your physical objects today can be turned into holograms in the future. Your TV, the perfect multi-display workstations, board games, and so on will no longer be physical objects assembled in factories, but holograms designed by creators from around the world."

The future of the metaverse goes beyond Zuckerberg's imagination. If digital transformation is a reshaping of current society, the metaverse is a construction of future society, presenting new horizons for human cognition.

The metaverse is no longer the "metaverse" as understood in *Snow Crash*. Its connotation is extended. It now incorporates artificial intelligence, VR (virtual reality), AR (augmented reality), MR (mixed reality) and other digital technologies, presenting the possibility of constructing a digital world that is both parallel to and assimilated with the real world. It promotes the interaction of information science, quantum science, mathematics and life sciences, and shifts scientific paradigms. It drives breakthroughs in philosophy, sociology, and even the entire human science system. It encompasses all digital technologies including blockchain technology. And it also enriches the digital economy transformation models by incorporating the digital finance achievements such as De-Fi (decentralized finance), IPFS (interplanetary file system), and NFT (non-fungible tokens).

In the future, the metaverse will no longer be limited to the current two-dimensional state that is accessed through intelligent terminals and perceived primarily through visual and auditory means. Instead, people will be able to enter a fully immersive and interactive three-dimensional world through human-computer integration and digital interaction, achieving continuous connectivity between the real and virtual worlds. In this world, people will be able to not only replicate the panoramic physical world, but also potentially achieve independence of consciousness from the physical body, and shuttle freely between the two worlds. This will engender a variety of virtual resource forms and diverse collaborations, labour divisions, and transactions. The resources developed and utilized in the metaverse will multiply that of the physical world, thereby expanding human cognition and activity domain. Through the mutual infiltration and integration of traditional culture and metaverse culture, human civilization will once again be transformed.

During the Age of Discovery, humans greatly expanded the known territory and global networks across continents and oceans through new sea routes, unifying the world. Eventually, the metaverse is likely to usher in the next Age of Discovery, where humans will exploit and thrive in a new virtual territory.

BRIDGING REALITY AND THE METAVERSE WITH NFTS

With the development of cutting-edge technologies such as 5G, VR, AR, IoT, blockchain, digital twin, and so on, assets, or even artworks, native to the digital world began to emerge, and NFTs gradually came into sight.

NFTs are unique encrypted crypto-currency tokens stored on the blockchain to represent digital assets that can be bought and sold. When thinking of blockchain, people may first associate it with Bitcoin. NFTs are also a type of crypto-currency. But unlike Bitcoin, NFTs are unique and one-of-a-kind, while Bitcoin is homogeneous with each Bitcoin being indistinguishable and interchangeable. While Bitcoin is scarce, interchangeable, and not unique, NFTs are unique and non-fungible.

Because of their unique, one-of-a-kind nature, NFTs can be used to represent something unique such as artwork. Artworks such as paintings, songs, films, and photographs have value because of their one-of-a-kind nature. However, if these artworks are turned into digital files, they can be copied. NFTs can 'tokenize' these files by converting tangible or intangible items into NFTs and granting digital ownership certificates that can be bought and sold. Based on the property of blockchain, the exclusive rights of NFT owners can be recognized.

Now, more objects have been forged into NFTs, such as Steve Jobs' job application handwritten at the age of 18, goals scored by famous athletes in NBA games, WeChat[15] or QQ avatars, land, real estate, the source code of the World Wide Web, Nobel Prize-winning papers, and covers of *TIME* magazine. Their prices are astronomical. Digital visual artist Mike Winkelmann, also known as Beeple, sold his collection of works *Everyday: The First 5000 Days* as an NFT at Christie's for a staggering $69.35 million. Jack Dorsey, the former CEO of Twitter, sold his tweet consisting of only five words, "just setting up my twttr," for $2.9 million.

NFTs establish a mapping between physical and virtual objects, turning virtual goods into highly liquid commodities and visual assets. NFTs also map the data content on the internet through chains, making NFTs the asset entities of data content, thereby enabling data content circulation. Through this mapping, virtual goods such as digital assets, game equipment, decorations, and land ownership all have a tradable entity and the traditional way of trading virtual goods is altered. NFTs enable users to produce and trade virtual goods directly, just like transactions in the real world. NFTs free users from gaming platforms to freely trade virtual assets.

NFTs are vital infrastructure for the metaverse and serve as a medium for native assets within the metaverse through virtual object mapping. Like keys in the physical world, NFTs are analogue digitalized keys in the metaverse. People can confirm users' permissions by recognizing NFTs through programming. This enables a virtual world to pivot to power decentralization and virtual property transactions in the absence of third-party registration institutions, greatly improving the efficiency of data asset transactions. This can financialize any rights of access, viewing, approval, construction and so on in the metaverse and facilitate the circulation, leasing, and trading of these rights.

NFTs are a bridge between reality and the metaverse, bringing the two worlds closer as NFTs deepen. A true parallel world may eventuate in the realm of blockchain.

AIGC: ACCELERATING TOWARDS TECHNOLOGICAL SINGULARITY

The ultimate form of the metaverse remains uncertain, and no one can provide a definitive answer. However, one thing is certain: the metaverse represents the seamless integration of technology and humanities, reshaping the economy and society through its technological advancements. As we step into the metaverse, more aspects of work and life will become digitized, leading to a greater demand for digital content and higher expectations for its form and interactivity. AIGC (Artificial Intelligence Generated Content), a novel content production method, has become a key force and accelerator driving breakthroughs in the metaverse.

In late 2022, the emergence of ChatGPT and its subsequent continuous iterations showcased significant advancements in artificial intelligence in the field of natural language processing, sparking a widespread AIGC trend across various industries. This phenomenon has continually refreshed people's understanding of artificial intelligence.

The evolution of content production methods on the internet has undergone generational revolutions, transitioning from Professionally Generated Content (PGC) to User Generated Content (UGC) and, subsequently, to AIGC.

During the Web 1.0 era, the dominant content production method was the PGC model, where specialized professionals were responsible for sophisticated and high quality content creation and production. While these experts possessed refined skills, extensive industry experience, and profound knowledge, the PGC model often required a certain production cycle and failed to meet the timely demand for real-time information. It also lacked the ability to customize content, leaving it powerless in the face of diverse user needs.

During the Web 2.0 and Web 3.0 eras, social media rose to prominence, giving rise to the User Generated Content (UGC) model. Users no longer merely consumed content but became creators, freely sharing their experiences, thoughts, and expertise through social media, providing valuable content for other users. However, the User Generated Content (UGC) model was not without flaws. Issues such as information overload, insufficient moderation mechanisms, and a lack of content quality assurance were prevalent. False information frequently permeated the entire network, and legal problems such as copyright infringement and personal privacy violations were widespread.

In the era of the metaverse, the need for content far exceeds that of traditional internet usage. Both PGC and UGC fall short of meeting this demand, leading to the emergence of AIGC as a new content production method. With the development of NLG technology and AI models (e.g. LLM), the automatic generation of massive, high-quality, and personalized content has become a reality. AI is now capable of not only assisting in information search and problem analysis but also in activities such as drawing, poetry writing, composition, editing, and translation. The influence of AIGC is evident in almost every content production field. At the 2022 Beijing Winter Olympics, an AI sign language anchor named 'Lingyu' reported on the Olympic events 24/7, using precise sign language gestures to help hearing-impaired individuals experience the nuances of winter sports. AIGC maintains the professionalism and high quality of the PGC model while avoiding the content quality and legal issues associated with the UGC model. Furthermore, AIGC can generate more personalized digital scenarios and content at a lower cost and faster speed, providing users with a better experience. This not only significantly accelerates the production speed of metaverse content but also expands its imaginative space and commercial prospects.

Throughout history, creativity has been a human prerogative, with exquisite Dunhuang murals and timeless Tang and Song poetry embodying artistic beauty that transcends eras and traverses past and present. Imagination and creativity, like two brilliant pearls, have illuminated the path of human progress and empowered humanity to drive social advancement. Today, AIGC possesses a similar level of creativity, intertwining technology and art, enriching our world with greater possibilities.

In 2005, renowned American engineer and technology writer Ray Kurzweil explored the future prospects of artificial intelligence development and the arrival of the Singularity in his groundbreaking work, *The Singularity is Near: When Humans Transcend Biology*. He defined the Singularity as the point in time when artificial intelligence surpasses human intelligence, leading to a monumental and irreversible change in human society. With the continual improvement of AIGC's ability to construct digital content, we have reason to believe that humanity is rapidly approaching the Singularity.

1.3 TOWARDS THE BOUNDLESS UNIVERSE OF DIGITAL CIVILIZATION

THE NEW WAVE OF DIGITAL CIVILIZATION HAS ARRIVED

The rapid advancement of technology has placed us at a brand new intersection in time.

Digital civilization is like an ever-flowing river, originating from the past and surging into the future. Propelled by this new wave, we bravely step into a digital age full of hope and confidence in the future of business, society, and human civilization. This optimism stems not only from the unprecedented ways the digital age will drive human development but also from native digital enterprises thriving in this new era.

Take Amazon, for example, which uses data assets to power its growth momentum.

Amazon's vast digital infrastructure underpins its expanding smart business empire. Central to its development philosophy is a self-propelling fast cycle, termed the "Growth Flywheel." Amazon's belief is simple: more customers lead to more sellers, better services, lower costs, competitive prices, and an enhanced user experience. As illustrated in Figure 1.3, this virtuous cycle, powered by AI derived from massive data, continually strengthens Amazon.

FIGURE 1.3
AMAZON'S GROWTH FLYWHEEL

According to the e-commerce data company Marketplace Pulse, Amazon, as the world's largest e-commerce platform, has nearly ten million seller accounts. As provided by Amazon CEO Jeff Bezos' 2021 annual shareholder letter, Amazon has 200 million Prime users. Leveraging this massive volume of consumer behaviour, Amazon employs algorithms to provide customers with personalized product recommendations tailored to individual preferences. Simultaneously, using pricing bots, Amazon automatically captures price data from multiple competitors across the web to offer customers the lowest possible prices, maximising user utility. At Amazon, AI and big data analysis serve as flywheel tools. By continuously outputting organizational knowledge and energy through AI, innovations incubated in a particular business sector can expand the boundaries of the company's AI capabilities, and the upgraded AI can then drive faster development in other business sectors. Initially, AI and machine learning at Amazon were primarily used by the product recommendation team to enhance their predictions of product sales. However, with the continuous improvement of technology and intelligence, the technical expertise accumulated by AI and machine learning is shared across the entire company, transforming into a growth flywheel for the organization's integration and operation.

Amazon's approach to data usage is linked to its founder Jeff Bezos' obsession with customers and his extreme proficiency in understanding digital realms. Amazon believes that a customer's perpetual dissatisfaction is the inexhaustible driving force behind its constant growth, and customer obsession is at the core of Amazon's corporate culture. In order to unwaveringly focus on customers, Amazon not only aims to satisfy customers but also strives to delight them. The company's understanding of customers often reaches levels that customers themselves may not be aware of. This deep understanding is the core capability of Amazon's artificial intelligence, underpinned by its profound comprehension and reverence for digits and algorithms. This approach has given rise to thousands of services and products with a mission to meet customer needs.

Amazon's data capabilities also drive continuous optimization in its operational management. A robust system of digital metrics and intelligent management tools helps the company's leadership achieve the automatic execution of routine decisions, freeing them from day-to-day operations to concentrate on future development.

Google is another company that drives its management and decision-making through data. As a major force behind the digital economy, Google's management approach is future-oriented. Using a numbers-driven approach, Google encourages employees to pursue the combination of personal and corporate values, striving for continuous improvement rather than settling for perfection.

Google firmly believes that all significant decisions should be data-driven. Among the myriad of Google-style operational decisions, an example that stands out is how data-driven human resources management is implemented. Google has a department called the 'People Analytics Department' within its global human resources system. This department assists the global Google organization in making human resources decisions through data analysis. In the past, Google eliminated all manager levels, defining employees as independent business units.

However, due to the inefficacy of this approach, Google then rehired these managerial-level employees. The company headquarters posed a management question regarding the effectiveness of managers to its People Analytics Department, to assess the performance contributions of managerial-level employees.

Within this department, there is an information laboratory formed by social scientists. These scientists analysed Google's existing data on the performance evaluations of managerial-level employees, including evaluations from superiors and employee surveys. The analysis indicated that, overall, managerial-level employees performed well. However, due to the existing data's inability to reflect the influence of more variables, they categorized the performance data of all managers along a dimension from high to low. They then separately analysed the upper and lower segments. Through regression analysis, these scientists found significant differences between managers in the upper segment and those in the lower segment in terms of job output, employee happiness, and employee retention rates. The employees of the good managers were more willing to stay with the company, demonstrating those managers' value. However, this data could not help with answering a more decision-worthy question: What makes a manager a good Google manager?

The scientists collected two sets of data: Google established an "Excellent Manager Award," where employees nominated recipients and detailed the good behaviours and abilities of excellent managers. This employee description became the first set of data. The second set of data was obtained through interviews conducted by scientists with managers in the upper and lower segments, aiming to understand their behaviours and management styles (the managers didn't know which segment they were in). The scientists coded and analysed the materials obtained from the awards and interviews. Through this analysis, they answered the question. Eight behaviours led to high performance and three reasons caused managers to underperform.

Google shared the analysis results with relevant employees and began to measure employees' performance based on these behaviours, developing a twice-yearly corresponding feedback mechanism. The encouraged behaviours were also incorporated into its management training courses. In this way, data-driven decision-making turned Google's human resources work into a scientific discipline.

Throughout human history, great companies and entrepreneurs have had grand visions, keenly seizing the advantages of their time and dedicating themselves to changing people's lifestyles. In the digital age, such entrepreneurs will continue to emerge, leading people to explore broader business prospects within the waves of digitization and intelligence.

EMBRACING CHALLENGES AND OPPORTUNITIES

The new era of digital civilization is filled with limitless possibilities. As we venture forwards, we will encounter challenges and uncertainties, but we will also find unexpected opportunities. We must confront and embrace these challenges and opportunities and continuously transform ourselves.

1. **Challenges and Opportunities of Cognitive Innovation**
   The development of society and the economy originates from continually deepening our understanding of the world. Based on this understanding, transformative scientific systems and technological achievements gradually emerge.

   In the era of scientific computation, human cognition of objective things evolved through processes such as observation, experimentation, and data collection and interpretation. Mathematical methods explained physical, chemical, and biological phenomena. The invention and application of computers expanded human cognition from scientific computation focused on singular problems, to business computation for complex operations, and further to societal computation for systematic global analysis. The process of recognizing the world will propel humanity to perceive nature and self from an entirely new perspective.

   In the era of the digital economy, big data is key to achieving new cognition and breakthroughs. The technical ecosystem of collecting, managing, analysing, modelling, applying, and securing data has become the most prominent innovation feature. The big data industry chain, supported by interdisciplinary cross-cutting and integrated technology research, continually extends and enriches, creating enormous opportunities for technological innovation and development in applications, with opportunities for leapfrogging progress and surpassing development.

For example, in the field of data mining and fusion, China's independently developed Yanyun DaaS technology creatively uses black box technology to rapidly acquire data without original software or developers. This demonstrates an opportunity to stand alongside the field's most advanced players and achieve leapfrog innovation.

In terms of data governance, new challenges and problems such as privacy leaks, data misuse, and unreliable data decision-making are emerging. There is a tremendous demand for technological innovations in data privacy protection, trustworthy transmission of data transactions and sharing, clear definition of data rights and usage rights, and valuation and pricing of data.

Big data accelerates the iterative speed of human cognition of new things and the reconstruction of new values. It reshapes the macroeconomic structure, production methods, consumption patterns, and management paradigms in the fields of nature, production, life, society, and politics. The generation and acquisition of data, cross-border transmission, integrated analysis and mining, capitalization, and market allocation will change the governance model of the traditional value chain division, creating a more equitable environment and distribution of benefits for market participants in the value chain division. This will drive the evolution of the global value chain division and the reconstruction of the division pattern.

Big data accelerates the pace of innovation in the integration of agriculture, manufacturing, services, and social governance, driving the transformation of traditional industry management methods, innovation in service and business models, and the restructuring of industrial value chain systems.

In agriculture, technologies such as big data and blockchain can be utilized to construct integrated agricultural credit. By digitizing agricultural assets and leveraging agricultural data, direct connections between agriculture and banking can be promoted, establishing a "data + e-commerce + finance" agricultural digital ecosystem and platform.

In manufacturing, big data's transformative ability is evident in various aspects of industry. In the design phase, it promotes the development of models like C2M, enhancing the level of personalization in industrial design. In the production phase, big data technologies optimize assembly line operations, strengthen fault prediction and health management, improve product quality, and reduce energy consumption. In the sales phase, also by using big data technologies, it promotes the integration and precision of industrial production and sales.

In the service industry, the use of big data analysis technologies, based on data capture, aggregation, analysis, consumer habit analysis, marketing strategy suggestions, inventory warnings, etc., can accurately analyse multi-channel user data. This helps enterprises fully explore the value of customer flow, accelerate sales and marketing conversion. While using data desensitization technology to protect sensitive data securely and legally, it covers the entire process of project management, including enterprise consulting and assessment, implementation, and deployment, customized development, system maintenance, and strategic cooperation, ensuring the maximum availability and exploitable value of data.

Throughout the digital economy, data, as a factor of production, is integrated into the economic system. With characteristics such as replicability, shareability, unlimited growth, and infinite supply, it is a key productive force that connects innovations, activates funds, nurtures talents, promotes industrial upgrading, and drives economic growth. Being the core in reshaping production relations, data has effectively promoted the formation of a "co-building, co-sharing, co-governance" social governance pattern. It drives regional digital economic construction through industrial digitization transformation and the "industry-city-people" integration development model, leading innovative practices in regional development models.

The outbreak of the global COVID-19 pandemic made the role of big data in constructing a shared future for the digital and physical worlds more significant. The digital economy became the starting point for a new type of globalization, constructing a completely new order of economic globalization and promoting sustainable development characterized by low carbon, circularity, symbiosis, safety, and intelligence.

2. Challenges and Opportunities of Technological Innovation

The evolution, competition, and selection of information technology, as described by Darwin's theory of evolution, is a process of development from the low level to the high level. The evolution of computing hardware, from computing scales, punched cards, vacuum tubes, integrated circuits, to CPUs (central processing units),

GPUs (graphics processing units), and FPGAs (field-programmable gate arrays), has seen an exponential growth in computing power and process complexity.

The evolution of a message-based internet core centred on information interconnection to a service-based commercial internet, will ultimately form a value internet core centred on trust and value connection. In the process of information technology evolution, software has also undergone its own differentiation, evolving from being subservient to hardware to forming products and industries represented by operating systems, and then to the "software defines everything" reality brought about by the internet and cloud computing.

The decoupling of integrated hardware infrastructure, achieving the virtualization of hardware resources and programmability of management tasks, dominates the reshaping of the information technology system. The foundation of the integrated innovation in the digital economy era, built on the "software defines everything" reality, has emerged with innovations such as autonomous driving, cloud phones, cloud terminals, and smart devices. This foundation will continue to yield more technological innovations.

In the digital economy era, cloud computing, through continuous technological evolution, plays a crucial role as the bridge between the industrial age and the digital age. The birth and development of cloud computing reflect the connotation and extension of "software defines everything."

Cloud computing initially addressed the fluctuating demand for information technology resources in the digital economy era through virtualization technology, providing digital productivity such as computing, storage, and network services.

The concept of cloud-native and the application of containerization technology make running applications on the cloud similar to cargo containers. It achieves the independent deployment of applications and serves decoupled services through micro-services in the form of APIs (Application Programming Interfaces). These emerging cloud technologies will continue to drive the emergence and iterative update of new computing paradigms.

In the industrial age, horizontal competition only led to minor iterative developments, trapping various fields and industries in competition. In the digital economy era, innovation must break free from the existing involutionary competitive mind-set. Emerging computing paradigms such as cloud computing, edge computing, blockchain, and neural computing will exponentially expand the scope, function, and industrial chain of cloud computing. This will provide us with opportunities for differentiated competition and developmental positioning, allowing us to lead and leverage advantages against competition.

3. Challenges and Opportunities of Scenario Innovation

The application of digital technology allows humanity to view the development of things from a new dimension in cyberspace, thereby redefining scenarios from a holistic system perspective.

Take Toyota's lean production model. Unlike other automobile companies that focus on expensive specialized production equipment and solely enhancing the performance of individual parts, Toyota, from the outset of any design, adjusts the technical standards of various components based on the maintenance conditions of parts from previously sold vehicles. This approach ensures the longest possible failure-free usage time, fundamentally redefining the automotive manufacturing model from a holistic perspective.

Guided by first principles, new technologies, and through innovative data scenarios, disruptive tools and methods will emerge.

Using digital currency as an example, the combination of digital currency + blockchain disrupts existing payment models with a "transactions are settlements" approach. As a result, inclusive finance and precision poverty alleviation will become more achievable. Digital currencies might not require assistance from third-party institutions or may foster new commercial forms, driving greater economic and social development through iterative innovation.

Amidst the COVID-19 pandemic, the digital economy, as a form of economic integration between digital technology and the global economic system, shaped a new order of economic globalization. New technologies, products, and finance are becoming new global growth points, forming a new globalization trend represented by the digital economy.

The convergence of technology, business, and scenarios reconstructed the relationships between individuals, humans, and nature, and individuals with themselves. This will introduce unprecedented ethical, moral, regulatory, and legal challenges. Building a new eco-system of safety based on proactive and passive security is essential to maximize the benefits of the digital economy and counteract negative impacts of change.

Creating new civilizations is a perpetual theme for humanity. In the future, humans will continually advance along roads leading from industrial civilization to digital civilization. At this historical turning point, we can sense the gears of progress. We are also facing enormous challenges, but we have to understand Alvin Toffler's views: "Pessimism is useless; it's better to contemplate the blueprint and navigate the treacherous sea. When the old situation no longer applies, and a new future hasn't yet been established, it's an excellent opportunity for growth and transformation!"

CHAPTER 2

RESHAPING DIGITAL THINKING THROUGH DATA SCIENCE

The arrival of the digital civilization wave has taken us from 'Internet Plus' to 'Intelligence Plus' and from traditional economy to digital economy. We are all set for a rapidly changing, upgrading age. While many talked about changes, few delved into the fundamental causes behind the cognitive revolution that propelled civilization's progression.

In the past, mathematics was a tool to understand the world. From Pythagoras to Isaac Newton, philosophers and scientists continually refined our mathematical systems. Enter the digital age, with data science offering us new insights that make a seamlessly connected and interactive world possible, further disrupting our cognition. This cognition has equipped us with systematic, holistic and true world views, bringing us closer to the essence of the world.

Data science has already brought new ways of thinking and a new perspective on data management. It made us realize that the advent of digital civilization has changed the world. And the disruption has only just begun. What cognitive change will the surging metaverse bring to humanity? This is something we could all benefit from contemplating.

2.1 THE POWER OF COGNITION

HUMAN EVOLUTION IS A SERIES OF COGNITIVE REVOLUTIONS

From apes to humans, standing upright to venturing into space, humans have experienced a tumultuous evolutionary journey, ultimately reaching the top of Earth's biological chain. Throughout the epic evolutionary process, humans gradually advanced towards higher civilizations as cognition was continuously disrupted and upgraded.

Cognition refers to the way we perceive and comprehend the world. For instance, in the early stages of limited mobility, people created world views based on what they saw. When they observed that the ground was flat, they believed the entire Earth was flat, covered by the inverted-cauldron sky coined by the Chinese idiom "the Earth was square, and Heaven was round." Later, people observed that celestial bodies seemingly revolved around the Earth, concluding that the Earth was the centre of the universe, or a "geocentric model." At that time, almost everyone believed this to be the true nature of the world. Today, it is common knowledge to even an elementary school student that the Earth is round and is a tiny standalone planet in our vast universe. This is a contemporary understanding of the world.

The inaugural leap of human society began in the 18th century. The two industrial revolutions have transitioned human society from agrarian civilization to industrial civilization, bringing leaps and bounds of societal productivity and drastic changes in our ways of life. As we enjoyed the conveniences brought by industrial civilization, our cognition of the world was also elevated. What cognitive changes will result from industrial civilization to digital civilization?

To answer this question, we need to go back to the beginning of human cognitive evolution to understand how humans have explored everything about themselves and related to the world.

Thanks to scientific thinking, modern society has aptly grasped the laws that govern the world and mathematical reasoning. Earth rotating from west to east, tides were caused by the gravitational force of the moon. Lunar eclipses are common knowledge today, but back then were perplexing phenomena – the omnipotent gods were imagined to rule over everything in the world. It was believed that the world was created by God, and humans were created by Nüwa; floods during the harvest season were caused by the anger of the gods, and diseases were the doom for offending the deities. Anything that could not be obtained required prayers to the gods and obedience to fate. For a long time, the deity-worshiping mind-set dominated human civilization.

Eventually, these mythical legends were questioned by some intellects. As the British writer Oscar Wilde said, "We are all in the gutter, but some of us are looking at the stars." Thales, known as the father of science and philosophy, was one of them. He believed that natural phenomena should not be explained by supernatural factors and attempted to explain the world through experience and rational thinking. He studied astronomy, identified Ursa Minor, measured the height of the pyramids using shadows cast by sunlight, and accurately predicted a solar eclipse that occurred in 585 BC. He also proposed the idea that everything originates from water, suggesting that the Earth was just a floating ball on water. Although not accurate, this viewpoint was far more advanced than the primitive cosmology of Thales' time, around 500 BC.

Thales was the first person to approach the natural world with rational thinking and a scientific spirit. Fifty years later, Pythagoras took it a step further. Known as the "father of mathematics," he proposed a mathematical system. Believing that the world follows mathematical laws, he revealed the relationship between numbers and the laws of things. He began to explore the mysteries of nature through mathematics, also known as the language of science. Pythagoras' ideas profoundly influenced later generations of thinkers. Among them was one of the most influential: Aristotle.

One of Aristotle's major contributions was treating nature as a scientific research objective from which natural and social sciences gradually branched into many subjects. Aristotle also proposed the First Principles, identified the three elements of scientific development, and pioneered an analytic methodology based on observation and reasoning, using qualitative methods instead of the quantitative ones we use today. He also emphasized logical reasoning and the rigorous use of mathematics, which formed the bedrock for many scientific developments.

Aristotle's thinking is a watershed moment in the history of science, dominating the views on nature during the Middle Ages until 1900 years later, when the scientist Galileo introduced science experimentation. Galileo's experiments were quantitative, the most renowned being the Leaning Tower of Pisa experiment. His conclusion that any two objects fall to the ground simultaneously overturned Aristotle's theory that "the speed of falling objects is proportional to their weight." This quantitative method opened up a new world.

In 1687, the groundbreaking scientist Newton used an apple to usher in a new era of science. He published *Mathematical Principles of Natural Philosophy*, which elucidated the concept of universal gravitation and the three fundamental laws of motion. Newton's laws allowed people to uncover the fundamental laws of the physical world. It is no exaggeration to say that Newton's laws explain everything we observe in the universe. After 2000 years of development, quantitative views of nature finally superseded Aristotle's qualitative views of nature. Today, Newton's theory is still widely applied in civil engineering, mechanics, hydraulics, and transportation, as well as cutting-edge technologies like aviation, space launches and interstellar exploration, leaving a lasting impact on social and science development.

Newton's transcendent achievements over his predecessors made the 18th century French mathematician Laplace exclaim that Newton was the luckiest because he found the only law that existed in the entire universe. The physics system constructed by Newton was once considered the only criterion to understand the world, capable of explaining all natural phenomena. Many even believed that physics no longer needed further additions. Among them was University of Munich's Head of Physics, who advised students in 1875 not to choose physics anymore because "this branch of knowledge is about to be matured."

Nonetheless, when the understanding of the world was deepened beyond the reach of a microscope, classical physics could no longer be applied. Atoms were too small to see and touch and were left to physicists' imagination. Such cognition went beyond human sensory experience, and we began to accept the existence of the invisible world. Scientific theories like quantum mechanics seemed gobbledygook because they described a world which can't be experienced. Quantum theory became a key to a new realm of human cognition.

In the early 20th century, scientists such as Planck, Einstein, Bohr, and Heisenberg initiated and refined quantum mechanics, and explored the structure, motion, and pattern of change in the microscopic world. They found a better explanation for the world through the lens of quantum mechanics: the world was distinctively different from that in our eyes. The universe was not singular but multiple; the world was complex, chaotic and permanent in its impermanence, so much so that qualitative changes caused by quantitative changes could not be totally predicted. The world is interlocked, as opposed to a true-false dichotomy, and does not exist in an objective space of time spanning past, present and future; rather, time is a man-made illusion.

The advent of quantum mechanics marked a major human progression in the 20th century, leading to the inventions of telephones, Magnetic Resonance Imaging, microwave ovens, and fluorescent lights. The studies of semiconductors were also founded on the principles and effects of quantum mechanics, ultimately leading to the invention of diodes and triodes that became a cornerstone for the modern electronics industry.

From the dominance of gods to applying observation and reasoning to explain natural phenomena, from qualitative views of nature to quantitative experimental methods, from Newton's three fundamental laws of motion to quantum mechanics, through one cognitive disruption after another, we have gained holistic and true worldviews. Cognitive revolutions propelled human progression. In return, human progression engendered technological advancements that elevated the methodology and tools of the cognitive revolutions. Nevertheless, the cognitive revolution remains the most fundamental driving force.

Looking back, the arduous trudge and scientific exploration across millions of years of human history are an awe-inspiring journey. The early humans who lived in caves and fed on wild animals crafted rough stone axes and weapons made from bone. Homo sapiens returning from a hunt carefully struck flint or fired sticks to cook their gains. People snapped tree branches to draw simple images of cattle and sheep on the ground, euphorically communicating these symbols to their clansmen. Our ancestors ascended human civilization firmly and stoically.

Ships drifting in oceans for months returned to Europe having discovered new continents. Steam locomotives slowly departed in low humming whistles, carrying people towards distant horizons. The first generation of computers carried out precise calculations under human instruction. Our predecessors entered the digital civilization with acceleration.

Civilization evolution or cognition disruption in any age is the fruit of prolonged cumulative progress. The digital age we live in is inseparable from the centuries-long cognitive evolution in human history, as well as science systems and technologies created by past sages with diligence and sacrifice. Only by standing on the shoulders of these giants can we gaze at the starry sky. The cognitive disruption and progression is the necessity of the progress in the digital age, as well as a historic mission that we must undertake.

BOUNDLESS COGNITION LED BY CONSTANT DISRUPTION

The knowledge acquired by our predecessors through relentless exploration has been passed down as a collective memory. Later generations inherit the knowledge to make discoveries and invent new technologies. In a way, the cognition in any era is at its apex of all time. Today, the scientific knowledge possessed by a junior secondary school student may far surpass that of the greatest scientists of the 17th century. Yet we may appear incredibly ignorant in the eyes of people a hundred years from now.

It is nothing shameful. Even the greatest science giants in history were bound by self-limitations.

Isaac Newton, one of the most iconic scientists in history and a prominent figure who ushered in the scientific era, was also a devout believer in theology. It was believed that Newton became obsessed with theology in his later years. In actuality, Newton was a devout but unorthodox Christian. According to historical records, from 1687 until his death in 1727, Newton devoted significant time and energy to the study of alchemy and biblical chronology. Newton's legacy is not confined to the history-defining three laws of motion, the law of universal gravitation, calculus, and optics; rather, he left behind millions of words of theological and alchemical notes.

Einstein, another great scientist, shared Newton's belief that the universal laws were the creation of God, who governed the celestial bodies' trajectories.

A reflection of Einstein's limitations lies in his series of renowned debates with Bohr about quantum physics. Einstein did not accept the new quantum theory based on "uncertainty" and "probability," advocated by the Copenhagen School led by Niels Bohr, and considered it a "wrong path." Einstein believed in classical philosophical thinking and the principle of causality. In his view, a complete physical theory should possess determinism, realism, and locality, as opposed to Heisenberg's uncertainty principle that violated determinism. For this, Einstein said a famous remark that is widely referenced today: "God does not play dice."

In later life, Einstein devoted himself to the finding of a unified theory that could explain all interactions, attempting to reconcile macroscopic relativity with microscopic quantum mechanics, even if it meant refuting his theory of relativity. This pursuit continued until he died in 1955.

Lao Tzu[1] said, "The Tao (道) that can be told of is not the Absolute Tao. The Names that can be given are not Absolute Names." This statement highlights the limitations of human cognition. The Tao is something that can never be fully grasped based on our current level of understanding. What humans comprehend at a certain stage is merely a provisional conclusion, referred to as the Li (理). As technologies advance, our cognitive capabilities will improve and this Li will strengthen and deepen, but we will never reach the eternal truth of Tao.

Recognizing the limitations of human thinking is the starting point for self-transcendence and cognition reconstruction.

History told us that humans always believed they had found the truth, only to realize that these truths could change or be completely overturned. For example, Copernicus revealed that the Earth we inhabited was not the centre of the universe but rather a speck in the universe. Darwin showed us that humans had evolved from other species so were not much different to other animals. Freud made us aware that our consciousness did not have complete control over the many unconscious behaviours we engaged in every day.

In facing every major change, humans courageously broke out of the thought limitations and expanded the cognitive boundaries, achieving a quantum leap in capabilities. Whether it is the invention of quantum computers, a grandiose infrastructure project, or relentless exploration into the universe, they are all salient testaments.

Today, digital civilization is rapidly transforming us. Technology development is no longer a linear progression. Rather, it is a progressive, leapfrogging, and explosive progress from which cognitive disruption inevitably ensues to shake up our thinking and behaviour.

The father of modern management, Peter Drucker, once said, "The greatest danger in times of turbulence is not the turbulence itself, but to act with yesterday's logic."[2] In this new era, we must proactively break free from the inertia and limitations of our thinking. We can't simply rely on past approaches, experiences, and logic for our future growth. Instead, we must embrace the digital age, reconstruct our thinking systems, achieve cognitive upgrades, and renew ourselves through continued iterations.

2.2 **THE WORLD IS DIGITAL**

FROM PYTHAGORAS TO NEWTON

Long before the digital age, mathematics had been an important tool for understanding the world and was the bedrock of scientific thinking. Mathematics is a cognitive system derived from initial assumptions and logical reasoning, and a formidable force for driving technological development and human progression.

Through millions of years of trailblazing and stumbling, our ancestors have made remarkable scientific achievements, but in the beginning, a lack of carrier meant that those brilliant scientific ideas could not be preserved and passed on. For a long time, later generations were unable to advance the scientific development built by their predecessors.

Pythagoras did find a carrier for the brilliant ideas: mathematics. He believed that a supreme force governed the entire universe by mathematical principles. Nothing was as rigorous, perfect, and harmonious as mathematics. A hundred years later, Plato inherited Pythagoras' ideas and took them a step further, claiming that mathematical concepts are innate and a priori, and it is between the sentimental and theoretical world, and is the only path to the theoretical world. Since then, both science and philosophy have been inseparable from mathematics.

Two thousand years later, when Newton astonishingly emerged and profoundly introduced universal gravitation, a concise yet captivating formula that explained the laws of celestial bodies' movements and why humans stood between heaven and Earth, people fully grasped the power of mathematics. With the power of mathematics, science began to thrive and the progress of human civilization accelerated.

Fast forward to modern days, and a plethora of achievements in natural sciences emerged rapidly. From Einstein's theory of relativity to Heisenberg's uncertainty principle, from Mendeleev's periodic table of elements to Mendel's theory of genetics, from computer to nuclear energy application, these achievements would not have been possible without the essential tool of mathematics.

During the first industrial revolution, James Watt improved the steam engine by leveraging the rapidly developing mathematics and calculus to calculate the correlation of the output power of the steam engine, the steam pressure in the boiler, and the angle of the connecting rod. As a result, internal combustion engines and electricity became hugely popular, leading to great inventions such as automobiles and electric lights. To some extent, mathematics hoisted human civilization.

In the 21st century, mathematics and computers have been closely integrated, unleashing tremendous power in breeding tech titans like Apple, Google, Amazon, Alibaba, and Tencent. These companies have quickly and successfully leveraged tools of mathematics and computers to amass a trillion-dollar market.

Throughout human development, tools have also constantly evolved. From stone to bronze, iron, gunpowder, steam engines, internal combustion engines, telegraphs, telephones, televisions, computers, satellites, the internet, the evolution of tools spurred the evolution of civilization. New tools constantly superseded old ones, just as vaiours video apps such as YouTube superseded television, and WhatsApp Messenger superseded text messages, and so on.

Each tool embodied human understanding and exploration of the world. The steam engine and internal combustion engine signified the development of mechanics. Behind telegraphs, telephones, televisions, computers, and the internet lay the informatization revolution. Mathematics is a tool for abstraction and a tool for many other tools. Mathematics is a key to the world of science and truth, empowering humans to break away from the perceived physical laws, to think further and closer to the truth.

Mathematics is also a language emerging from the tangible world and transcending it. It is seemingly irrelevant to physics, chemistry, economics, and culture, yet it can encapsulate the entirety of existence. As Galileo sad, "The universe is a grand book that records all knowledge and wisdom, available for humans to read at any time. However, only those who understand the language of the book can comprehend its mysteries, and this grand work is precisely written in the language of mathematcs." Similarly, as Richard Feynman sad, "To those who do not know mathematics, it is difficult to get across a real feeling as to the beauty of nature ... If you want to learn about nature, to appreciate nature, it is necessary to understand the language that she speaks in."

Throughout the ages, mathematics accelerated social and technological progress and advanced human civilization. I believe that the application of mathematics will not end in the digital age. Mathematics will continue to demonstrate its prowess in scientific and technological research, cultural studies, and the research of economic theories. Mathematics will prompt us to excel, achieving a greater societal and human civilization.

Nonetheless, mathematical analysis focuses on the quantitative relationships and spatial forms in the real world. In the digital age, digitalization expanded the possibilities of space, taking us from two-dimensional and three-dimensional physical spaces to online virtual spaces, which inevitably altered our spatial cognition. Mathematics as a cognitive tool started to show its limitations, and data science emerged to reconstruct our cognitive system.

DATA SCIENCE UNIFYING THE WORLD ANEW

As the technological revolution deepens, particularly in digitalization and networking technologies, through creative activities using computing technologies, humans cultivated an entirely new domain on the internet: cyberspace.

In the past, we only owned the physical space we inhabited. The advent of cyberspace enlarged our activity space. As cyberspace rapidly assimilates into production, consumption, and cultural systems, people's lifestyles and ways of thinking have transformed. Among them is a cognitive shift from mathematics to data science.

The leap to the digital civilization from the industrial civilization also instigated a shift in the value of social resources. In the industrial age, the most valuable resources were energy and raw materials; oil was deemed the highly sought after "lifeblood" of industries. But in the digital age, data became a novel factor of production, dubbed the "new oil" of the digital age.

To some extent, the history of human development is a continual process of data generation and data accumulation. We can even claim that the scale of data indicates the level of human civilization and socio-economic development.

From ancient counting methods using stones and sticks, and record-keeping by tying knots, to the modern big data technologies, the means of data acquisition, data recording and storage ballooned, and the volume of data grew exponentially. The Library of Alexandria in 300 BC collected all the books in the world. However, if we were to equally distribute all the information available in the world today, each person's share of information would far exceed the knowledge contained in the entire collection of the Library of Alexandria. As another example, each smartphone can generate 1GB of data in a single day, which is roughly equivalent to the size of 13 sets of electronic files of *The Twenty-Four Histories*.[3]

During the digital age, data become tightly intertwined with our lives. Every action we take on the internet, from browsing news, to online learning, shopping, and entertainment, generates data, and smartphones and various smart home devices silently collect it. We are marking our life-history by using data every day. However, unlike traditional data records, these data records have a life of their own. To some extent, they are an extension of ourselves, forming a 'virtual me' in cyberspace in the form of data. Internet companies gain deep insights into us by analysing this data.

We are also consumers of data. Digital consumption has become the foremost expenditure today. Over the past 20 years, the scale of internet users in China has undergone a tremendous transformation. In 2000, the number of netizens in the country was 16.9 million, and by June 2023 this figure had soared to 1.079 billion. The average weekly internet usage time per person also increased from approximately 16.4 hours to 29.1 hours. This means that every day each of us spends roughly four hours online. Whether we are using payment methods, hailing a ride, taking high-speed trains, or purchasing airline tickets, data traffic charges are involved. Digital consumption during the purchasing process has become an integral part of everyone's daily life.

Changes on the supply side reflect a similar trend. In the 1990s, the top ten companies by global market value were those in the traditional businesses such as General Electric, Walmart, ExxonMobil, and only IBM stood out as the only representative of high-tech companies.

By the early 2010s, high-tech companies such as Apple, Microsoft, and Google rose with astonishing speed and were regularly listed. As the wheel of time turns to the present, the proportion of high-tech companies continues to rise. Taking PricewaterhouseCoopers' (PwC) "Global Top 100 Companies 2023," which ranks global, publicly listed companies by their market capitalization as of March 31, 2023, as an example, the top ten companies are Apple, Microsoft, Saudi Aramco, Alphabet (Google's parent company), Amazon, Nvidia, Berkshire Hathaway, Tesla, Meta (Facebook's parent company), and Visa, with 70% of them being high-tech companies.

It was once joked that: "Perhaps in future meetings, we won't ask how much assets and capital you own, but ask how much data you have. When evaluating the strength of a company, we won't just consider its technology and business model, but also the amount of data it posesses." This is no longer a joke. As we entered the digital age, the prowess of data became prominent. The plethora of big data is unleashing immense value and is pervasive in economic activities covering production, distribution, exchange, and consumption, catalysing across diverse sectors of socio- and economic development.

At the same time, data-related technologies are also flourishing, spanning across data collection, transmission, integration, fusion, storage, processing, analysis, application, visualization, security, and data rights. Subsequently, data science as a new knowledge system emerged, integrating mathematics, computer science, software engineering, statistics, engineering, informatization, and other related disciplines, as shown in Figure 2.1.

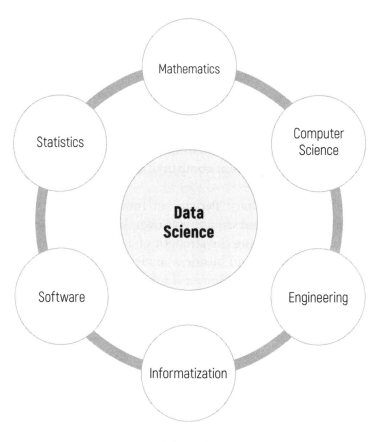

FIGURE 2.1
DATA SCIENCE: MULTI-DISCIPLINE INTEGRATED KNOWLEDGE SYSTEM

Data science is not purely theoretical mathematics or purely applied mathematics. It is a knowledge system that specializes in the study of data itself. It can be seen as an extension and upgrade of traditional statistics, aiming to explain the underlying rules behind various phenomena presented by data.

In trying to understand what the world is made of, early sages proposed many concepts. Some said the world constituted five key elements: gold, wood, water, fire, and earth. Some said it was made up of particles, while others believed it was composed of numbers. Newton believed that the world consisted of absolute and relative space-time, with absolute space-time being unrelated to human cognition, while relative space-time being closely related to humans. The ideal tool for defining relative space-time is numbers. Both mathematics and data science are number-related cognitive tools. In this sense, the world is made of numbers.

Knowing this, we realize that our understanding of the world is dictated by our cognition and application of numbers. Data science is growing more sophisticated with the advancement of digitalization technology. The digitization process guided by data science is also deepening our understanding of the world, which inevitably leads to cognitive disruption.

Speaking of which, we must re-emphasize the great contribution of mathematics to humanity. From Pythagoras to Newton, people gradually became accustomed to explaining various phenomena using mathematical methods. The evolution from simple units to systems, to uncertain systems, and then to complex and uncertain systems, constantly disrupted and elevated human cognition. These mathematical methods prepared us with a mind-set for understanding the world in the big data age. Without this solid foundation built by mathematics, data science would probably have difficulty fulfilling its role.

Just as astronomical telescopes allow us to glimpse the vast and mysterious universe, and microscopes enable us to observe marvellous microorganisms, data science, based on the collection and analysis of massive data, offers us a new perspective to comprehend the world and revolutionize traditional human cognition and methodologies of understanding.

Many phenomena and systems in real life are living, evolving, random, and too complex to be explained by simplified theories. This is where data science becomes pertinent. We can simulate complex systems by constructing various computer models, superimposing them, importing various relevant variables, and then deduce and predict using simulation. For example, earthquake prediction and weather forecasting are the typical data science applications. Data science is a comprehensive knowledge system that, in a way, resembles great wisdom.

Data flows like water, ceaselessly streaming and merging without boundaries; data stands like a mountain, precise and accurate, rational and dependable. Literally everything in the digital age can be expressed by structured data, and it can be connected through structured data interaction. In other words, data science can make the interconnectivity of everything and panoramic interaction a reality.

Rather than simple, boring symbols, data becomes a driving force for a closer, more vivid, and smarter world.

Data science is not as mysterious to fathom and complex to apply as many imagine. It is close to our lives, and everyone can benefit from it. By mastering the tool of data science we can better understand the world and anticipate trends. We often cannot see, go quick and far in the dark, but data science equips us with a vision of the essence of the world in darkness.

In the transition from the industrial age to the digital age, many things underwent fundamental changes through the lens of data science. Mobile phones as communication tools became mobile terminals for shopping, entertainment, and online working; cars as transportation means became mobile scenes and mobile living spaces. In the industrial age, products were just products with decreasing marginal utility. In the digital age, however, products are not purely functional but possible intellectual property (IP) imbued with personality and emotions. Such products can interact and grow with consumers, thereby possibly increasing marginal utility. In the industrial age, enterprises were commercial organizations that provided products and services, and the relationships of enterprises, employees, customers, and partners were one-way and linear. However, in the digital age, enterprises experiencing radical and disruptive change gradually evolved into platforms that incubate industrial IP and cultivate industrial ecosystems. The relationships among enterprises, employees, customers, and partners become two-way, nonlinear, and collaborative.

In the industrial age, the world was siloed by design. In the digital age, data science reunited the world, bringing us closer to its essence with a more systematic, holistic, and accurate understanding.

THE UNCHANGING, UNDERLYING LOGIC: FIRST PRINCIPLES

As the ancient Greek philosopher Heraclitus said, "All is flux," and, "You cannot step into the same river twice, for new waters are constantly flowing past you." In essence, the only thing that remains unchanged in the world is the change itself.

Everything is impermanent, and that includes human evolution, civilization progression, the rise and fall of nations, enterprise development, and the inevitable cognitive evolution from mathematics to data science.

Yet one important law in physics, the Law of Conservation of Energy, states that energy neither appears nor disappears. It only transforms from one form to another, or transfers from one object to another, while the total amount of energy remains constant. Therefore, when kinetic energy disappears, it may have transformed into potential energy; when potential energy disappears, it may have transformed into thermal energy.

Energy is varied and dynamic in form, and it exists in perpetual flux, but its total quantity remains constant and enduring. It is evident that all changes stem from the unchanging, and the unchanging is the most fundamental aspect behind change.

But what is the invisible hand that governs the myriad changes?

From the industrial age to the digital age, from leaps and bounds of our civilization to the cognitive revolutions, one thing that has remained constant is the underlying logic, or First Principles.

Aristotle, the ancient Greek philosopher who lived in the same period as Confucius, had many propositions that profoundly impacted humanity. Two thousand years ago, he defined First Principles as the "fundamental principles by which things are known." He stated that for every system's exploration, there exists First Principles – foundational propositions or assumptions that cannot be overlooked, omitted, or violated.

In simple terms, First Principles tell us that everything has a primary essence, from which everything develops. Whether it is the foundation of a nation, the vision of a company, or the aspirations of an individual, First Principles directly address the essence of things. To solve problems, we must see through phenomena to the core, dissect problems into their basic components, and seek solutions from the primary essence.

The entrepreneur Elon Musk is an exemplar of innovation and disruption. He launched tens of thousands of satellites into space to form the Starlink constellation, creating a global space communication system. He invested heavily in rocket development and successfully launched them. He introduced the disruptive product Tesla, which redefined the concept of automobiles. When asked for the secret to his success, he summed it up as "First Principles." He once said, "By using First Principles, I trace things to their fundamental truths and reason from here ..." It is crucial to apply First Principles rather than using comparative thinking. In life, we tend to compare and do what others have already done or are doing, which only leads to incremental development. The thinking approach of First Principles is to view the world from a physics perspective, peel away the layers of appearances to see the underlying essence, and then move upwards layer by layer. This requires a great deal of mental effort.

In 2002, Musk embarked on his space exploration journey and set a goal for himself: to send rockets to Mars. To achieve this goal, Musk visited aerospace manufacturers worldwide in search of suitable part-ners. However, he found that buying the ready-made launch vehicle would cost as much as $65 million. Due to the high cost, Musk began to rethink how to address this problem.

He started reasoning from First Principles. When he thought about the problem from the essence of things, he realized that a rocket is essentially an industrial product made of aerospace-grade aluminium alloys, titanium, copper, carbon fibre, and other materials. He calcu-lated the cost of all the materials used in rocket manufacturing and found that compared to the selling price of a rocket, this cost was neg-ligible. At this point, he had a somewhat unconventional idea in the eyes of others: to purchase inexpensive raw materials and manufacture a rocket himself.

Then, Musk founded the now well-known company SpaceX. By applying First Principles, Musk traced the problem he faced back to its fundamental question, and found effective solutions.

As an entrepreneur, no matter what challenges he encountered, Musk always applied First Principles thinking. When Tesla was in the early stages of developing electric vehicles, the high cost of batteries became a problem that seemed impossible to overcome. At that time, the price of energy storage batteries was $600 per kilowatt-hour, and the price of an 85-kilowatt-hour battery would exceed $50,000.

However, Musk firmly believed that there must be a solution to this problem. He began to think from the essence: What materials are batteries made of? What is the market price of these materials? He discovered that if Tesla purchased raw materials from the London Metal Exchange and produced batteries themselves, the cost would be only $80 per kilowatt-hour. As a result, Tesla established its battery factory, significantly reducing costs after production.

A building is most stable when constructed on First Principles. In the digital age, our cognition is ever-changing or even disrupted, but the underlying logic remains unchanged. The digital age is an era of data explosion filled with a myriad of chaotic, unstructured data and information. But by following First Principles and utilizing data science to unravel the layers of haze, we can see the essence under the surface. By possessing a steadfast soul, firm beliefs, and a long-term mind-set, we can hold on to the fundamentals in this ever-changing digital age.

2.3 A REAPPRAISAL OF DATA AND ITS GOVERNANCE

THE NEW ATTRIBUTES OF DATA: FACTORS OF PRODUCTION AND ASSETS

Data did not emerge in the digital age; rather, it was rediscovered during this era. Can our past understanding of data meet the demands? The answer is unequivocally negative. We must reconceptualize data based on data science and First Principles, and establish a novel digital mind-set.

Data is a topic on everyone's lips, but what exactly is it? We must have a clear understanding of the definition and concept of data to better comprehend its value and impact on individuals, businesses, and society.

There are numerous definitions of data: The Data Management Association International (DAMA) views data as a representation of facts in formats such as text, numbers, graphics, images, sound, and video; the Data Element White Paper released by the China Academy of Information and Communications Technology in 2022 considers data to be a record of facts/activities and other phenomena; the International Organization for Standardization (ISO) define data as "information represented in a formal manner suitable for communication, interpretation, or processing." Data is a symbolic description with a rich and diverse range of expressions: it can be a string of numbers, a video, a piece of text, an image, or a myriad of other media.

With the advent of the digital age, data has been endowed with two new attributes: one as a factor of production and the other as an asset.

Productive forces, composing of factors of production, provide a fundamental driving force for the economy and society's development. Factors of production are the necessary resources for conducting social production and business activities: in layman's terms, without them, production cannot proceed, and economic development would be severely impacted. In the traditional economy, land, labour, capital, and technology are all critical factors of production but, in the digital age, data is a new critical factor of production.

Being a new type of factor of production, data not only participates in various aspects of social production, playing a significant role in driving the development of productivity and improving social efficiency, but also promotes the digital transformation of traditional factors of production such as land, labour, capital, and technology, thereby empowering the transformation and upgrading of traditional industries. Data is not only a factor of production but also a new asset. In accounting, assets are defined as the resources formed through past transactions or events, owned or controlled by the enterprise, and anticipated to yield economic benefits. Land, factories and capital are all assets. In the digital age, data is also an asset. Our personal information and the experience and knowledge formed during our lives, studies, and work are presented in the form of data, which are essentially our assets, providing vital support and continuous momentum for our survival and development.

Companies generate vast amounts of data in the process of production, operation and management, such as business system data, management data, process data, data in contracts, and patents. These datasets have become important strategic assets for enterprises, contributing to enterprises' sustainable development and forming a crucial competitive edge. It can even be said that the amount of valuable data an enterprise possesses directly determines its market position. Companies like Apple, Google, and Tencent have world-leading competitive advantages precisely because they own and control unimaginable amounts of data.

Data has gradually permeated every aspect of any country's socioeconomic fabric. In particular, sensitive data in politics, economics, diplomacy, military, science, and technology, and biology profoundly affect economic development, national security, and social stability. Therefore, data is both a fundamental strategic resource for a country and a core asset that must be possessed. Take China as an example. In August 2023, the Ministry of Finance officially released the "Interim Provisions on Accounting Treatment of Enterprise Data Resources,"[4] which stipulate that data used internally by enterprises that meet the criteria for intangible assets can be defined as intangible assets; data owned or held for the ultimate purpose of sale in the ordinary course of business, if they meet relevant regulations, can also be recognized as inventory, that is, data assets can be recognized as inventory. These provisions will come into effect on January 1, 2024, meaning that, from 2024, data elements will be officially included in the balance sheet.

Data scientist and authoritative expert Viktor Mayer-Schönberger, in collaboration with Kenneth Cukier in their co-authored work *Big Data: A Revolution That Will Transform How We Live, Work, and Think*, stated, "Although big data has not yet been listed on the balance sheets of businesses, it is only a matter of time." Today, this prediction has become a reality.

The inclusion of data on balance sheets represents a groundbreaking milestone, signifying that data has evolved from a natural resource to an economic asset, and it will become a crucial pillar for government and corporate reporting, as well as fiscal revenue in the future. This transition is an inevitable outcome of societal progress and is poised to exert a profound influence on the development of future societies.

Once data asset is included in the balance sheet, its significance to enterprises necessarily increases. So, where do a company's data assets originate?

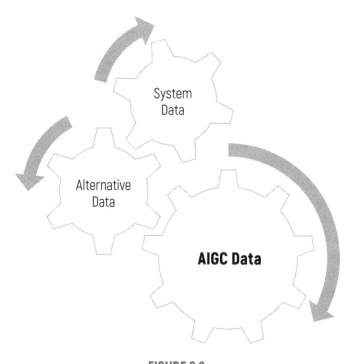

FIGURE 2.2
SOURCE OF ENTERPRISE DATA ASSETS

Traditionally, a company's data comprises two segments: first, system data, such as data automatically collected and generated by financial, sales, ERP, and production systems; second, alternative data, which is supplementary information required to fully depict a scenario, not generated by systems but acquired externally. For instance, the financial sector often needs to augment traditional financial data with non-financial valuable information that aids investors in making investment decisions when constructing marketing or risk-control models. Historically, companies have innovated in product, service, and business process development by leveraging systems data and alternative data. For example, banks would gather and analyse various financial data, aligning it with clients' risk preferences and asset holdings to continuously offer suitable new products. The advent of AIGC (Artificial Intelligence Generated Content) has introduced a third type of new data, namely, data generated by artificial intelligence.

Every strategy a company formulates is fundamentally aimed at innovation. Economist Joseph Alois Schumpeter described innovation as "establishing a new production function," i.e. "recombination of factors of production," which entails introducing a "new combination" of factors of production and conditions into the production system. According to Schumpeter's perspective, business innovation was previously understood as the reconfiguration of products and services. However, in the digital age, as data becomes a crucial factor of production, innovation has transformed into the reconfiguration of data elements.

AIGC has accelerated the reconfiguration process of data elements, as well as the speed at which businesses gain insights into their customers, operations, and products, thereby hastening business innovation. AIGC can fully leverage system data and alternative data, which autonomously generates more data, leading to new perceptions and, consequently, the creation of novel products and services. If data accumulation in the past was measured in years or months, with AIGC, it is now measured in minutes and seconds. Thus, AIGC represents a significant revolution in the digital economy. The tight integration of AIGC and data assets enables businesses to accumulate data assets at a much faster pace.

The continuous accumulation of AIGC data benefits from the use of general purpose large-scale models. These models contribute new data every second, seemingly propelling the accumulation of corporate assets into a perpetual motion era. However, relying solely on general purpose large-scale models is insufficient, as those models are akin to a high school student possessing basic knowledge and intelligence but lacking specialization, which preventing the models from sharing professional expertise. To maximize AIGC's role in specialized domains, it requires a tool – knowledge graph management. By continuously training large language models through knowledge graphs, they can become experts in specific fields.

Over the past few years, Digital China Group has been dedicated to researching industry knowledge domains and has developed a platform for constructing knowledge graphs across various industries – it's called SmartVision (Shen Zhou Wen Xue in Chinese). I created this name with the vision that "A teacher is one who answers questions and solves doubts." As we should consider AI (artificial intelligence) as our teacher, the SmartVision platform continuously accumulates knowledge by asking questions of the large language model. The professional knowledge accumulated finally becomes the data assets of each enterprise, supporting them in accelerating innovation through Generative AI, by lowering the development entry barriers and cost.

SmartVision distinguishes itself from other platforms by providing enterprises with the capability to connect models, computing power, data and applications. It serves as a one-stop operational platform for large language models, offering comprehensive, multi-level platform capabilities. It enables the integrated invocation of computing resources, the integrated invocation of large language models, data/corpus governance and knowledge management, rapid low-code application construction, as well as effectively addressing numerous issues such as large language model security, application scenarios innovation, data and corpus issues, agile AI application development, unified model management, and the continuous release and management of models and applications. In short, SmartVision allows enterprises to quickly integrate their business needs with large-scale model technology to achieve intelligent business operations.

SmartVision demonstrates excellent results when used in the enterprise real-life environment. Take, for example, a multinational medical equipment company: traditional FDA certification typically requires six revisions and ten months of repeated communication with third-party agencies. However, with SmartVision, this time can be reduced to one month. Behind this, SmartVision enables AIGC to relearn all the historical declaration materials and even the regulator officers' approval preferences, allowing the company to pass at the first attempt.

The value of data lies not only in its magnitude but also in its scientific and effective governance and use, which is our fundamental starting point for re-understanding data. Only by acknowledging the attributes of data as both a factor of production and an asset can enterprises continuously accumulate data assets, activate the value of data, and seize the opportunities brought by a new round of technological revolutions and industrial transformations.

WHO TRULY OWNS THE DATA?

Data is mined and utilized, distinct from the traditional factors of production such as land, labour, capital, technology etc., its economic value far exceeds them. As Viktor Mayer-Schönberger has said, "Data is like a magical diamond mine that keeps on giving long after its principal value has been tapped. Data's true value is like an iceberg floating in the ocean. Only a tiny part of it is visible at first sight, while much of it is hidden beneath the surface."[5] To better utilize data and tap into its value, a scientific and efficient approach to data management must be acquired. As technologies of artificial intelligence, blockchain, and cloud-native advance, the old rules of data application and management will be overturned, and new rules will emerge.

Understanding the new rules of data management begins with data rights.

The story of former U.S. President Trump fully illustrates the significance of data rights.

In the 2016 U.S. presidential election, Donald Trump unexpectedly defeated the favourite presidential candidate Hillary Clinton and was elected as the new President of the United States. The world was aghast. When some dug deep into the story behind the scenes, a company hidden behind Trump called Cambridge Analytica gradually emerged.

Cambridge Analytica is a data company that collects and analyses data from the internet and provides data insights to companies. In the 2016 U.S. presidential election, Cambridge Analytica used the data of 50 million (Facebook admitted ex post facto it was 87 million) users stolen from Facebook to conduct a targeted marketing campaign, pushing Trump's political advertisements to target voters on Facebook, contributing to Trump's winning of the U.S. presidency.

What Cambridge Analytica did during the presidential election confirmed the concerns of David Carroll, an American scholar who has been closely watching the data breaches in society at large. In 2018, he came up with an idea: if personal data on Facebook is all in the hands of Cambridge Analytica, can individuals request the return of their data from the company?

In August 2018, Carroll sued Cambridge Analytica for the return of his personal data. He believed that data rights should be a fundamental respected right of individuals. David Carroll won his lawsuit in 2019, and the parent company of Cambridge Analytica, SCL Group, pleaded guilty.

In one interview, David Carroll raised a profound question: "What does it mean when we are treated as a commodity that can be mined?"

This inevitably makes us wonder: Who does data belong to? Who has the right to use it? How can privacy rights be protected?

Our behaviours are extensively recorded, generating a large quantity of data through frequent online activities. The fast-growing integration of digital industrialization and industrial digitization makes data a fundamental resource. The future development of the digital economy relies on orderly and secure data flow, making data rights a non-negligible essential right. Data rights confirmation became an immediate imperative.

Data rights confirmation refers to determining the rights holder of data, possession, usage, and benefits, as well as liability for privacy protection. Beijing Big Data Trading Service Platform defines 'data rights confirmation' as clarifying the responsibility, rights, and mutual relationships on trading data for both trading parties; protecting trading parties' respective legal rights and interests; providing guidelines on confirming data holders, data rights, data sources, acquisition time, utility period, data usage, data volume, data format, data granularity, nature of data industry, and data trading methods to ensure that data transactions are scientific and methodological, unified and secure.

The difficulty of data rights confirmation lies in its nature that is unique from tangible or intangible property rights.

For example, data comes in various types, and so do different data rights. Generally speaking, data can be categorized into three types based on the origin: government, commercial, and personal. Government data refers to data created or collected by government departments in the process of fulfilling their duties. Commercial data refers to data created or collected by commercial entities during their operations. Personal data refers to data that reveal personal information. Personal data may overlap with the first two types if they involve personal information, and such data should be classified as personal data. The scope of data rights differs for each. Despite the attributes of property rights that all three types possess, government data is generally considered a social public resource, so its notification, access and usage are granted to the general public. Commercial data rights include property rights, intellectual property rights, trade secret rights, and other rights relating to the legitimate interests of businesses. Because personal data rights also include property rights in addition to name rights and privacy rights, personality rights are also an important right associated with personal data. Data rights are not static. It can change as application scenarios evolve and give rise to new rights, which further complicates the pre-definition of rights ownership.

Furthermore, there are multiple participants in the data production process, each contributing to the value of data in its respective stage, and the rights must be divided among them. For tangible assets, rights confirmation is clear-cut. Whether it is a house, a car, a cup, or a chair, their property rights are well-defined. The ownership of products belongs exclusively to manufacturers at the production stage because the production process is irrelevant to consumers and is acquired by consumers through purchase once these products enter the market. However, the production process of data is entirely different. Online consumption produced a myriad of data. E-commerce platforms as data controllers utilize the data to serve their business, such as providing personalized product recommendations. Yet the production process of this data is not solely completed by the e-commerce platform – it only provides a platform where data is generated through users' actions like registration, browsing, subscribing, purchasing, and reviewing. The e-commerce platform and the users co-participate in and co-contribute to the production process of this data, presenting a challenge of confirming the data rights and usage rights.

Data rights confirmation for complex data interests is a conundrum we must confront in the digital age.

The government plays a crucial role in tackling this challenge. Now, governments worldwide are undergoing explorations for data governance.

In China, on August 31, 2015, the State Council issued the 'Action Plan for Promoting the Development of Big Data,' which clearly stated a series of ideas and measures to enforce market development mechanisms, such as a "guide to cultivate big data trading markets; conduct pilot projects for application-oriented data trading markets; explore the trading of big data derivative products; encourage data exchange and trading along the industrial chain; promote data resources circulation; establish sound data resource trading and pricing mechanisms and regulate trading behaviours." Driven by a collective effort of national policies, local governments, and industries, big data trading mechanisms were actively explored in many provinces and cities. The establishment of Guiyang Big Data Exchange, Donghu Big Data Trading Centre, Shanghai Data Trading Centre, Beijing International Big Data Exchange, and so on made significant contributions to data asset registration and rights confirmation, data asset integration, and the establishment of a credit assessment for data exchange.

In the United States, in 2016, the Federal Communications Commission (FCC) approved a consumer privacy protection rule that explicitly stated that consumers own the data generated on broadband internet, and broadband service providers must obtain consumer consent before using consumers' search history, software usage, location, and other personal data.

In 2017, the European Union released the 'Building a European Data Economy' report, which established data producer rights for anonymized data that are non-personal and computer-generated, prohibiting unauthorized use and access to such data.

In 2018, the European Union enacted the General Data Protection Regulation (GDPR), which stipulates that users have autonomous control over their relevant data and that data subjects have the right to request data controllers to delete their personal data and prevent its dissemination.

On December 15, 2020, the European Union announced two legislative proposals, the Digital Services Act and the Digital Markets Act, targeting data platforms and large technology companies. The Digital Services Act aims to govern platforms and protect the data rights of users within the platforms, while the Digital Markets Act focuses on platform competition to create a fair platform competition environment.

In the digital age, a country's data industry is inseparable from the country's economy, people's interests, and societal development.

Data rights confirmation is the absolute foundation of the entire data industry chain. Treating data as a commodity with an effective property rights confirmation will provide unequivocal institutional guarantees for data security, enable a standardized evaluation system for data property disputes, and unleash data's potential to innovate and promote socio-economic development.

ADDING A STRAITJACKET TO DATA SECURITY

In the digital age, all industries are accelerating digital transformation. Electricity, factories, parks, cities, transportation, and finance are growingly intertwined with data, resulting in an exponential growth in global data volume. According to the Data Age 2025 report by IDC, the global total data volume generated annually will grow from 33ZB in 2018 to 175ZB in 2025. Behind the gargantuan amount of data are the salient challenges of data security.

Frequent data breaches in recent years spoke volumes for the importance of data security. The Facebook data breach mentioned in the previous section was fined USD $5 billion by the U.S. government (equivalent to 9% of Facebook's annual revenue) for violating users' privacy rights. Alphabet, the parent company of Google, was fined €50 million for violating the E.U.'s GDPR in handling personal data. These substantial fines underscore the necessity and importance of data security.

Traditional security models mainly focus on networks and known threats, and face significant challenges when the IT focus of new digital enterprises pivots to business applications. These challenges include advanced persistent threats (APTs);[6] weak protection against zero-day vulnerabilities; inability to address internal threats due to changing network boundaries; and the ever-unattended human factor that became a key uncertain and influencing factor in the security system.

Data security is no longer limited to the prevention of destruction, tampering, and unauthorized use of data in the traditional information security realm. In the new era of data security, orderly flow, compliant use, and the secure integration of data are paramount in addition to the above objectives to maximize data insights and their value.

Data in silo has limited value and the digital-native era would end if there were concerns of data security risks.

The first practical criterion for a secure data flow and usage is often data masking. This criterion is common in most enterprises. The data discoverers and users do not need to know the sensitive parts of the data content; they only need to understand the overarching logical relationship of the dataset. When techniques are deployed to obfuscate the predetermined sensitive parts of the dataset, the value of the entire dataset can be fully realized without a loss. This presents a major obstacle to unleashing the data value before the data masking technique is available.

The TDMP (Tara Data Masking Platform)[7] system developed by Digital China Group exists to achieve this exact purpose for enterprise customers.

As with all innovative technologies, the success of implementing the data masking technique is based on two things: technical efficacy, and its adaptation to real enterprise environments. TDMP enables high-concurrency and high-performance data masking in the condition of petabyte-scale data and complex enterprise data sources. The built-in artificial intelligence scanning engine can largely transform and shield sensitive data, while preserving the high fidelity and consistency of business data to keep business semantics unaltered. The data consistency remains through multiple masking or masking in different systems, ensuring a continual consistency of business data across all business operations.

These two key factors have led to the widespread recognition of Digital China Group's product among many financial enterprises and its rapid expansion into industries beyond finance.

Data masking is just one technology used to achieve data security in the digital-native era. We should recognize that from data decomposition, classification, and identification at the data source to the deployment of big data sandboxes, and the technical implementation of data masking, multi-party security computation, privacy computation, trusted computation, and so on, the governance of data security in the entire digital-native era has become the key anchor for data flow security and data value optimization. The governance of data security has amassed a boundless market. Digital China Group is further investing in this space together with our partners, promoting the data security capability building of Chinese enterprises.

Data security has transcended beyond the realm of traditional information security. In addition to technologies, comprehensive law-making is the indispensable guardrail for data security. In recent years, various jurisdictions have issued a series of data security-related regulations and standards, such as the European Union's General Data Protection Regulation (GDPR), the California's 2018 California Consumer Privacy Act, the Cybersecurity Law of the People's Republic of China, and the Personal Information Protection Law of The People's Republic of China.

In the big data era, the development, utilization, mining, sharing, and integration of data bring us the benefits of big data as well as the hidden data security issues. Only by imposing a straitjacket on data security through regulations and technologies can we achieve data value optimization through a secure data flow.

COUNTERING DATA DOMINANCE WITH DATA SOVEREIGNTY

Israeli historian Yuval Noah Harari proposed the concept of "data dominance" in his book *Homo Deus: A Brief History of Tomorrow*. He said that, as more data flows from our bodies and brains to smart devices via biometric sensors, enterprises and governments can understand and manipulate you, and make decisions for you. More importantly, they may also decipher the underlying mechanisms behind the human body and brain, possessing the power to engineer life itself.[8] In Harari's view, today's technology giants have access to the data of billions of global users. By analysing this data, they grasp a comprehensive understanding of users' lifestyles, even more so than the users themselves. For companies that possess this level of big data, the world has no real secrets. Powered by a vast data trove, abundant computing resources, and advanced analytical capabilities, these companies not only profit handsomely but also expand their borderless business empires. Harari concluded that those who control the data also hold "data dominance."

In agrarian societies, land was the most important asset and battles revolved around land grabs. Those who owned more land acquired more power. In the industrial society, the importance of machines and factories superseded land, and battles shifted to the control of these factors of production. In the digital age, the importance of data has gradually superseded land and machines. And the intensifying battle will centre on data control.

Internet giants such as Google, Facebook, Amazon, ByteDance, Alibaba, and Tencent have established a preeminent dominance in data collection and data control.

A classic example of data dominance is the payment dispute between Google, Facebook and the Australian media. Since February 18, 2021, Facebook has suspended the news functions for Australian users on its platform, including official accounts of the Australian government.

The above actions of the high-tech giants reveal the near untamed power they possess. This power is not granted by public authority such as the state or the law but is bestowed upon them by their users unconsciously. This power is built upon the unprecedented information monopoly of the internet age and has almost boundless influence.

In 2019, economist Shoshana Zuboff in her book *The Age of Surveillance Capitalism* revealed how large technology titans generate enormous profits by monitoring users' behavioural data, thereby dominating capitalist society and reshaping power structures.

In August 2019, Christopher Wylie, co-founder of Cambridge Analytica, also revealed in his book *Mindf*ck* how social media data was deployed to manipulate the 2016 U.S. presidential election and the Brexit referendum. He issued a warning to the public that "The most powerful technology titans that control information are manipulating the thoughts of the masses in unimaginable ways."

As cyberspace and the real world converge, the technology giants that acquired immense power in cyberspace are gradually shaping the real world as the feasible new rulers. This data dominance is like the sword of Damocles hovering over our heads.

The traditional societal power structure and governance system are commensurate with information dissemination in the traditional media era. In the digital age, the societal power structure and governance system will be reconstructed, and data sovereignty cannot be neglected in this process. Only by elevating data security to the sovereign level and fostering a new value of data sovereignty can data dominance be balanced.

Data sovereignty does not advocate sovereignty's absoluteness, supremacy, and exclusivity, like traditional sovereignty, because the sovereign state doesn't possess all data, nor does it have the ability to mine all data. The actual rulers of the data world are those high-tech giants. Data sovereignty primarily targets them, followed by countries where the rulers are located and asserts the protection of privacy and security. When protection cannot be achieved by general legal supervision, sovereign states will take direct control of data, using storage localization, data trusts, cross-border flow control, etc. However, regardless of the specific measures, both privacy and security are legitimate bases of data sovereignty.

Because of this, in July 2020, the European Union released two reports on data sovereignty. On July 14, the European Parliament published a research report titled 'European Digital Sovereignty,' which elaborated on the background of the E.U.'s proposal for digital sovereignty and on the new policy of strengthening the E.U.'s strategic autonomy in the digital field. It also clarified 24 specific measures that had been undertaken. On July 30, the European Council on Foreign Relations (ECFR) published 'Europe's Digital Sovereignty: From Rulemaker to Superpower in the Age of US-China Rivalry,' which argued that the E.U. cannot simply rely on strengthening regulations to defend its digital sovereignty, just as referees can never win the football game. The E.U. must not only be a rule-maker but also directly participate and become a leader in the digital field amidst U.S.-China technological competition.

China is also vigorously defending data sovereignty and building its national data strategy, and there are a number of areas it can explore to strengthen that strategy. For example, it should clarify national data sovereignty by law and provide a legal basis for regulating the entire data lifecycle.

2.4 PLANNING FOR THE FUTURE WITH DIGITALIZATION

DIGITALIZATION IS A NECESSITY FOR THE EVOLUTION OF THE ERA

The cognitive evolution from mathematics to data science has profoundly impacted all aspects of human society, with businesses being among the most affected. As the value of data is being deeply extracted and widely applied, there have been qualitative changes in the enterprises' business processes, management decisions, organizational structures, and industrial chain collaboration methods. Digital transformation has become an inevitable choice for enterprises.

During a conversation I once had with the chairman of a leading shipbuilding group, he shared some immensely enlightening insights about the digital transformation of enterprises. One remark resonated deeply with me: "Enterprises that do not undergo digital transformation will perish."

I wholeheartedly agree. I believe that economic vitality and momentum stem from two aspects: entrepreneurial spirit and synchrony with the world's industrial revolutions. If the leaders of an enterprise lack entrepreneurial spirit, the enterprise will surely lack vitality. Similarly, if an enterprise deviates from the main theme of the industrial evolutions, it will be very difficult to gain new momentum.

In the spring of 2022, several of our directors of the Yabuli China Entrepreneurs Forum had dinner with Yu Minhong,[9] the founder of New Oriental.[10] At that time, due to severe business challenges, New Oriental was facing a transformation. After adjusting its business, New Oriental vacated some of its campuses, leaving many brand new desks and chairs unused. Minhong decided to donate these desks and chairs to rural schools in remote areas, a decision that surprised many. According to Minhong, New Oriental donated nearly 80,000 sets of desks and chairs at that time. That period was the darkest moment since the establishment of New Oriental, with its stock price once falling below one U.S. dollar. However, we all believed that New Oriental would rise again.

Sure enough, six months later, Dongfang Zhenxuan, under Minhong's leadership, caught the short video trend and experienced an unexpected surge in traffic. Driven by Dongfang Zhenxuan, New Oriental's stock price began to rebound, achieving a miraculous resurgence. This is a manifestation of the entrepreneurial spirit and the synchrony with the pulse of the era, by capturing a disruptive opportunity to innovate the business.

The second story pertains to NVIDIA. Following the release of ChatGPT by the American artificial intelligence research company OpenAI, ChatGPT rapidly ascended to become the most sought-after large language model, thereby igniting a fresh wave of artificial intelligence technology spearherded by AI's large language models. In this latest surge of productivity revolution symbolized by AI's large language models, NVIDIA, which has long been rooted in the realm of AI computing infrastructure, emerged as the victor. In August 2023, NVIDIA disclosed its most recent quarterly financial statement up to July 31, 2023. The report revealed that the company's quarterly revenue had soared to an all-time high, reaching $13.51 billion, a 101% increase year-on-year; the net income reached $6.188 billion, an 843% increase year-on-year; and its gross margin hit an astonishing 70.1.[11]

NVIDIA's narrative is testament to entrepreneurial spirit and a synchrony with the zeitgeist. NVIDIA's founder, Jensen Huang, a Chinese-American entrepreneur, is hailed as the Steve Jobs of the graphics world. Since its inception, NVIDIA has been dedicated to the research and development of graphics chips. In its early days, due to betting on the wrong technological direction, NVIDIA faced multiple failures, and the investment Huang painstakingly secured from venture capitalists depleted. Fortuitously, the Japanese gaming titan SEGA approached him, providing $7 million in funding for the development of a game console chip. Although this project ultimately failed, SEGA still paid the money. This funding allowed NVIDIA to survive, paving the way for the subsequent creation of the GPU[12] and NVIDIA's dominance in the graphics chip sector. A few years ago, before the advent of AI's large language models, NVIDIA was not as active as it is today. However, with the fully-fledged explosion of artificial intelligence, NVIDIA skyrocketed, becoming the world's first chip company to exceed a market value of one trillion dollars.

An interesting episode occurred in 2016 when Huang donated the world's first AI intelligent computer, the DGX-1, to the then relatively unknown OpenAI. Its computing power reduced OpenAI's training time from one year to one month. On the intelligent computer's body, Huang inscribed the following message: "To the future of Computing and Humanity. I Present You The World's First DGX-1." The AI trend that caused NVIDIA's market value to surge began with that engine.

From NVIDIA's success, we can appreciate Huang's entrepreneurial insight and his acute predictions for the future, as well as how high a company can fly on the winds of the era.

Digital transformation has become the main theme in the development of the digital economy. This signifies that every enterprise must accelerate its digitalization and make effective use of data, an essential factor of production. Enterprises that fail to do so, that reject digitalization, are without a future.

This is a profound lesson drawn from numerous failed business cases, such as Kodak, which built a century-long foundation but was ultimately left behind by the times.

In January 2012, Kodak declared bankruptcy. This institution, established in 1880 with a century-long glorious history, was the trailblazer of the film era, the preeminent global manufacturer and supplier of photographic products and services, and an unrivalled colossus of imaging. Yet, regrettably, this leviathan of an age fell from grace, ultimately succumbing to the relentless surge of digitalization.

At the beginning of the 21st century, an unparalleled digital tempest engulfed the traditional imaging sector, delivering a formidable shock to the industry's entire value chain. The global digital market rapidly burgeoned, while the market share of film cameras plummeted at an alarming rate. Despite experiencing first-hand the contraction of the film business since 1998, Kodak's executives failed to grasp the transformative impact that the swift evolution of digital technology would have on the industry. They hesitated to double down on digital businesses and did not pivot their strategy in time. By 2002, only about 25% of Kodak's offerings were digital, in stark contrast to its competitor Fujifilm, which had achieved a digitalization rate of 60%.

It was not until 2003 that Kodak's leadership came to an epiphany, shifting their strategic focus from film to digital. In the following year, Kodak launched six digital camera models and acquired a host of digital technology firms. However, these measures were insufficient to reverse the company's decline. As a latecomer to the digital age, Kodak could no longer compete with titans such as Sony, Canon, and Konica, and was left to struggle for survival in the interstices of the market. By 2012, years of losses had driven Kodak to a dead end.

Ironically, the digital imaging technology that toppled Kodak's empire was invented by Kodak itself. In fact, Kodak had always possessed formidable technical prowess in digital photography. As early as 1975, a Kodak engineer invented the world's first digital camera, which was deployed in the field of space exploration. In 1991, Kodak developed a professional-grade digital camera with a resolution of 1.3 million pixels. In 1995, the company released its first consumer-friendly digital camera, which quickly became a favourite of amateur photographers. Of the more than 10,000 patents held by Kodak, 1,100 pertain to digital photography, far surpassing any of its peers. "Either success or failure boils down to the same person,"[13] leaving a lingering sense of sadness to many.

Kodak is not alone; the decline of industry giants such as Nokia and BlackBerry in their mobile device businesses can also be attributed to their failure to adapt to the digital transformation.

All enterprises aspire to enduring success, yet the destiny of businesses is fraught with uncertainty. One thing, however, is certain: the times will leave behind those who lag, and only those enterprises that discern the trends of the era and act accordingly will avoid being cast aside. As the entrepreneur Zhang Ruimin[14] stated, there are no successful enterprises, only enterprises of their time.

In the past, discussions of business development typically categorized companies as either traditional or internet-based. With the ongoing deepening of digitalization, in the future, all enterprises will be digital, irrespective of their industry, the nature of their operations, and whether they are trillion-dollar behemoths or small and micro businesses. In the digital age, those unable to undergo digital transformation will find no room to survive, akin to horse-drawn carriages being no competition to high-speed trains.

DIGITALIZATION ≠ INFORMATIZATION

As business digitalization ceases to be an elective and becomes an imperative, entrepreneurs must cultivate a digital mind-set and grasp the true nature of digital transformation.

Digitalization has been discussed across various sectors for years, and a common refrain echoes: "Digital transformation is challenging." Many corporate leaders acknowledge the significance of digital transformation, yet they encounter a haze of confusion, unsure of what it is or where to commence. It is often said that thought precedes action, and only by revisiting the First Principles to achieve a lucid and precise understanding of digital transformation can one dispel the fog of confusion and clarify the path to successful execution.

To this end, it is crucial to delineate two concepts – informatization and digitalization – which are frequently conflated, leading to a murky comprehension of the latter. In reality, these two are distinctly different. In my lectures within 'Corporate Digital Transformation – A Practical Course' at the University of Science and Technology of China's Business School, I begin by differentiating between digitalization and informatization. A similar perspective was shared by the chairman of a leading shipbuilding group, during our exchange: digital transformation is a business topic, not an Information Technology topic. Businesses need to pursue digitalization, not informatization.

The concept of informatization was introduced in the 1960s, and our understanding of it has since become quite profound. Claude Elwood Shannon, the founder of information theory, precisely defined information as "that which eliminates uncertainty." Norbert Wiener, the originator of cybernetics, described information as "the content and name that people exchange with the outside world in the process of adapting to and influencing that world. Information is information, not matter or energy, yet it can be transformed into either." With the rapid advancement of information technology and the increasing ubiquity of the internet, businesses embarked on the journey of informatization – transferring information from the physical world, such as offline business processes, to online systems, and to be stored and recognized by computers, and leveraging various IT systems like OA, ERP, and CRM to optimize, solidify, and automate processes, as well as providing decision-making support.

Informatization enhanced the efficiency of enterprises but did not alter the logic of real-world business operations. In terms of thought processes, we still predominantly employ a physical-world mind-set when contemplating and managing business activities.

Throughout this process, the deployment of information systems has yielded a distinctive by-product: data. Yet, in the age of informatization, businesses have failed to recognize the pivotal role of data, nor have they implemented strategies to manage and exploit it. This marks the demarcation between informatization and digitalization. To put it simply, if an enterprise still perceives data as mere information, then its endeavours are confined to the construction of informatization, not digital transformation.

What, then, constitutes true digitalization? It revolutionizes the conventional mind-set, regards data as an asset to be harnessed, and constantly extracts value from transactional, user, and product data. Such data insights are then embedded into enterprise operational management and are applied in mathematical models to construct and optimize business logic, which, in turn, guides the enterprise operations. In essence, this is a process analogous to machine learning, where the system iteratively learns from operational data and models, thereby identifying deficiencies and shortcomings. Drawing from the definition provided in Huawei's 2019 White Paper on Industry Digital Transformation Methodology, digitalization leverages cutting-edge digital technologies such as cloud computing, big data, the Internet of Things, and artificial intelligence to construct a fully perceptive, connected, scenario-rich and intelligent digital world. Built on an acute digital representation of the physical world, it seeks to optimize and reinvent physical business operations, by innovating and reshaping traditional management, business, and commercial models. Hence, I assert that digitalization is essentially a disruption of the technological paradigm, with data as the core element of digital transformation.

Take China Merchants Bank as an example. Its total asset scale is approximately one-quarter to one-third of that of the Industrial and Commercial Bank of China, yet their market capitalizations are remarkably similar. This is primarily due to China Merchants Bank's extensive accumulation of data assets, particularly concerning high-net-worth clients, for whom it has developed over 2,000 application scenarios. These applications not only amassed consumer and high-net-worth client data, but also evolved into premium services products.

Thus, it is evident that data as a novel factor of production, has become a water shed between digitization and informatization.

For this reason, we no longer emphasize informatization; instead, we've introduced the concept of digitalization.

It is inevitable that informatization will be superseded by digitalization. The entire field of information technology has been in a state of constant disruption, evolving from elementary electronic process handling to intelligence-based tasks backed by structured data, to interconnected systems relying on networked computing, to platforms linking upstream and downstream use of the internet, to enterprise system optimization governed by big data management. Emerging technologies are constantly disrupting their predecessors. As computational architecture has evolved from standalone computing to network computing and cloud computing, enterprises are now designing systems grounded in both data and reality, whether binary or multivariate systems. Drawing a parallel to humans, who can be perceived as a trinary system with an energy system centred on the heart and blood vessels, a mobility mechanism reliant on bones and muscles, and an intelligence framework driven by the nerve system and brain, an enterprise's binary system is composed of an intelligent or digital framework anchored in the cloud and smart terminals, together with a physical framework that centres on movement and energy.

The advent of cloud computing has brought these two systems closer. Just as the human organism is an effective integration of multiple systems, the continuous evolution of digital technology is fostering an effective convergence of data and physical systems, thus laying the groundwork for the evolution of enterprise digitalization. Furthermore, the analytical and reconstructive capabilities of cloud-native and digital-native technologies are creating fertile ground for enterprise digitalization.

Against this backdrop, digitalization has supplanted informatization, for informatization serves merely as an enabling tool, whereas digitalization entails the sharing of data assets. The core assets of a business, once transformed into data assets, can be sharable and accessible, creating a new network for value circulation.

It is evident, therefore, that digitalization fundamentally involves the continuous embedment of digital technology into every facet of enterprise operations throughout the entire industry chain. It enables the mapping and interaction between the physical and digital worlds, integrating "data + algorithms" throughout the management lifecycle to form a cohesive loop that enhances organizational efficiency and efficacy. The ultimate goal of digitalization is to ceaselessly accumulate the data assets of an enterprise, and continuously enhance and even redefine its competitive edge.

In a contemporary view, the past corporate transformations were merely accumulations of quantitative changes. In the digital age, however, enterprises are undergoing qualitative transformation. Through digital transformation, enterprises can ascend to a higher dimension to disrupt the marketplace.

This has already become a reality: in the transportation industry, ride-hailing services have revolutionized traditional taxi-hailing; in retail, live-streaming sales have emerged as a new shopping paradigm, to the extent that even JD.com[15] and Taobao,[16] which once revolutionized traditional brick-and-mortar retail, were nearly upended by this trend; in finance, banks have constructed a series of digital platforms, evolving from financial service providers to integrated financial ecosystems encompassing financial, lifestyle, and travel services; even in the most traditional sector of agriculture, companies are deploying data analysis of soil, seeds, and climate to optimize inputs and maximize production efficiency and yield.

Before the second industrial revolution, people could not fathom the changes that electricity would bring to the world. Prior to the information revolution, the profound impact of computers and the internet on human society was beyond comprehension. Similarly, today, the potential of digitalization is beyond our wildest imaginations. The changes it will bring will undoubtedly exceed our expectations. Seizing the opportunities presented by digitalization, accelerating digital transformation, capturing new market opportunities, experimenting with new business models, and gaining a foothold in the market ahead of others, are the pathways to the future for all enterprises.

CHAPTER 3

DIGITAL TRANS-FORMATION DRIVEN BY DATA CLOUD INTEGRATION

The process of digital transformation requires reconstruction of business models and corporate values. It is about enhancing an enterprise's competitiveness – from understanding customer needs to product development, from brand-building to supply chain management, and from internal managerial decisions to external industry chains. In order to achieve these goals, there are four possible approaches: data assets accumulation, inter-industry data sharing, AI-powered decision-making, and boundaryless organization. These four elements are intricately linked, mutually complementary, and even causally related.

The proverb "a nine-storey tower rises from a heap of earth" suggests that the journey of digital transformation requires a gradual and systematic approach. Only by the use of proven transformation methodology and continuous self-upgrading, can enterprises truly seize development opportunities in the digital economy, and evolve into enterprises that are suited to the digital age.

3.1 DATA CLOUD INTEGRATION: CREATING A NEW ENGINE FOR DIGITALIZATION

DIGITAL TRANSFORMATION IS A CORPORATE STRATEGY

For enterprises, digital transformation is not a matter of choice, but the only way forwards. Many businesses continue to be perplexed by the question of how to transform and struggle to establish a clear course of action, despite widespread acknowledgement that failure to do so will result in obsolescence.

How can digital transformation be executed with efficacy? It is my conviction that the establishment and execution of digital transformation as a fundamental corporate strategy is of paramount importance. Digital transformation encompasses considerably more than the mere adoption and implementation of digital technologies, or the digitization of equipment and systems. This endeavour necessitates a thorough transformation, inside and out, demanding strategic consensus and complete commitment across the organization.

It is essential to understand digital transformation through the lens of business strategy, and it is imperative to define the term 'corporate strategy.' In my book *The Power of Time*, I explored the concept of strategy. I believe that strategy pertains to the allocation of corporate resources and the formulation of corporate development goals. It is a comprehensive plan for achieving increased profitability and sustaining long-term survival and growth, based on a thorough and scientific examination of internal and external circumstances. At its core, the objective of a strategy is to enhance an organisation's competitiveness and establish an enduring competitive edge. Digital transformation embodies the essential elements of a strategy, and operates towards the identical end goal. We can therefore be sure that a digital transformation strategy is, at its core, a corporate strategy.

When considering corporate development, it is imperative to treat digital transformation as the core strategy for the organization. In Chapter 2, I discussed Schumpeter's views on innovation, where he posits that innovation entails "recombining factors of production" to introduce a unique novel amalgamation of factors of production and conditions into the production system, thereby "establishing a new production function." Schumpeter further identified five forms of innovation: the introduction of a new product; the adoption of an innovative method of production; the entry into a new market; the acquisition of a new source of supply of raw materials or semi-finished goods; and the implementation of a new corporate structure. These were then summarized as five types of innovation: product, technology, market, resource allocation, and organizational innovation. By understanding Schumpeter's insights into innovation, we can comprehend the strategic significance that digital transformation has for organizations. Through digital transformation, enterprises integrate data, a crucial factor of production, into their business, management, and technological architectures, as well as into every process and aspect of the value chain, thereby generating various "new combinations" and the ongoing attainment of product, technology, market, resource allocation, and organizational innovation.

For this reason, enterprises ought to prioritize not only the application and transformation of digital technology, but also a transformational change of mind-set and the development of a corporate digital culture that re-injecting a renewed gene of innovation into the business. It is crucial to acknowledge that digitalization serves as a catalyst for new business and consumption models, offering fresh avenues for production, sales, service, innovation, and management, and spurring profound changes in production methods, organizational structures, and business models. In the industrial age, a company's size determined its strength, as larger enterprises possessed greater capital, labour, and resources, which allowed them to manufacture and distribute a greater quantity of goods, reach a more extensive market, and exert substantial influence over their business partners and clients. In the current digital age, scale ceases to be a substantial competitive edge for businesses. More crucial is a transformational change of mind-set, if not a complete disruption, and the degree to which digital tools are employed to enhance the capabilities of personnel. In order to drive operational efficiency improvements, enhance product value, re-engineer processes, and construct ecosystems, organizations must recognize and capitalize on emerging patterns, values, and opportunities that arise with a digitalization perspective.

Recognizing digital transformation to be a corporate strategy is essential to synchronize with the overarching development strategy of an organization, and to devise a scientifically sound digital transformation strategy that considers the unique attributes and needs of the business. This involves setting unambiguous objectives, trajectories, and courses of action for digital transformation, integrating digital cognition and mind-sets into the core of business operations, and embedding digitalization mechanisms into the overarching enterprise development strategy. By driving the transformational change of business processes, management mechanisms, organizational logic, and the technological innovation framework, this approach comprehensively enhances sustainable development capabilities.

When formulating a digital transformation strategy, it is vital to start with the enterprise's original intent and capabilities, anchored by contemporary trends. This requires an understanding of its founding principles: "what we want to do," an evaluation of the organization's capabilities: "what we can do," and an alignment with the requirements of the present era: "what we must do." By incorporating these three components into the digital transformation strategy, the organization will be steered in the right direction and ensured of a solid implementation and delivery.

Of course, it is of paramount importance for the digital transformation strategy to have an unambiguous strategic goal. It is only when business leaders elevate their vision, making it crystal clear to all members of the organization in which direction they should be moving, that all forces can be fully mobilized. This ensures the optimal allocation of the organization's resources.

Many organizations maintain divergent perspectives. McKinsey, for example, identifies a single objective for digital transformation: capturing growth and augmenting value. This should guide the development and implementation of all digital technology applications and implementations. In contrast, Huawei's goal for digital transformation is even more precise: internally, to achieve industry-leading operational efficiency by bridging informational gaps across domains, and digitalizing and servicing diverse business areas; and externally, to improve customer satisfaction by streamlining, enhancing, and securing business interactions with customers.

In my opinion, the most essential and fundamental goal of an enterprise's digital transformation is the continuous production of systematic data, alternative data, and AIGC (Artificial Intelligence Generated Content) data. This process accumulates more data assets for the enterprise. Simultaneously, the aforementioned data assets are employed to reconfigure offerings and provisions of products and services, thus attaining business innovations. As illustrated in Figure 3.1, these two processes mutually reinforce and advance one another, culminating in the formation of a growth flywheel for the organization that sustain a steady stream of development momentum for the enterprise.

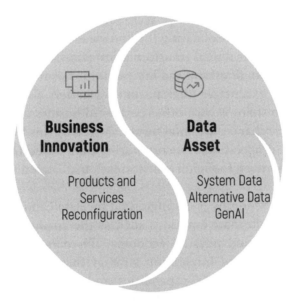

FIGURE 3.1
BUSINESS INNOVATION AND DATA ASSET AS CATALYSTS OF THE GROWTH ENGINE

Positioning oneself as a future industry leader and gaining a competitive edge in the current era are contingent upon the accumulation of data assets. Maintaining an uninterruptable dedication to the accumulation of data assets is critical for the success of an enterprise's digital transformation strategy, because only by doing so can the enterprise steer itself towards a more prosperous future.

DATA CLOUD INTEGRATION: AN INNOVATIVE STRATEGY FOR DIGITAL TRANSFORMATION

Digital transformation is a huge challenge in the current era that every enterprise must confront. Diverse organizations have offered a range of responses to this challenge, and I, too, have been consistently involved in my own exploration and practice.

Over the last two decades of development, Digital China Group has provided diverse information services to China's various industries. From traditional data networks to today's cloud, data modelling, artificial intelligence, and intelligent computing centres, a plethora of solutions has catered to clients' needs. In the realm of digital transformation, we have accumulated solid expertise. I have always envisioned consolidating the knowledge and insights we have gained through our digital transformation efforts, as well as the lessons learned from domestic and international businesses, to develop a systematic, executable digital transformation framework. The objective is to share it with other perplexed business managers and collaboratively shape the digital future. Driven by this initial vision, I put forth the proposition of incorporating Data Cloud Integration as a strategic approach to digital transformation at Digital China Group in 2022.

The digital economy is distinguished by Data Cloud Integration. In contrast to alternative notions such as the amalgamation of the digital economy and physical economy, this data-centric and value-driven Data Cloud Integration strategy furnishes organizations with ubiquitous, agile IT capabilities and integrated data-driven capabilities, and develops cross-discipline innovative digital business scenarios and new business models, aiding enterprise clients in the establishment of future-oriented core competencies and competitive edges. This approach promotes digital and intelligent transformation and the upgrading of all of society. A panoramic view of the Data Cloud Integration strategy is illustrated in Figure 3.2.

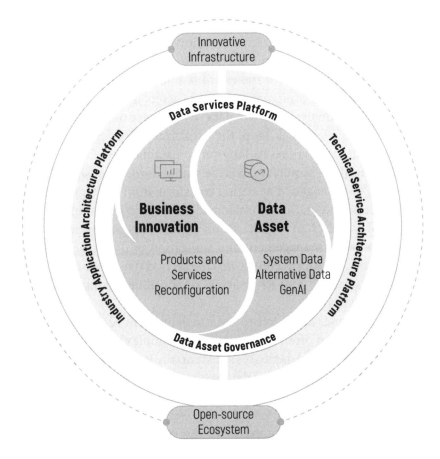

FIGURE 3.2

DATA CLOUD INTEGRATION: A NEW STRATEGY FOR DIGITAL TRANSFORMATION

At the heart of the Data Cloud Integration strategy is the growth flywheel generated through the convergence of data assets and business innovation. The fundamental nature of the digitalization process is to make expertise and knowledge "computable." Our experience as a provider of services to businesses has taught us that rapid deployment or iteration of business operations is the most fundamental objective of virtually all organizations. Banks, for instance, consistently pursue novel financial management products, augmenting their clientele base and streamlining operational procedures, thereby rationalizing customer service. The primary objective of banks transcends mere data accumulation and management. But in order to achieve such transformation, digitizing the business is essential, which means completing the digital business transformation procedure.

Data is a representation and reflection of business. To generate new business opportunities and expedite implementation, continuous accumulation and reconfiguration of data assets is critical for the rapid integration and amalgamation of data. When these two elements interact in a positive feedback loop, the organization generates a growth flywheel, which guarantees its long-term sustainability.

Following data acquisition and accumulation, how should these data assets be managed? The digital transformation strategy, as driven by Data Cloud Integration, must consider this emerging subject, as the extent and scope of an organization's digital transformation are contingent upon the management and utilization of data assets. Hence, the data service platform constitutes the second tier of the Data Cloud Integration strategy, with its principal responsibility being the administration of data assets.

The traditional approach to data management relies on symbols or information and often results in highly complex code-writing. The invention of relational databases substantially improved the efficiency of code writing, but relational databases often prove inadequate when confronted with a particular subject or object. This has prompted the development of object-oriented databases, which are alternatively referred to as analytical databases. In response to the insufficiency of large-scale analytical databases, data warehouse technology emerges.

Today, data has evolved from symbols and information to become an asset. The primary distinction between data and traditional commodities lies in the repeatability of data and the creation of new value with every utilization. In the process of utilization, variability between the price paid and the value obtained adds to the complexity of pricing and classifying data assets. Moreover, the expeditious accumulation of data assets via AIGC (Artificial Intelligence Generated Content) poses substantial challenges to data governance. Consequently, enterprises are required to transition from simple management to effective governance of data, necessitating the establishment of a data service platform as an integral component of the digital ecosystem of the organization.

Data governance is not an easy task. In light of the difficulties and pain points associated with the management of data assets, and taking into account their fundamental attributes, Digital China Group have developed the Liu He Shang Jia data assets platform. Integrating AIGC (Artificial Intelligence Generated Content) automatic generation technology with DataOps and DataFabric principles, Liu He Shang Jia is a one-stop, intelligent big data, full lifecycle research and development platform. This unified platform enables users to execute a wide range of data and intelligence scenarios, encompassing tasks such as data collection, development, governance, analysis, and sharing. It facilitates the integration of diverse data assets value systems for the benefit of businesses, by continuously transforming data into assets. Ultimately, it streamlines efficient administration of data assets and propels enterprises towards data-asset-centric digital transformation and innovation.

After establishing a data service platform, enterprises have to swiftly innovate their services. Under the cloud architecture, we have provided them with an application infrastructure architecture, i.e. an aPaaS.[1] This architecture is a toolbox based on applications. Through the provision of various specialized capability tools, these platforms facilitate the reorganization of products and services. These tools inject the digital innovation capabilities needed by enterprises in various industries, helping them to better understand and meet user needs, enhance data quality, ensure data security, and deeply mine their existing data resources to realize the value of data assets.

An aPaaS is distinguished by its features which are attributed to application scenario based on industry usage situations. It decomposes and reconstructs the business capabilities of various industries. For example, historically, banks have prioritized fundamental core business systems to serve functions such as deposits, loans, and remittances. However, driven by business transformations in the financial sector, the requirements for these systems have evolved. At the beginning of 2022, regulatory documents demanded the construction of digital middle platforms in the financial industry. Consequently, a multitude of technical and business operations of the banks were divided into diverse tool constituents, enabling their recomposition or more effective utilization in support of business model and operational model innovations. Concurrently, with shifts in concepts and business models, banks' demands for cloud solutions have intensified. With the advancement of digital transformation, cloud computing has evolved from being a mere technological implementation to functioning as a highly efficient support system for agile banking operations.

To address the evolving demands of the banking industry, Digital China Information Services developed the Jiu Tian Lan Yue Cloud-Native Financial PaaS Platform.

This platform enables the conversion of banking functions into APIs and mini programs, allowing bank personnel to innovate in business processes with the same ease as creating PowerPoint presentations, based on linguistic and textual descriptions. By leveraging AI technology, novel products and services can be generated through voice commands. The architectural evolution and data asset transformation in the banking sector have been substantially propelled by this.

Historically, the telecommunications network operator sector provides services based on communications platforms and, nowadays, they provide cloud platforms or even application platforms. To better enable these operators to serve their clients, we have launched the Pan Yun Data Centre. We are developing various tools and platforms for different industries and enterprises, exploring digital transformation strategies for diverse application scenarios.

To support these tools, the Data Cloud Integration strategy furnishes enterprises with a GPaaS[2] (General Platform as a Service) general-purpose toolbox. This toolbox comprises almost all key technologies and PaaS services that businesses would require during digital transformation. By using these general-purpose tools, businesses can complete the reconfiguration process, entailing faster innovation.

PaaS, composed of aPaaS and GPaaS, forms the third layer of the Data Cloud Integration strategy. Beyond this layer, there is a critical layer serving as public resources ('public utility'), called IaaS[3] (Infrastructure as a Service), which is the digital infrastructure. It can be further classified into two overarching categories: open-source and public cloud. The public cloud transcends its initial implications, with projects such as National Computing Network ("East Data, West Computing" to channel more computing resources from eastern areas to less developed western regions in China), signifies a commercialized approach. In the same way that the ubiquitous mobile payment systems and Global Positioning System (GPS) are used to deliver services to any smartphone or automobile, these public resources, leveraging cloud technology, are an integral component of the digital infrastructure.

Digital China Group has taken the initiative to establish two ecosystems: a cloud ecosystem and an open-source ecosystem. Considering the constrained resources of organizations and the difficulty of effecting transformation exclusively through internal endeavours, the establishment of an ecosystem assumes paramount importance. By leveraging the cloud and open-source ecosystems as cornerstones and collaborating effectively within these ecosystems, organizations can consistently obtain sufficient resources to accomplish their strategic goals throughout the digital transformation process.

The Data Cloud Integration strategy represents a complex system framework characterized by a multifaceted framework architecture that incorporates even the behaviour of living organisms. It starts with a growth flywheel comprising data assets and business innovation, and expands into a larger, exponential growth flywheel driven by the establishment of data-service platform, general-purpose toolboxes, digital infrastructure, and cloud and open-source ecosystems.

Within this strategic framework, assetizing data to support pervasive and agile business innovation capabilities is the key to completing digital transformation. The proliferation of AIGC (Artificial Intelligence Generated Content) large language models serves as a catalyst for content generation and knowledge discovery, transforming into an essential technological breakthrough that propels digital-native progress. The "data + cloud" native platform disrupts established technological paradigms at its foundational architecture level, ushering in a new era of data and knowledge emergence through enterprise digitalization.

I often liken a strategy to a play-script, wherein the latter entails delineating every conceivable scenario in addition to establishing objectives. A goal devoid of these scenarios is nothing more than a conceptual castle in the sky. The Data Cloud Integration strategy is succinctly delineated with "onepage," thereby converting it from a slogan to a practical road map. This process promotes the attainment of strategic consensus and guarantees the effective execution of the strategy. 'Onepage' should be utilized by every organization to assess its digital transformation strategy.

By implementing this strategic framework, it is possible to successfully disrupt an organization and rebuild it.

Consider a leading shipbuilding company in China. It has historically operated as a manufacturer; however, in the current digital age, it is undergoing a transition to reposition itself as an integrator and supply chain manager.

The organization's digital transformation strategy entails the conversion of data assets, which includes the design of diverse ship components and the client interaction process. By transitioning from digital twin to digital-native and integrating AIGC, a novel process is established for construction, integration management, and supply chain management. The blueprint for the forthcoming metamorphosis of shipbuilding enterprises, as illustrated in Figure 3.3, was collaboratively conceived by its chairman and myself, employing the Data Cloud Integration strategy and architecture.

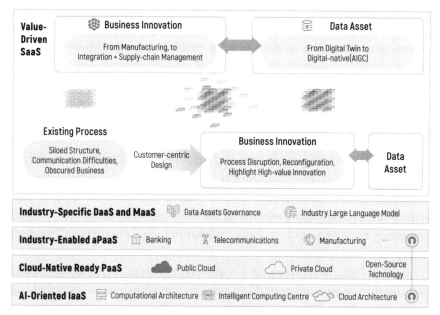

FIGURE 3.3

BLUEPRINT FOR TRANSFORMATION OF FUTURE SHIPBUILDING ENTERPRISES

The banking industry is another example of digital transformation using Data Cloud Integration strategy. Banks are the ballast of China's financial system, and to facilitate the country's modernization and better cater to the real economy, the digitalization of banks is unavoidable and, indeed, inevitable. To restructure their fundamental competitiveness, adapt to the contemporary era, access untapped avenues for growth, and attain expansion in both asset and market value dimensions, banks must embrace digitalization.

Since their inception until their current prosperous state, the fundamental purpose of banks has been to facilitate the monetization of assets. This phenomenon expedites the circulation of credit throughout temporal and spatial dimensions, thereby fostering economic dynamism and supporting expansion. Monetization facilitates the circulation and appreciation of assets, which is a fundamental aspect of economic progress. According to data provided by the People's Bank of China, China's M2 money supply (defined as the aggregate value of money in circulation during a specific time period) was a mere ¥0.18 trillion RMB in 1980. However, by the end of 2021, it had escalated to ¥238.29 trillion RMB, representing the most explicit indication of economic expansion. As economic digitalization progresses, the magnitude of data assets held by corporations will progressively grow. Consequently, the overall value of assets in the economy will increase, and the monetization of data assets will facilitate the emergence of novel growth opportunities and business models.

In the context of data scenarios in the real economy, banks, being major asset management institutions, can significantly increase the scale of their asset management operations by delving deeply into data asset management services. This could provide banks with growth opportunities that are tenfold or even one hundredfold. The digital economy presents both prospects for exponential expansion in the banking industry and challenges to the digital capabilities of the banks.

I have thought deeply about the subject of digital transformation in the banking industry, an area in which Digital China Group has amassed an abundance of practical expertise. The digital transformation of banks, which operates under the umbrella of the Data Cloud Integration strategy, primarily encompasses two critical domains of endeavour:

Firstly, augmenting the comprehension of digitalization, which is different from informatization. It is imperative to acknowledge that the conventional industrial economy and industrial civilization are being disrupted by the digital economy and digital civilization. A new digital-centric way of thinking is required to usher in the digital transformation.

Secondly, the path of digital transformation can be described as follows: Setting Strategy, Consolidating Foundations, Constructing Frameworks, and Nurturing Talent. The term 'setting strategy' pertains to formulating a development plan that is primarily focused on the acquisition and accumulation of data assets. To achieve a radical shift in productivity, it is critical to rapidly digitize core capabilities and amass data assets, construct a data middle platform, and emphasize that data is central to transformation.

'Consolidating Foundations' entails the construction of the infrastructure and technical architecture required for Data Cloud Integration. The cloud has emerged as the fundamental building block of contemporary technology architecture. Constructing a dual-mode transition technology solution that safeguards investments while facilitating a swift migration to cloud infrastructure is viable. When combined with an organization's capabilities to construct a multi-cloud management platform, this strategy guarantees security and reliability.

'Constructing Frameworks' pertains to the establishment of a data-driven business innovation framework, facilitating the shift from datafication of businesses to making businesses out of data. Scenario-based finance constitutes a fundamental model of making businesses out of data. The process entails the datafication of some segments under industry scenarios or major chains, and the integration with the data capabilities of the bank. This results in the formation of identifiable, evaluable, and risk controllable data assets, thereby facilitating inclusive financial services.

'Nurturing Talent' is concerned with bolstering the digital competencies of personnel to surmount transformation obstacles, with employees fulfil the role of implementing digital capabilities. Technical departments should, on the one hand, provide intelligent, low-code, and no-code tools. Conversely, it is imperative that business personnel acquire fundamental digital competencies in order to proactively enhance their digital literacy and data-oriented thinking abilities. By doing this, business departments can entirely achieve their innovative and leading roles in digital transformation.

The Overall Layout Plan for Digital China Construction, issued by the State Council of China, was officially unveiled in February 2023. This plan established a precise framework for the development of Digital China in accordance with the 2522 layout. This requires establishing two foundations – digital infrastructure and data resource frameworks – for promoting the five-in-one deep integration of digital technology with the construction of economy, politics, culture, society, and ecological civilization. They will enhance "two capabilities," namely, the innovation system for digital technology and the barriers to digital security, while optimizing the 'two environments' – the domestic and international contexts – for digital progress. The Data Cloud Integration strategy is specifically designed to advance the development of Digital China. It signifies a way of thinking and a set of methodologies for investigating the trajectory of digital transformation for enterprises. Moving forwards, it will also function as a catalyst for the redefinition of corporate value and the new engine of a novel economic paradigm.

BUILDING SUCCESSFUL PATHWAYS FOR DIGITAL TRANSFORMATION

Strategy is fundamental to the lasting sustainable success of any organization, which is also contingent on the efficient execution of these strategies. A strategy that remains unimplemented is merely a slogan. Many businesses do not lack strategies, but rather lack a well-structured and systematic approach to implementation. Data Cloud Integration strategy isn't just a strategic blueprint; it entails a holistic restructuring of business operational procedures, including conceptualization at the highest level and pragmatic execution. As depicted in Figure 3.4, this consists of data assets accumulation, inter-industry data sharing, AI-powered decision-making, and boundaryless organization.

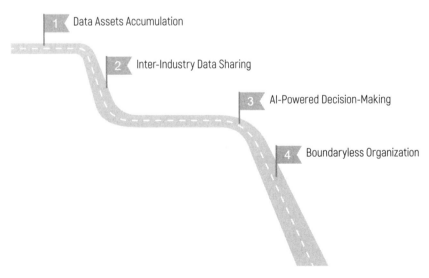

FIGURE 3.4
SPECIFIC PATHWAYS FOR ENTERPRISE DIGITAL TRANSFORMATION

Data assets accumulation forms the core part of the Data Cloud Integration strategy. It is also the foundation of enterprise digital transformation. Data assets accumulation serves as the fundamental requirement for every intelligent and digital transformation with an organization. Datafication of corporate assets can substantially amplify the fundamental competitiveness of a business. It forms a digital asset ecosystem and generates new value networks through the circulation of data assets, thereby enhancing innovation capabilities during the data assets accumulation process.

Inter-industry data sharing represents the value network's further metamorphosis. A revolution in value networks is catalysed by any changes that asset datafication induces in customer demands, technology research and development, business models, and asset management. Inter-industry data sharing facilitates the integration of internal and external resources, the prompt adaptation to front-end business changes, the response to market demands, and the efficient collaboration of the industrial chain – all of which contribute to the acceleration of enterprise development.

Decision processes are empowered by AI-powered decision-making. In the digital age, intelligent decision-making should be highly efficient and streamlined, even automated, as driven by data. The primary importance of AI-powered decision-making resides in its capacity to furnish enterprise managers with decision support through the correlation and analysis of data. This, in turn, enhances the accuracy and effectiveness of operational decisions while optimizing the inherent capabilities of individuals. As algorithmic and data support become more prevalent, the significance of AI-powered decision-making will grow.

Boundaryless organization transforms businesses into platforms for showcasing talent and capability. Physical constraints frequently dictate the scale of an enterprise in traditional sectors, thereby establishing distinct boundaries. However, these distinctions will inevitably become less clear as value networks develop. By leveraging digital infrastructure, organizations can expand upon their inherent capabilities and transform into platform-based enterprises.

The Data Cloud Integration strategy paints a digital landscape, which provides enterprises with a feasible, transparent road map along the path of data assets accumulation, inter-industry data sharing, AI-powered decision-making, and boundaryless organization.

By adhering to this trajectory, organizations can re-establish their worth, materialize ambitious goals, and genuinely emerge as 'enterprises of the era.'

3.2 **DATAFICATION OF ALL ASSETS**

EMPOWERING ASSETS THROUGH DATA ASSETS ACCUMULATION

We often say that the future is here. However, many enterprises find themselves ensnared between the two. Such enterprises face challenges on two fronts: they are burdened by traditional and, in some cases, obsolete business models, and they must confront the effects of new technologies and emerging paradigms. In order to achieve core competitiveness and sustainable growth potential in an increasingly competitive market, these businesses must undergo digital transformation. And the key to this lies in data assets accumulation.

Datafication of assets is at the heart of enterprise digital transformation. The recent proliferation of AIGC (Artificial Intelligence Generated Content) large language models has expedited the generation of data, and as a result, organizations are facing an ever-increasing imperative to do data assets accumulation.

Asset datafication refers to the process of converting tangible assets from the physical world into a digital format and mapping them onto the virtual world, thereby converting them into data assets.

The process doesn't alter the inherent actualization of the value of assets; their existence still fundamentally relies on their physical counterparts. By mapping the assets of physical enterprises – those generated from real-world transactions – to the virtual world, the nature of existing credit relationships is altered. However, the intrinsic and utilitarian value of the assets remains unchanged. Due to the one-to-one anchoring of tangible assets to their digital counterparts, digitized assets retain various attributes akin to their offline circulation, such as transferability and ownership. Consequently, the value exchange process is enhanced, making transactions more convenient.

Datafication of assets has made asset management more intelligent, efficient, and streamlined. Once assets are converted into data, various aspects of asset management become interconnected. Managers can grasp real-time data on the dynamics of assets, enabling them to achieve holistic lifecycle management and precise operations for these assets. Significant improvements are made to the safety, specificity, timeliness, and efficiency of asset utilization and regulation. In this era of inventory rich economy, businesses will possess a stronger competitive edge.

The chairman of a leading shipbuilding group has spoken about his company's exploration and practices in the realm of asset datafication, thus presenting a role model.

It is widely acknowledged that the shipbuilding industry is a profession that spans several centuries. Traditional shipbuilding techniques are extraordinarily complex, encompassing a multitude of stages, and communication and collaboration between these stages are particularly challenging. For instance, during the design phase, designers utilize three-dimensional modelling to form design plans. However, what's handed over to the shipyards are two-dimensional blueprints. The shipyard then uses these plans for production design, planning both how to build the ship and how to organize the shipbuilding. In this process, the two-dimensional design is converted back into a three-dimensional model. Finally, there is yet another conversion on the production side from three-dimensional to two-dimensional on the production side, because the manufacturer's work is based on these blueprints. This trend isn't just limited to the manufacturing process; when a new ship is delivered to a client, they typically receive paper manuals that are sometimes so voluminous that they could fill a truck.

Constant conversion from 3D to 2D and back again fundamentally binds the complex and cumbersome shipbuilding industry together through inefficient, expensive means. This reduces the efficiency of shipbuilding and introduces redundant labour. Various stages, including design, production, and after-sales, frequently encounter issues in seamless data integration and empowerment due to communication barriers and a lack of a uniform language.

Recognizing the drawbacks of these ineffective methods, this ship-building group implemented a radical transformation. They promoted digital shipbuilding using a 'single digital model.' The goal was to create a foundational platform for digital shipbuilding within a single system, achieving a high level of coupling among people, processes, and data. In 2019, this leading shipbuilding group successfully manufactured a ship which stood out as the world's first large steel navigational vessel constructed paperless. This ship was rooted in a single digital platform from design to construction. Any modification in one stage would instantly be relayed to the subsequent stage, serving as the foundation for further processing in that stage. Each step intertwined seamlessly with the next, with all those involved contributing value to a singular digital model. This enabled concurrent design, construction, and experience. The digital platform could easily generate three-dimensional digital blueprints at the manufacturing phase. Workers could access these via intelligent terminals equipped with large touch screens, making the manufacturing process more efficient and standardized.

Through digital shipbuilding, this leading shipbuilding group not only reduced the time required for information transfer and technical communication across various stages but also lowered operational costs. Moreover, they achieved interoperability throughout the entire supply chain, leading to mutual benefits with their partners. In doing so, it amassed a vast quantity of digital assets.

The leading shipbuilding group is the industry leader in China's shipbuilding sector. Its unwavering dedication to digitalization and constant innovation positions it as a model for the exploration of a suitable model of digital transformation not only for the shipbuilding industry, but for the entire manufacturing sector. It serves as an influential benchmark for other traditional manufacturing companies that aspire to reinvent themselves through digitalization.

The Group's digital shipbuilding strategy demonstrates how datafication of assets can reshape business models. It provides comprehensive, multi-tiered solutions to problems encountered across various operational stages of a business. It also addresses a company's core needs in production, market expansion, and brand building, laying the groundwork for a virtuous cycle.

For instance, in the production and sales phase, through asset datafication, businesses can presell digital assets anchored one-to-one with physical goods. This locks in customers, facilitates production based on specific demand, and reduces manufacturing costs.

In the operational management phase, costs are reduced, and cross-departmental communication, which traditionally might have posed challenges, becomes seamless.

In the brand building phase, by using the features of blockchain, such as its openness, transparency, and traceability, the credibility and influence of a company are enhanced. This strengthens the brand's reputation.

For cash flow management, consumers can purchase relevant data assets in advance. This allows businesses to retrieve capital funds ahead of schedule, thereby accelerating cash turnover, and subsequently infusing more capital into reproduction. Without relying on third parties, businesses can truly have sovereignty over their assets.

This possibly encapsulates the essence of asset datafication's value: by reconstructing business models, it addresses the overarching structural and systemic challenges faced by enterprises and encourages cyclical growth.

Companies that achieve this sustainable growth can craft new customer experiences, produce unprecedented value, and cultivate new ecosystems. Consequently, businesses that take the lead in data assets accumulation could emerge as industry pioneers, thereby eliminating those traditional, self-complacent enterprises as obsolete. Such evolution, despite being ruthless, is inevitable.

FROM UN-LEARNABLE TO LEARNABLE

There's a popular best-selling book titled *Things You Can't Learn from Haidilao*.[4] The book argues that Haidilao's rise in the restaurant industry was propelled by its unique competitive advantage, which is based on abilities that others cannot master. Using this analogy, one can suggest that a firm's core assets are precisely those elements that competitors cannot learn, steal, or acquire. These assets, tangible or intangible, give the firm a sustained competitive advantage, enabling it to establish a consistent capability in market exploration, product development, profitability, and the execution of progressive and efficient operational mechanisms. Of all a company's assets, these core assets are the most precious.

Why do customers choose your business over competitors? It's due to your unique core assets that other enterprises lack. Only by the datafication of these core assets can the true potential of a company's data assets accumulation be realized.

The very reason we choose to datafy core assets is to make them learnable for others. Only when data assets are circulated and shared can they reach their utmost efficacy.

Circulation is a prerequisite for the development of the modern economy; it creates value. Since the Stone Age, circulation has been a fundamental component of human civilization. The roads we traverse, which have evolved from non-existent to spanning across lands, oceans, skies, and outer space, have always served to facilitate circulation. Whether it is the Silk Road connecting East to West, air routes bridging different time zones, or the ubiquitous global digital network, all are forging myriad connections, promoting circulation, and driving economic development. In the current digital age, circulation is the backbone of constructing new value networks.

In recent years, the surge in popularity of companies like Meituan,[5] Uber, and DiDi[6] can be attributed to asset circulation and sharing. The datafication of assets is by far the quickest method for this circulation. Through the datafication of assets, we can expedite their continuous circulation, and achieve exponential development. A new value circulation network emerges when businesses choose to share their core assets and these assets are digitalized and shared.

Why did Amazon rise to prominence? Because it datafied its core assets and, with sharing as a premise, established a new network for value circulation.

In 2002, Tim O'Reilly stepped into the office of Amazon's CEO, Jeff Bezos. This brief encounter not only changed the trajectory of Amazon but also the human understanding of data and assets.

Tim O'Reilly, a pioneer of the internet, introduced and popularized the concept of Web 2.0. He viewed Amazon as an overly-isolated website and sought collaboration. He hoped that Amazon would make their book sales data accessible, enabling publishers to monitor book purchasing trends and thereby determine future publications. However, Bezos did not recognize data as a core asset of Amazon at the time, nor did he recognize the potential benefits of offering such data services. Consequently, he initially gave O'Reilly's proposal little consideration.

Shortly thereafter, however, O'Reilly presented Bezos with a complex tool they had developed called 'Amarank'. This tool allowed O'Reilly to scrape Amazon's website every few hours for rankings of books published by his company and competitors. Nowadays, writing such a web scraper might seem straightforward. However, back in 2002, this type of data collection could only be accomplished using rudimentary screen scraping techniques. Bezos was advised by O'Reilly to develop a suite of online tools known as Application Programming Interfaces (APIs) that would allow third parties to easily retrieve product prices and sales ranking data.

Bezos was eventually convinced. Embracing the idea of open internet, he began advocating within Amazon for the development of tools accessible to external developers, with the motto, "let them surprise us". In the spring of that year, Amazon hosted its first developer conference which attracted numerous IT titans, marking it a resounding success. During the conference, Amazon released its API and named it Amazon Web Services (AWS), marking the start of what would become Amazon's cloud computing offerings.

Amazon continued its journey in the digitalization of core assets. On its brand-registered accounts, Amazon added the 'Amazon Attribution' feature. This streamlined the process for sellers promoting Amazon products through Google or YouTube ads and assessed the effectiveness of their advertising. Previously, sellers would employ a three-tiered funnel approach to determine whether or not to continue specific advertising campaigns. With 'Amazon Attribution', the process was streamlined: direct advertising with special links to collect data, facilitating the re-strategizing of advertising campaigns across platforms. This feature enables sellers to track metrics such as page traffic, click-through rates, and sales in a streamlined manner for sales activities occurring outside of Amazon.

Amazon amplified the inherent value of digital assets with skill. Amazon has made its vast dataset accessible to collaborators via the AWS platform, integrating it seamlessly into their business model whilst embarking on a brand-building journey.

The datafication of Amazon's core assets has generated enormous returns. In 2020, Amazon Group's revenue reached $386 billion, with a net profit of $21.3 billion; AWS's cloud computing business generated $45.3 billion in revenue, with a net profit of $13.5 billion. Although AWS cloud computing revenues accounted for only 11% of the group's total revenue, they contributed over 60% of the group's profits. This data underscores why Bezos proclaims that Amazon is not merely an e-commerce company but also a technology-driven high-tech company.

Utilizing the datafication of core assets for digital transformation is also evident in the renowned Wall Street investment bank, Goldman Sachs, which has consistently been one of the world's most profitable commercial enterprises. For many years, Goldman traders, armed with a mysterious trading weapon, generated a $1 billion annual profit whilst avoiding losses of billions of dollars. SecDB, the proprietary trading engine of Goldman Sachs, is this enigmatic money-maker. SecDB is a database platform that not only made Goldman's traders among the most intelligent on Wall Street, but also enabled the company to navigate the 2008 financial crisis more adeptly than its competitors.

With the advancement of digital technology, Goldman Sachs decided to embark on a digital transformation journey. One of its significant moves was to open-source a previously strictly confidential technology. Goldman unveiled hundreds of APIs, allowing users to directly interface with SecDB, facilitating data extraction, pricing engines, and other functionalities. Users can use Goldman's historical data to assess whether a trading strategy is genuinely profitable and to assemble bespoke securities to hedge their portfolios. Most of these APIs are available on GitHub, a platform for developer collaboration. Furthermore, Goldman commits an annual fund of $100,000 to support the development of applications using its code – however, Goldman retains ownership of the resulting intellectual property. This shift positions Goldman Sachs from a stance of exclusivity to one of inclusivity, transforming its core assets from private to public. This not only creates value within the organization, but it also actualizes external sharing. The circulation of these data assets is poised to bring Goldman Sachs even more value.

Seeing the immense benefits of datafying core assets, Goldman Sachs' competitors also began exploration in this field. For instance, JPMorgan Chase began granting users access to specific Athena features. Athena is JPMorgan's trading engine, created by some of the same engineers who created SecDB in the 1990s.

Datafying a company's core assets can effectively catalyse the integration and flow of data assets, making the opening, sharing, and trading of data a reality, thus making the most of the datafication of assets.

Establishing shared digital assets is a significant characteristic of a company's digital transformation. This type of sharing nourishes the enterprise, enhancing its innovative capabilities and core competitiveness throughout the data assets accumulation process.

3.3 INTER-INDUSTRY DATA SHARING, MUTUAL GROWTH, AND MUTUAL BENEFITS

HARNESSING INTER-INDUSTRY DATA SHARING: THE PATH TO INDUSTRIAL SUPPLY CHAIN PROSPERITY

Datafication of assets has resulted in changes in multiple areas such as customer needs, technological research and development, business models, and asset management. This has given birth to the value network's transformation. Based on the new value network, the connections, collaborations, and organizational structures both within and outside of enterprises have undergone huge transformations. Among them, the evolution of external organizational methods has manifested as inter-industry data sharing.

We live in the era of mobile socialization and interconnection. Socialization refers to the phenomenon where, with the rapid rise of social networks, social media, and social marketing, online-based social behaviours are deeply ingrained in all human activities. It has altered the production relationships and lifestyles of people and transformed the development of enterprises and industries.

Through data integration, enterprises achieve a socialized and networked organizational structure, allowing every employee to connect with others and share resources, information, skills, and knowledge. This facilitates communication and connection with customers, upstream and downstream supply chain partners, and other stakeholders. Using socialized service platforms, businesses can establish a digitally interactive ecosystem, giving designers timely access to customer data and feedback, thereby providing invaluable direction for product development. Without such interactive community and the ensuing data and ecosystem feedback, the enterprise's product design would resemble the Chinese idiom 'the blind men and the elephant' – groping in the dark.

This digitized external organizational approach contributes to the synergistic effect of inter-industry data sharing. The mode of collaboration between enterprises and their external symbiotic partners evolves from the original linear, tree-like hierarchical structure to a three-dimensional network structure. Sharing and interaction become seamless tasks, driving the restructuring and value enhancement of the supply chain.

Take a leading shipbuilding group as an example. The traditional ship design process typically began with contract and basic design, followed by detailed design, production design, and manufacturing. The upstream and downstream industries operated in a sequential fashion, marked by protracted cycles and coordination challenges, where issues in a single area could potentially impact the entire operation. However, because of the inter-industry data sharing made possible by digital transformation, design institutes, equipment manufacturers and ship-owners became integrated into the ship design process. By incorporating production design into the contract and fundamental design stages, the shipbuilding group is now able to mitigate the recurrent coordination obstacles that plague the design process and therefore enhance the efficiency of the design workflow and manufacturing.

Another classic example in the field of inter-industry data sharing is Rolls-Royce. Rolls-Royce provides power to 35 types of commercial aircraft worldwide. With over 13,000 of its engines in use, in 2020, it reported revenues exceeding £20 billion. While Rolls-Royce sells engine products to airlines, the operational data remains with the airline. Without this data, the progression of engine products is challenging. To combat this, Rolls-Royce positioned itself as a Customer Operation, or Customer Data Operator, harnessing socialization techniques to collect and obtain client data. Using this information, they refine their products to better serve their customers, resulting in mutual benefits.

Rolls-Royce collects real-time engine data from customers and simulates its performance in the 'cloud' to reduce unneeded aircraft maintenance and unscheduled groundings. To manage this massive data influx, Rolls-Royce developed a new platform. With the consent of airline customers, this platform collects pertinent data for Microsoft's Azure Data Cloud. The data is then transferred to the Lakehouse platform of Databricks, where it is analysed using machine learning and AI tools provided by Databricks. This analysis serves as a backbone for improvements to flight delays and cancellations. As a result, the reliability of flight scheduling has improved, with customers reaping the greatest benefits.

Rolls-Royce has established a direct communication channel with its customers via inter-industry data sharing. By integrating engine production and maintenance with customer feedback, they can continuously improve their products and services. This approach has garnered them an increasing number of business opportunities.

Inter-industry data sharing has created a collaborative supply chain ecosystem. As depicted in Figure 3.5, it empowers businesses via three fundamental elements.

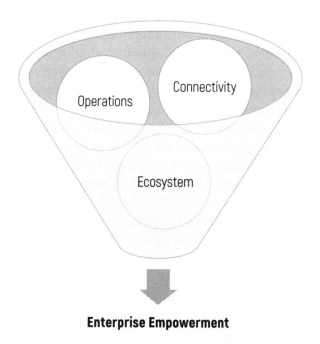

Enterprise Empowerment

FIGURE 3.5
THREE CORE ELEMENTS OF ENTERPRISE EMPOWERMENT
FOR INTER-INDUSTRY DATA SHARING

Element 1: Connectivity
Through the internet, enterprises have expanded their business relationships. This connection no longer remains confined to an enterprise's internal staff and operations but now extends to include supply chain partners, corporate customers, and distributors. The business value of connectivity is manifested when all departments, employees, and supply chain partners can serve customers. Through digital technology, a genuinely customer-centric operational model has been constructed, thereby facilitating enterprise transformation.

Element 2: Operations
Data drives the business operations and processes of organizations. But data is no longer restricted to a company's internal structured transactional or predictive data; it now originates from the company's customers, employees, and markets. It encompasses specific industry and market insights, customer behaviour, and sales activity. Enterprises strive to capture a broader range of market intelligence, customer feedback, and business communication information, which, in turn, assists them in making informed decisions, and effectively mitigating risks.

Element 3: Ecosystem
Collaboration between enterprises and their business partners is no longer limited to business processing or unidirectional information transfer. Instead, there is a heightened emphasis on communication, interaction, and process management centred on customer operations and services. Through inter-industry data sharing, companies consolidate both offline and online business communication and processing, aggregating data dispersed across various business systems based on roles and business requirements. Therefore, they achieve a manifold increase in business processing efficiency and collaborative service capability.

It is noteworthy that achieving complete inter-industry data sharing is not instantaneous. Every enterprise within the supply chain needs to digitize its individual segments, followed by digitally connecting businesses to other enterprises. Inter-industry data sharing often initiates in specific segments of the industrial chain and then progressively extends and develops across the entire industrial chain.

MIDDLE PLATFORM:
THE NUCLEUS OF ENTERPRISE DIGITALIZATION

Inter-industry data sharing drives businesses to integrate more internal and external resources. It facilitates a more effective response to rapidly changing front-end businesses, a faster response to market demands, and enhanced collaboration with upstream and downstream industry chains. The 'middle platform' aptly satisfies these demands.

The concept of the 'middle platform' derives from the operational system of the United States military. On the front lines, the U.S. military, through its efficient, flexible, and unified rear system, supports its mobile front-end units to increase operational efficiency and reduce redundant investments. Later, Alibaba adopted and expanded this concept, proposing in 2015 its strategy of "large middle platform, small front-end." The middle platform strategy of Alibaba was inspired by the Finnish company, Supercell. Despite having only 300 employees, Supercell consistently launched hit games, cementing its position as one of the most profitable game companies. Supercell pioneered the middle platform strategy and implemented it to the extreme. This relatively small business established a robust middle platform to support multiple small game development teams. In this configuration, each team could concentrate on innovation.

Today, many discuss the 'middle platform,' but interpretations vary. Although analogies are frequently used to simplify explanations, they are sometimes necessary to comprehend a concept.

Despite Dutch football genius Johan Cruyff advocating an "all-out attack, all-out defence" football strategy as early as in the 1970s, and achieving commendable success, this strategy did not immediately gain widespread acceptance. Only after Spain won the World Cup and the European Championship did this strategy receive attention. The crux of this strategy is the midfield. The midfield not only connects the team, but also serves as the team's command centre. Spain's midfield dominance exemplified the sophistication of contemporary football. The precision in their strategic execution, the speed of their rhythm, and the display of individual player abilities were astounding. This elevated the competitiveness and aesthetics of the game to unprecedented levels.

The middle platform of enterprises is analogous to the midfield in football. How to shift a company's 'engine' from the front-end to the mid-end, and how to manage a company's risk control during or even before an event, rather than after, lies in achieving integrated management of the company's core capabilities on the middle platform.

Digital technology has presented enterprises with the necessary tools for constructing robust middle platforms. Process digitalization enables businesses to achieve comprehensive visualization and intelligent automation across all managerial facets. Advanced big data analytics provides continuous insights into core competitive advantages, thereby facilitating a deeper understanding of the shifts within the entire industrial value chain and their consequential impacts. Consequently, the enterprise's core capabilities are continually enhanced. Furthermore, cloud-native technologies allow businesses to achieve digitalization and systematization of their entire operational processes, establishing hyper-connectivity and fostering integration with the broader environment. This offers enterprises the opportunities to exploit new growth avenues.

The middle platform is not just a simplistic platform; it functions as the strategic command centre of an enterprise. It is a platform for the collection, storage, computation, processing, and amalgamation of vast quantities of data. The platform signifies a transition in which business production materials are converted into data-driven productive capabilities. This nourishes business operations, creating a cyclical, iterative, closed-loop process. The digital age necessitates organizational restructuring, process reinvention, and technological upgrading, all of which are embodied by the middle platform. A commonly observed procedure within enterprises involves the middle platform delineating objects based on various business scenarios. As depicted in Figure 3.6, this is followed by micro-processes, micro-services, and data layer adaptations tailored to specific products and services. With the middle platform's solid support, the front-end business operations and innovation become efficient and agile. Enterprises are able to conduct diverse experiments and adjustments in accordance with the latest market trends. Having identified and validated new market opportunities, they can rapidly deploy the formidable capabilities of the middle platform to gain a competitive edge and secure market share.

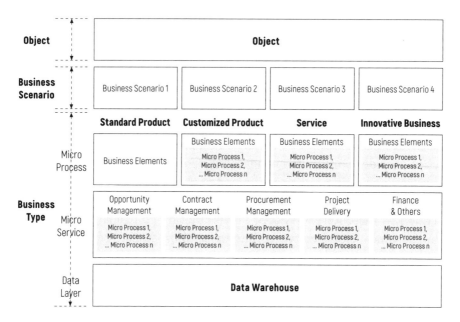

FIGURE 3.6

COMMON MIDDLE PLATFORM PROCESSING FLOWS IN ENTERPRISES

The middle platform can also centralize the processing of digital procedures. Similar to our brain and neural system, the middle platform can always adjust and revise, enabling the actualization of intelligent decision-making. Based on insights derived from strategy and beyond, it ensures that the organization can maintain its agility to promptly discover problems and adjust accordingly.

The middle platform also serves as the organizational fulcrum, empowering individuals to face competition with collective strength. Individuals within the enterprise acquire the proverbial 'keen eyesight,' 'sharp ears,' and 'mighty strength' of ancient Chinese legends in every aspect of the business, from customer requirements to service delivery. Through the data and networks of the middle platform, every employee can quickly contribute their expertise, thus fostering a streamlined operation.

The importance of the middle platform cannot be overstated. Over the last 20 years, innovation has emerged as the strategic linchpin for businesses. Observing leading companies at the forefront of this wave, such as Amazon, Haier,[7] and Huawei, it is clear that their capacity for rapid responsiveness and sustained complex innovation is supported by a comprehensive middle platform.

Use the ubiquitous example of the Meituan's food delivery service as an example. Meituan's food delivery platform includes tens of millions of merchants and delivery riders. So, how does Meituan mobilize this massive workforce to quickly and safely deliver food? If they relied on human coordination, they would likely need more dispatchers than delivery riders, which is inconceivably inefficient. Meituan has therefore established a data middle platform. Through data analytics, it assists users who order food on the platform to match with appropriate restaurants, and it assists restaurants in matching them with riders as quickly as possible. The result? Food is delivered to consumers with great efficiency.

Middle platforms can be classified in various ways, including Business Middle Platform, Technical Middle Platform, and Data Middle Platform, as illustrated in Figure 3.7.

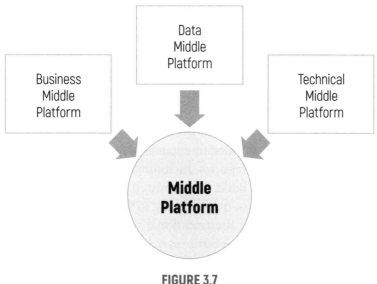

FIGURE 3.7
MIDDLE PLATFORM CATEGORIZATIONS

The Business Middle Platform derives from and serves the business, facilitating the reuse of business elements and a rapid response to business demands.

The Technical Middle Platform provides technical support for the Business Middle Platform's implementation. It comprises technical components from various domains, such as micro-services development frameworks, DevOps platforms, container clouds, PaaS (Platform as a Service), and additional application technologies. The Technical Middle Platform offers the front-end, the business middle platform and the data middle platform a straightforward, user-friendly, and efficient infrastructure for application technology, as well as foundational technical, data, and other support.

The Data Middle Platform is data-centric and processes, analyses, and models diverse types of data derived to support the usage of the Business Middle Platform. Typically, raw data, related data, and processed data (such as organized thematic data, algorithms, and models, etc.) are collected from various business systems or data lakes, for the use of the Data Middle Platform. In the context of an e-commerce website's recommendation system, for instance, the Data Middle Platform provides the algorithms upon which the Business Middle Platform relies to support associated recommendations.

The construction of these middle platforms lays a solid foundation for corporate data services and data sharing, acting as a catalyst for businesses transitioning from 'data' to 'value.' In addition, a comprehensive middle platform makes inter-industry data sharing a reality. For instance, Beike Real Estate achieves the goal of inter-industry data sharing through the development of a middle platform, thereby revolutionizing the business model of the industry.

Beike Real Estate[8] was officially established in April 2018 and offers services in a variety of categories, including used homes, new homes, rentals, and renovations. Beike is committed to providing comprehensive service connections for quality living to families across the nation. Beike's mission to digitize the traditional real estate service industry has presented it with complex business models and increasingly refined operational challenges, thereby placing significant demands on the platform's overall service capabilities.

Beike has on-boarded over 200 new broker brands and welcomed numerous business teams with research and development capabilities, and the platform needs to accommodate their diverse business needs. The expansion of platform integrations has resulted in the coordination of formerly parallel businesses under a comprehensive platform, thereby ensuring the optimal addition of services. Hundreds of thousands of brokers, shop owners, functional staff, photographers, transaction managers, and other service roles are gathered on Beike's platform. Beike intends to provide each of these service roles with the appropriate workstations to carry out their duties. Furthermore, it is essential to ensure the iterative independence of these workstations while maintaining efficiency and stability.

Beike established a resource-sharing middle platform to meet the diverse needs of brands, businesses, and service providers through business streamlining and fundamental capability integration. This system consolidates formerly dispersed resources onto a re-usable platform that supports front-end business operations robustly and provides unified SaaS solutions. It continually improves the company's overall efficacy, fostering industry collaboration and integration in order to better serve the customers.

A second-hand property transaction entails over a dozen stages involving various agents – from listing a property, measuring the size, taking photographs, to coordinating buyer visits, price negotiations, contract signings, bank loan arrangements, property transfers, and final inspections. Previously, a single real estate agent would oversee this entire process. On the Beike platform, however, it is a collaborative effort involving more than ten individuals.

Beike dissects each phase of the second-hand property transaction procedure and assigns distinct responsibilities to various people. These individuals may have originated from Lianjia[9] (which incubated Beike) or other real estate brokerage firms. On the Beike platform, all data is shared, allowing everyone to view each other's work. Once a transaction is completed, the system divides the commission proportionally to the value contribution of each broker role. This establishes a refined mechanism for measuring and distributing value.

In the past, Lianjia operated internally in a similar fashion, where all participants being Lianjia employee. However, Beike was the first to initiate large-scale collaboration across the entire industry and production chain, thereby forming an organizational ecosystem. Within this ecosystem, every enterprise can participate, and contribute to the actualization of inter-industry data sharing.

The middle platform serves as the nexus of corporate digital transformation, signalling the inevitable transition from being business-driven to data-driven. It transcends conventional perceptions of the boundary of corporate management, accelerating organizational growth through an integrated and collaborative approach.

3.4 PROPELLING MANAGEMENT THROUGH AI-POWERED DECISION-MAKING

EMPOWERING SMARTER ENTERPRISES THROUGH AI-POWERED DECISION-MAKING

Herbert Simon, an esteemed American management theorist famously coined the phrase "Management is decision-making." Throughout the management process, managers are confronted with a multitude of challenges. Irrespective of the characteristics of these challenges, decision-making is always vital. All of these management functions – planning, organizing, leading, and controlling – are all dependent on decision-making. As a result, AI-powered decision-making emerges as an essential pathway in the digital transformation of an organization. The implementation of intelligence and digitalization in decision-making processes facilitates the digital transformation of the internal structure and management approaches of an organization.

Decision-making is subjective and perceptual in nature, hence inherently full of complexity. Managers are required to evaluate potential risks, balance diverse interests, and make decisions amidst circumstances that are dynamic and constantly evolving. The question of whether such decisions are scientific or correct is addressed by Simon's theory of bounded rationality. American economist Kenneth J. Arrow initially proposed the notion of bounded rationality, which asserts that human behaviour is "consciously rational but rational to a limited extent." Simon expanded upon this and illustrated the effect of bounded rationality on decision-making with an apt metaphor:

In an endeavour to reach its nest, a small ant crawls across the beach along a twisted and winding pathway. This is due to its sensory abilities, which allow it to only approximate the location of the nest and then head in that hazy direction. The ant is incapable of anticipating potential obstacles it may face during its return journey to the nest. It confronts countless obstacles along the way, including stones, shells, puddles, and so forth. As a result, the ant is compelled to alter its course continuously.

Human decision-making, according to Herbert Simon, is comparable to the actions of this ant. People are dependent on their cognitive capacities and form assessments predicated on their restricted knowledge and incomplete comprehension. Consequently, such decisions exhibit a limited capacity of rationality.

To overcome this predicament, Simon proposed a resolution. He emphasized the significant role of information obtaining and processing in decision-making. This was defined by Simon and his colleagues as "any procedure through which information is transmitted from one organization member to another." In addition, they argued that, in an age of information overload, filtration, processing, and management of information are more critical than its production, storage, and distribution.

Simon's series of theories form the cornerstone of my proposed concept of AI-powered decision-making. Simon's perspective suggests that information processing and handling can enhance the accuracy of decision-making. With the advent of the digital age, there has been a significant enhancement in the capability and efficiency of businesses to process and handle information. Entrusting this information and data to artificial intelligence and big data processing facilitates AI-powered decision-making, ensuring that management issues of varying magnitudes within enterprises are resolved more effectively.

Businesses that have adopted AI-powered decision-making on the pillars of big data processing, machine learning, and artificial intelligence, can extract information from vast amounts of internal and external data. By also synthesizing a comprehensive analysis of the entire business, patterns emerge, market demands can be predicted, workflows can be improved, better decisions can be made, and more effective strategies can be formulated. This underpins digital sales and marketing, brand development, product innovation, smart manufacturing, sales, distribution, and channel management, ultimately creating end-to-end business value, resulting in sustained growth and efficient operations.

Digital Intelligence is the integration of Data and Intelligence, as depicted in Figure 3.8.

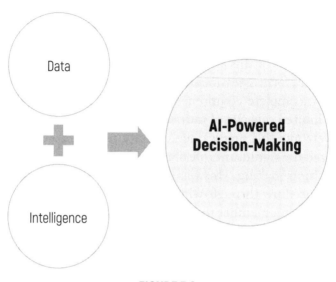

FIGURE 3.8
KEY ELEMENTS OF AI-POWERED DECISION-MAKING

Data encapsulates the comprehensive, pervasive, and seamless digitalization from the consumer end to the supply end. This includes the digitalization of business elements such as brand, products, sales, marketing, channels, manufacturing, services, finance, supply chain logistics, organization, and information technology. This development enables precise market demand response, real-time optimization, and intelligent decision-making. In the past, enterprise decisions were largely contingent on managerial experience or reliant on inefficient methods of information collection, such as surveys or distributor and channel summaries. In contrast, AI-powered decision-making today exemplifies efficiency and, in many cases, automation.

The most salient advantage of AI-powered decision-making lies in its ability to form a self-iterating decision feedback loop. Take a common business scenario involving sales and marketing: real-time data and feedback from sales and marketing scenarios are collected and then algorithms are employed to train sales and marketing models on this data. Once the models are deployed, they can accurately and immediately predict the needs of individual customers. Furthermore, customer feedback can be obtained via online decision-making and real-time interaction. The model then recalibrates itself through its self-learning capabilities, continually adapting to the evolving business scenarios.

As data from various business units continuously flows into the company's decision-making 'brain,' there is growth in the company's overall intelligence level. This intelligence, informs and nourishes all business aspects, allowing the company to make even more accurate forecasts and decisions, and becoming 'smarter.'

Google exemplifies this paradigm of AI-powered decision-making. It has created an environment in which every employee's innate creativity serves the company's objectives through data-driven processes. While Google offers substantial benefits to its employees, it concurrently underscores that these are reciprocations for their contributions to the company's innovative endeavours. Employees' performance will not be limited by external constraints; those who do not meaningfully contribute will become irrelevant and face the prospect of redundancy. Google has pioneered a meticulous evaluation of internal employee value by using digital process management, thereby significantly reducing managerial expenses. Consequently, Google has become one of the most creative companies in the world.

It is important to note that decisions can be classified either as non-routine or routine. Non-routine decisions are those that are made in unexpected, incidental, or unprecedented circumstances, and they are highly contingent on the decision-maker's experience, abilities, and personality. Conversely, routine decisions are frequent choices that managers must make. These decisions manifest in similar forms and may be resolved by employing established procedures, models, parameters, or benchmarks. The primary focus of enterprise AI-powered decision-making pertains to routine decisions, wherein the implementation of digital technology can be utilized to improve efficiency of the decision-making.

Whether in large corporate conglomerates or small and medium-sized enterprises (SME), AI-powered decision-making is an indispensable strategy. Only by early adoption and upgrading to this data and intelligence-driven paradigm can businesses keep up with the times.

AI-POWERED DECISION-MAKING: THE MULTIPLIER OF LABOUR PRODUCTIVITY

Many people may not yet recognize the significant implications of AI-powered decision-making for humanity – it will spark a productivity revolution.

Before the mid-18th century, the evolution of society was rather sluggish, as evidenced by the history of labour productivity. In the 1860s, however, the Industrial Revolution ushered in a new epoch. From the beginning of the Industrial Revolution to the present day, a span of two centuries, the change has been astounding. Our modern conveniences, for instance, the structures in which we inhabit, and the electronic goods we use, are products of this relatively brief 200-year period.

The ramifications of the Industrial Revolution were unprecedented, manifesting as a tenfold augmentation in per capita labour productivity over the past 200 years. For nearly 3000 years before, labour productivity remained largely stagnant

Why is there such a disparity? Humanity's monumental progress can be largely attributed to a fundamental shift in our *modes* of labour. Various modes have varying efficiencies. Pre-Industrial Revolution, humanity's efforts to shape the world relied predominantly on manual labour, resulting in low productivity. The Industrial Revolution was characterized by the substitution of human physical exertion with energy and machinery.

After the Industrial Revolution, humanity's endeavours became less dependent on physical strength and more dependent on skills. This resulted in significant changes to labour structures. In agrarian societies, farming comprised the majority of the workforce. As industrial societies evolved, however, fewer people remained in agriculture, and the value generated by manual labour decreased. In the United States, agriculture's contribution to the GDP is only 0.84%, compared to roughly 3% globally. In the early stages of the Industrial Revolution, the UK's textile industry comprised 85% of the world's capacity. If these capacities were to be met using conventional methods, 40 million workers would be required – a number double the estimated British population at the time. This massive textile industry was made possible by the strength of industrial manufacturing.

Pre-digital age, many engaged in skill-based jobs, such as driving and cooking. However, as digital transformation deepens, the proportion of skill-based labour in the workforce will decrease, placing a greater emphasis on innovative labour. The ultimate significance of AI-powered decision-making in enterprises is to liberate the most creative individuals from repetitive, low-value tasks, allowing them to engage in more insightful and creative activities.

More precisely, in what ways does the implementation of AI-powered decision-making within organizations improve labour productivity?

To begin with, AI-powered decision-making increases efficiency and substantially decreases expenses. Take JD.com as an example; in its Dongguan sorting centre, where more than 3,000 people once worked, there are now only 20 employees and 300 sorting robots. These robots work tirelessly around-the-clock, boosting the centre's productivity and cutting costs by 86%.

AI-powered decision-making can also enhance service efficiency. Alibaba reported that artificial intelligence handles 94% of its customer service. Even more astonishing is that customer satisfaction rates for AI-driven customer service exceeded that of human operators by three percentage points.

RPA (Robotic Process Automation) is a technology that interacts with user systems based on predefined scripted procedures. It exemplifies the integration of AI and automation in modern business operations through its software-based nature to facilitate the completion of repetitive tasks.

Initially, RPA was exclusively deployed in general contexts such as invoicing, ticket affixing, and account transaction recording. When addressing cross-system and cross-page invoicing and ticket affixing, for example, employees would manually log into the taxi software backend, and input relevant tax numbers and expense details. Subsequently, they would download and upload invoices to internal systems, thereby making the process rather cumbersome. With the implementation of RPA, a substantial proportion of these intricate steps can be eliminated. Multiple system-wide operations are autonomously performed by software robots that emulate human employees.

In an environment where labour cost is escalating rapidly and internal corporate structure is becoming increasingly complex, optimizing resources and increasing employee productivity have emerged as paramount concerns. RPA is proficient at simulating human-computer interactions on the front end by capturing user actions such as keystrokes, mouse movements, system triggers, and application calls. Upon capturing a specific procedure, RPA can automatically execute these steps based on predetermined rules; tasks such as reading emails, reconciling accounts, and generating reports can be handled by robots without a hitch.

Within the e-commerce domain, RPA's application increases efficiency. On numerous e-commerce platforms, freight insurance is prevalent, and some merchants even consider it complimentary. However, the compensation process for this insurance often confuses operational staff. The tedious tasks of tracking orders, synchronizing reimbursement progress with insurance firms, and inspecting policy details consume a considerable amount of their time. RPA emancipates them from such tedium. It can autonomously search, download, and aggregate information, as long as utilization rules are set in advance.

Merging RPA with AI is equivalent to Intelligent Process Automation (IPA). RPA can be compared to human hands, while AI can be compared to the human brain. In this symbiosis, IPA uses AI as the brain, directing RPA to accomplish tasks. With minimal human intervention, the convergence of RPA and AI to form IPA promises to expand and deepen the scope of automation.

In comparison to current business management approach, this AI-powered decision-making evolution distinctly accentuates productivity enhancement. This disparity must be acknowledged, and we must redouble our efforts accordingly.

RESHAPING DECISION-MAKING MODELS THROUGH AIGC

The progression of digital technology has improved the efficacy of enterprise management, empowering managers to make decisions and lead the organization. Especially since the proliferation of AIGC (Artificial Intelligence Generated Content) commenced in 2022, the capability of AI-powered decision-making has been substantially enhanced.

Before the advent of AIGC, data needed to be structured prior to its effective utilization in an enterprise application environment. However, the tremendous volume of data generated during business operations could not be structured. These consist of comprehensive internal meeting minutes, weekly and quarterly reports that encompass in-depth analyses and discussions pertaining to particular business issues, an abundance of contract texts and project acceptance materials that composed of intricate transaction details, and online interaction texts between customer service representatives and customers that offer direct feedback on products and services. Additionally, product user manuals, fault analysis documents, and technical materials for product services and support are abundant; they all contain the in-depth information necessary for technical support. Previously, this valuable information and knowledge was limited to random and discrete use by only a few experts or managers. Standard and traditional approaches to data processing and analysis encountered considerable difficulty when confronted with so much unstructured textual data. The incapability to efficiently extract valuable information resulted in the potential omission of critical decision-making foundations, market insights, and opportunities for innovation.

Progress has been made as a result of the emergence of large language models, exemplified by the advancement in natural language processing technology. By integrating artificial intelligence technology with human management experience, AIGC enables organizations to develop industry-specific or domain-specific management assistance tools. This has resulted in a generative management decision-making model that combines the strengths of both AI and human experience. By means of automated analysis, categorization, and knowledge extraction from unstructured data, this decision-making model furnishes decision-makers with powerful assistance. For example, employing automated text analysis techniques to examine customer service and sales correspondence, businesses gain a more precise comprehension of customer requirements and discontentment, thereby facilitating additional enhancements to their products and services offerings. Enterprises can use these technologies in conjunction with knowledge graph technologies to link information dispersed across various documents and systems, forming an enterprise brain that spans across organizational structures, business domains, and time dimensions. This provides an integrated platform for knowledge inquiry and even consulting and advisory. It becomes a super sales assistant, customer service assistant, or management assistant.

Digital China Group's SmartVision AI large language model integration platform significantly contributes to the enhancement of enterprise decision-making intelligence. As an illustration, a major manufacturer of home appliances utilized SmartVision to effectively optimize its decision-making processes. This company, which has amassed decades of industry experience, offers an extensive range of products encompassing both residential and commercial appliances. Annually, it processes a substantial volume of data and documents pertaining to product design, manufacturing, sales, and after-sales operations across numerous countries and regions. Despite experiencing substantial growth, the organization encountered a number of obstacles, with challenges related to decision-making devoting particular attention.

The organization had amassed an immense quantity of unstructured data through years of operation, including engineering design documents, product manuals, market analysis reports, customer feedback, and more. Nonetheless, the dispersion of this invaluable data among numerous departments posed a challenge in attaining organic knowledge sharing. When employees encountered problems or needed to make decisions, they often had to spend a significant amount of time searching for documents and data, or consulting with managers, resulting in low work efficiency and prolonged decision-making cycles.

The implementation of the SmartVision platform now assists this with this issue. By utilizing SmartVision, the organization successfully incorporated and organised their unstructured data from across diverse internal departments. These data comprised engineering designs, market reports, customer feedback, and other forms of text-based information. The platform then refined and conducted an in-depth analysis, automatically extracting and categorizing crucial information and knowledge by business domain and theme. Using such data, the organization trained a customized large language model to compre-hend its products, business operations, and industry-specific terminol-ogy and knowledge. Employees can consult this large language model when they need to quickly make decisions or locate information and answers; this increases the company's overall efficiency.

The use of AIGC in management decision-making allows manag-ers to push past cognitive boundaries, providing insights and foresight that are beyond the scope of human capabilities. This enables enter-prises to make faster and more accurate decisions, better equipping them to navigate the complex and dynamic business environment.

As AIGC technology advances and improves, so will its ability to process enterprise knowledge in terms of precision, breadth, and depth. This could eventually lead to the creation of a Super Enterprise Operation Brain capable of comprehending the entire scope of enter-prise business operations. We must fully utilize AIGC's potential to guide organizations towards a more intelligent and innovative future.

THE ULTIMATE GOAL OF AI-POWERED DECISION-MAKING: MAXIMIZING HUMAN VALUE

AI-powered decision-making is an inevitable trend in the development of our era and an unavoidable phase for businesses. I must emphasize that the purpose of digital intelligence enhancement is not intended to completely replace human roles but, rather, to maximize human creativity and value. This is the ultimate goal of AI-powered deci-sion-making and the core motive behind my advocacy of this theory.

During my visit to Europe, one of my itinerary items was to tour the Louvre Museum, where I was accompanied by a Chinese student studying abroad. This student, majoring in engineering, had held a deep interest in history since childhood and had accumulated an extensive knowledge of world history. Following his academic pursuits in France, he observed that a considerable number of Chinese tourists visiting Europe went to renowned sites like the Louvre or the British Museum, but it was uncommon to encounter guides offering explana-tions in Chinese. By using the internet, he identified tourists in need of Chinese explanations and used his historical knowledge to provide them with engaging tours. His narratives were indeed captivating;

at the Louvre, he took us through various exhibits, eloquently explaining the historical context, anecdotes, and vivid details of each piece, making the experience immersive. He was also willing to fly to New York to guide his clients through the cultural treasures of the Metropolitan Museum of Art, should they require his services.

The narrative surrounding this student aptly exemplifies the unique approach to work exhibited by the younger generation. They operate with complete autonomy in terms of time and location, allowing them to apply their intellect and abilities in domains that captivate their interest. This made me think that the growth of both individuals and businesses is intrinsically linked to the actualization of their inherent capabilities and that the advent of digitalization enables freedom: it activates the value of each individual within the organization by fully harnessing their individual creativity.

In the past, the prevailing approach in business management was for the boss to issue directives and employees to comply. At the time, this strategy substantially contributed to business growth, but times have changed. The environment in which businesses operate today is becoming more complex and uncertain. Being innovative is vital for sustainable development under such a context. According to Peter Drucker's book *Innovation and Entrepreneurship*, innovation is "the task of endowing human and material resources with new and greater wealth-producing capacity", implying that innovation is the act of providing value and satisfaction for the customers by enhancing products and services. In what ways can products and services be enhanced? Exclusively depending on the counsel of the boss or a selected few senior executives is inadequate. Harnessing the potential of every employee within an organization is vital. When this is achieved, the employees' creativity can be truly astounding, resulting in revolutionary developments.

For the development of a business, factors such as corporate culture, organizational structure, strategy, leadership, and talent are far more significant than technology alone. These facets are all human-centred, and even the most cutting-edge technology cannot guarantee business success if it fails to place importance on human value. A human-centric approach is essential not only in the realm of AI-powered decision-making, but in all aspects of corporate progression; talent remains at the centre of digital transformation.

Entrepreneurs must realize that personal creativity and curiosity is the most important thing. Digitalization and artificial intelligence can only replace repetitive or memory-driven work; truly creative works will never be replaced.

We find ourselves in a period of rapid change. Yet, it is not the change itself that is intimidating; rather, it is the peril of treading old paths and persisting with obsolete logics. Entrepreneurs must recalibrate their mind-sets, behaviours, and paradigms on the path to digital transformation, empowering their organizations and placing unwavering emphasis on the intrinsic value of humans, thereby reinvigorating every employee.

3.5 ONLY BY ELIMINATING BOUNDARIES CAN ENTERPRISES ACHIEVE THE IMPOSSIBLE

THE FUTURE ENTERPRISES SUCCEED THROUGH BOUNDARYLESSNESS

Inter-industry data sharing and AI-powered decision-making are the 'double helix' that digital enterprises of the future must possess; they are the DNA of the new business world. Their transformative effect on businesses is fundamental, propelling businesses towards a boundaryless horizon. As illustrated in Figure 3.9, contemporary society's engagement is predominantly facilitated through social media platforms. This results in an unavoidable erosion of organizational boundaries and an ongoing proliferation of data and sources of consumption.

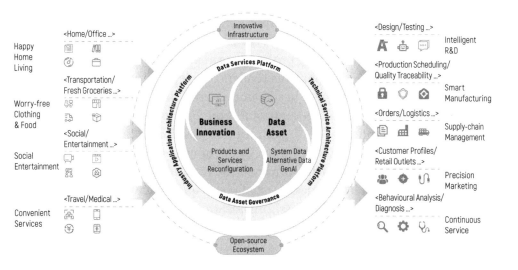

FIGURE 3.9

CONTEMPORARY SOCIETY'S ENGAGEMENT IS PREDOMINANTLY
FACILITATED THROUGH SOCIAL MEDIA

Boundaries have been the linchpin of business success. In traditional economic theory, it was widely held that business operations had definable boundaries. Given that the essential factors of production that comprise a business are tangible entities – land, labour, and capital – the theory of corporate boundaries said that once a business's scale of production reached a certain level, its boundaries are thus established.

While one cannot disregard the profound insights that traditional economic theories offer, it is important to recognize that such theories were formulated against the backdrop of the industrial age. Does this boundary theory still correspond to the requirements and characteristics of our digital era?

The answer is a resounding "no." In the digital age, the conventional economic theory of firm boundaries put forwards by traditional economists has become obsolescent, losing its foundational basis for applicability.

In the external environment of corporations, the integration of data related to the industrial chain is achieved through inter-industry data sharing, thereby gradually blurring the distinctions between entities operating in the industry. AI-powered decision-making for routine matters is made possible within the corporation through the digitalization of decision-making processes, primarily through the construction of knowledge graphs; this renders obsolete traditional corporate metrics such as employee headcount and revenue scale, which served as boundary markers. As soon as a "boundaryless" state is achieved, the intrinsic value of an organization is positioned to increase substantially through multiplication. By opening up its asset management platform, Goldman Sachs surpassed the traditional corporate boundaries delineated by metrics like staff count and revenue turnover. The transition to a "boundaryless" organization indicates that the assessment of these entities cannot be limited to a single metric.

The ethos of "boundaryless operations" is not a new concept; it was originally introduced by the former CEO of General Electric, Jack Welch. In 1981, Mr. Welch, widely recognized as a leading entrepreneur of the 20th century, assumed control of General Electric. Over two decades, he successfully transformed the organization from a bureaucratic and hierarchically intricate commercial behemoth into a nimble and efficient enterprise, escalating its annual revenue and net profits from $25 billion to more than $100 billion and $1.5 billion to $9.3 billion, respectively. This extraordinary expansion led to a market capitalization that increased by a factor of thirty, elevating the organization from 10th to 2nd on the global stage. This remarkable achievement of General Electric during Welch's tenure can largely be attributed to the implementation of "boundaryless operations" principles.

Welch postulated that the essence of "boundaryless operations" in a corporate context, involves immersing managerial philosophies and technological innovations in an environment devoid of boundaries. This requires going beyond traditional operational thinking and embracing a global outlook on resource allocation and market expansion to attract a diverse range of talent and promote the creation of innovative brands, thereby enabling an expansion of the enterprise' scope of development. Furthermore, Welch contended that the framework of a boundaryless corporation enables the development and exchange of cutting-edge methodologies and ideologies, both among employees and in collaboration with external entities.

During the period of industrialization, traditional enterprises distinguished themselves from their competitors through stringent demarcations. In the future, the success of a business will depend on its capacity to function beyond the traditional limitations of a boundary.

Why is it crucial? In the current digital age, it is crucial that we apply novel concepts and methods to recognize, evaluate, and address the obstacles that arise. Firstly, the transition to a consumer-centric era necessitates a substantial reorientation in the strategic thinking of corporations, to correspond with the ever-changing demands of consumers. Secondly, an attribute that truly defines the digital age is the process of datafying assets, thereby reducing the significant divide that existed between businesses and consumers. This necessitates that corporations dismantle their traditional organizational boundaries and incorporate consumer input into every aspect of product design, research and development, and production.

For example, the tremendous success of Xiaomi[10] smartphones is testament to the fruitful interaction between the producer and the consumer. By utilizing online interactions, the company compiles extensive consumer feedback regarding design and development elements, thus aligning the product features more closely with consumer preferences. Xiaomi's success has evidently been facilitated by the elimination of conventional organizational boundaries and the promotion of consumer participation.

With the progression of the digital economy, competition amongst enterprises is expected to intensify. In contrast, the traditional industry environment remains comparatively immobile, as markets approach a state of saturation. It is critical for corporations seeking to grow that they engage in innovation that transcends current limitations and boundaries. Such innovation cannot be insular or half-hearted. Kodak, the creator of the first digital camera, was ultimately forsaken by consumers and the market for clinging to film products. Automotive giants like Toyota and General Motors, with nearly 90% of the global market share, have made their best breakthroughs by perfecting hybrid electric vehicles, yet they still confront limited growth prospects within the industry. This has allowed Tesla, from outside these boundaries, to distinguish itself and establish a dominant position in the pure electric vehicle market. Apple invested $150 million in 2004 in developing the first-generation iPhone, which, upon release, achieved total sales of 6.1 million units. The iPhone's success as an innovative product exemplifies the triumph of a company continually expanding into markets beyond its traditional borders.

The future course of corporate growth and operations will involve more and more indistinct organizational boundaries, in which boundarylessness and flattening hierarchies emerge as critical attributes. In a deeper sense, future corporate operations will encompass not only the coordination of internal resources but also the utilization of external resources, employing every feasible entity connected through the internet, thereby obviating traditional organizational boundaries.

Gary Hamel,[11] American strategic research and management guru, pointed out that: "Enterprises must break free from antiquated mental constructs, thinking with a proactive and open mind-set, embracing diverse business frameworks, grasping future trends, establishing strategic frameworks, and organizing core competencies to secure a competitive edge in innovation." Businesses should strive to apply the concept of boundaryless business operations, insisting on innovation and development through openness. By welcoming the world with enthusiasm, they can greatly expand their external collaborations and partnerships, moving towards sustained rapid growth.

IN THE TERM 'BOUNDARYLESS,' WHERE DOES 'LESS' OR ITS ABSENCE RESIDE?

Faced with the digital economic tide, Chinese businesses must adopt advanced international management practices to achieve boundaryless operations in order to establish a foothold on the market and enhance their core competitiveness.

Where is the boundaryless nature of an enterprise manifested? It is evident in the absence of boundaries in resources, industries, products, customers, and organizational structures, as depicted in Figure 3.10.

FIGURE 3.10

FIVE MANIFESTATIONS OF ENTERPRISE BOUNDARYLESSNESS

1. **Resources, Boundarylessness**

According to the book *Wikinomics*, losers create walled gardens, while winners create a public space. Zhang Ruimin once remarked that by dismantling a corporation's boundaries, it will become a platform for the fluid accumulation and distribution of resources. The ultimate goal is to cater to a comprehensive user experience. Keeping this in mind, Haier introduced the philosophy of "boundaryless enterprise, leaderless management, and scale-less supply chain." This was actualized by the platformization of the company, the entrepreneurial spirit of the employees, and the customization of its services for individual users. By adhering to these 'three no's,' Haier has taken the global lead in establishing an IoT (the Internet of Things) ecosystem brand. It was the only Chinese company chosen for the initial batch of 'Lighthouse Factories' and introduced the 'Ren Dan He Yi' management model in the internet era, providing a case study for other companies to follow.

For resources to be truly boundaryless, business owners should adopt platform thinking, ecosystem reasoning, and a win-win mind-set as their business management philosophy. The ability to connect, aggregate, and integrate resources should be a core competency of any enterprise. Building, utilizing, and leveraging platforms, along with fostering an ecosystem, integrating into it, and ensuring its sustainable growth should be essential pathways for progression.

2. **Industries, Boundarylessness**

The founder of Xiaomi, Lei Jun,[12] once stated that a Xiaomi that only manufactures smartphones has no real future because its influence would soon be diminished. As a result, Lei Jun broke industry boundaries, leading Xiaomi to expand into other sectors. A review of Xiaomi's business landscape reveals that beyond smartphones, Xiaomi has also extended its reach into industries like home appliances, beverages, and clothing.

The concept of boundaryless industry compels businesses to venture into new territories and transcend traditional industry categories and limitations. This approach involves the consolidation and reorganization of value chains that formerly belonged to different industries, thereby creating new growth opportunities.

3. Products, Boundarylessness

Johann Wolfgang von Goethe once remarked that every idea initially presents itself as an unfamiliar visitor but, once it is recognized, it can become a transformative societal force. This concept applies to product innovation. Through shared consumer experiences and boundaryless innovation, numerous companies have set precedents. Huawei initially only had two primary business lines: telecommunications carrier and network operator infrastructure business and corporate data networking business. It later incorporated smartphones into its product lines, thus entering a new business arena. Jeff Bezos founded Amazon with the sole ambition of making it the largest bookstore in the world. However, two decades later, Amazon became the world's largest online retailer and later diversified into new products and services including the cloud computing services business AWS, creating a vast commercial empire. As product boundaries are continually redefined, enterprises adopting cross-industry and platform-centric approaches become the norm. This persistent breach of product boundaries further blurs the boundaries of corporate evolution.

Executives must recognize this fact. It is imperative not to confine oneself within preconceived notions or regard mature products as invincible boundaries. They should, instead, expand their horizons, continuously innovate, and adhere to the principles of customer-centricity and value maximization. Businesses should courageously drive product and service innovations by focusing on the ever-changing needs of customers, proactively integrating resources, and mobilizing internal and external forces.

4. Customers, Boundarylessness

Throughout history, businesses have tended to identify their target customers, which inherently sets boundaries for their customer base. In contrast, enterprises without boundaries do not adhere to a predetermined criterion for selecting customers. Instead, they strive to reach potential customers whose needs are unmet, as well as those who are not typically in their line of sight. These boundaryless businesses guide, educate, and cultivate these consumers in their consumption orientation. Simultaneously, by focusing on fluctuating or changing customer needs, they broaden the scope of their customer search.

More importantly, businesses should reduce or abandon competitions with competitors in the Red Sea market, focusing on traditional non-customers to explore or create new demand. As long as they move beyond existing customers and convert original non-customers into customers, businesses will have a world full of possibilities.

5. Organizations, Boundarylessness

In the industrial age, the organizational structure of businesses was based on departmental specialization, resulting in a pyramidal hierarchical structure. However, in the digital age, the ultimate goals of business management are to satisfy customer needs throughout the entire process and enhance their experience. Traditional organizational frameworks are no longer adequate, as they're unable to swiftly and accurately respond to customer demands.

Furthermore, businesses undergoing digital transformation will evolve into open ecosystems, blurring the distinction between their internal and external environments. This change mandates businesses to overturn their organizational structures and managerial processes, adopting boundaryless management. Only by doing so can a business achieve optimal resource allocation and maximize value creation. Haier's tremendous success in expansion and strengthening its position can be attributed to its approach in constructing a chain-group ecosystem, fostering a new organizational form that is boundaryless, mutually beneficial, and open for collaboration. This strategy is instructive for all businesses.

It's worth noting that, although an organization without boundaries allows business philosophies, data, and various other resources to flow freely within and outside the enterprise, this does not imply that the boundaries are completely open or non-existent. If they were, businesses would reach a state of disorganization.

EMPOWER THE INDIVIDUAL, ENABLE THE ORGANIZATION

The management of both the internal and external aspects of a business exemplifies this boundaryless nature as a result of the development of boundary-free business. Boundaryless management eliminates barriers between various functional departments within a company, allowing for better inter-departmental communication and collaboration. It tears down external walls, integrating suppliers and customers into a single process. It prioritizes teamwork over individual contribution, advocating for collective decision-making and highlighting the 'team spirit.' In the past, businesses were required to constantly revise their strategies based on the foresight and vision of entrepreneurs. However, in a boundaryless enterprise, real-time data supports strategies, meaning that the company's development is not solely dependent on an entrepreneur's vision.

The management approach of business organizations has changed. The new trend in organizational transformation is self-organization, which has quickly risen to prominence.

This notion of self-organization represents a cognitive revolution ushered in by the digital civilization. Now, some visionary business owners are adopting this business management model. They streamline organizational hierarchies, decentralize, and empower employees to have ownership within the organization, allowing them to become managers, decision-makers, and even shareholders. This not only fosters creativity but also encourages motivation.

Eric Schmidt, the former executive chairman of Google, and Jonathan Rosenberg, its former senior vice president of products, presented an idea in their book *How Google Works*: the pivotal function of future organizations is to assemble a group of "Smart Creatives" who can quickly perceive customer needs and develop products or services with a sense of joy. Who exactly are the "Smart Creatives"? In essence, they are individuals who do not require micro-management but simply a conducive environment for thought. Traditional management principles do not apply to them, and any attempt to impose them could stifle their creativity, provoke their resentment, or even cause them to leave. These individuals crave interaction, transparency, and equality. The authors emphasize that unless prohibited by law or regulation, Google prefers to share information with all of its employees, including core business matters and performance. Adopting such a model naturally attracts top talent, enabling Google to maintain its innovative capabilities and leading industry position.

The agile task forces at Digital China Group serve as a prime illustration of a boundaryless enterprise. Digital China Group has strategically implemented cross-departmental agile task forces, which have effectively eliminated departmental silos of management and expanded employees' cognitive horizons. This approach promotes increased self-awareness and cultivates a more resilient, systematic mind-set.

Digital China Group, apart from establishing internal agile task forces, has endeavoured to transcend corporate boundaries in an industrial ecosystem-based manner. By employing big data profiling and a comprehensive scoring system, Digital China Group has established the Digital China Services Alliance in collaboration with willing and capable collaborators in its network of more than 30,000 partners. The Alliance, established in November 2020, has primarily concentrated on the enhancement of business operations. Constantly dismantling organizational barriers, it enables the expansion of new business models, technologies and applications of co-development, and the development and sharing of solutions. This approach has established a pragmatic, executable path within the digital ecosystem, fostering collaborative development among member enterprises.

Many businesses are gravitating towards self-organizational management reform. Microsoft has transformed its hierarchical structure, postulating that individuals at any level have the potential to become integral to the company's operations and the centre of resource allocation. Huawei has consistently championed the notion, "Let those who can hear the gunshots make the decisions." During Xiaomi's nascent phase emphasizing efficiency, its over-20,000 employees were categorized into just three tiers: a senior executive team composed of the company's founders, each of whom oversaw a major department that housed several smaller teams. Each of these teams, which typically consisted of five to ten individuals, had an appointed lead. Depending on project requirements, team members could be reassigned flexibly to ensure rapid, customer-centric responses.

Incorporating a self-organising management paradigm within a corporation is no trivial task. During this process, several aspects warrant particular attention:

The first is to place the emphasis on individual initiative and motivation. Greater authority must be conferred to the business departments.

Adopting a project contract approach can transfer operational autonomy to respective departmental managers, delineating their responsibilities, rights, duties, and prospective returns. This will transform corporate projects into "personal projects," increasing departmental motivation and dynamism.

The second is to clarify job responsibilities, territorial boundaries, and allocatable resources. Departments should be held accountable for tangible results. Criteria for assessing departmental performance should be unequivocally outlined, as should standards and regulations for bonus allocation. This transformation of corporate roles into "my roles" contributes to the increased motivation and dynamism of functional departments.

The third is to establish a comprehensive corporate system, which is crucial for any enterprise. Prior to delegation, managers should ascertain if the company's business management has an integrated and robust system in place and whether it is standardized. This clarity enables managers to discern their precise authority and responsibilities, determining what can and cannot be delegated. This clarity also mitigates risks of unwarranted delegation or misallocation of authority. For those entrusted with new responsibilities, such clarity delineates the breadth and magnitude of their duties, facilitating optimum utility of their conferred powers to achieve predetermined objectives. Only then can delegation become systematic and meaningful. Underpinning this with systematic and standardized measures ensures that this delegation remains under effective corporate scrutiny, enhancing transparency, and offering a clearer demarcation of rights and duties between delegators and delegates, thereby facilitating the smooth execution of authorization management.

In order to sustain vitality and attain sustainable growth, enterprises should thoroughly revolutionize themselves along the path of data assets accumulation, inter-industry data sharing, AI-powered decision-making, and boundaryless organization. Upon the conclusion of this revolution, it will be apparent that the enterprise's value has undergone reconstruction, whereas the business processes, management approaches, and organizational models have been disrupted. Through such disruption and reconstruction, enterprises can establish a "moat" that is impregnable and thereby gain sustainable competitive advantages.

CHAPTER 4

ACCELERATING DIGITALIZATION WITH CLOUD-NATIVE TECHNOLOGY PARADIGM

The advent of a new era and cognitive disruption has driven us to a new phase of digital transformation. However, traditional technology paradigms can no longer support enterprises' business model innovation and business development. All enterprises, whether industry giants or small and micro businesses, face the challenge of uncertainty – what will the next technology paradigm be, and how will it evolve?

The cloud-native technology paradigm addresses this issue. It not only integrates and restructures various technological innovations, but also comprehensively upgrades the service capabilities of cloud computing and the internet system architecture. This paradigm shift realizes the concept of software-defined everything, profoundly changing the IT foundations of the business world.

4.1 TECHNOLOGY PARADIGM DISRUPTION IS INEVITABLE

CLOUD-NATIVE EQUIPS DATA CLOUD INTEGRATION WITH THE ESSENTIAL FOUNDATION

The Data Cloud Integration strategy has enabled companies to create a continuously accelerating growth flywheel, empowering the speed of development and competitive edge of the enterprises. The driving force behind this growth flywheel is the continuous evolution of technology, which propels operational and business advancements. It becomes the primary force for business innovation and growth.

From a management perspective, the sustainable development of an enterprise relies on three essential architectures, as illustrated in Figure 4.1.

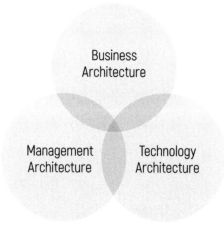

FIGURE 4.1
THREE ESSENTIAL ARCHITECTURES FOR ENTERPRISE DEVELOPMENT

An architecture is crucial for any business, as it addresses the provision of products and services to customers. Different business logics or processes form the unique business architecture of each enterprise, but they all share a common goal: make products and services more effective. To ensure the smooth operation of a business architecture, a management architecture comes into play. The management architecture, based on business processes and procedures, focuses on the effective management of internal personnel, aiming at providing the aforementioned services to customers.

However, it's not enough to have only business and management architectures–both of them require the support of technology architecture. In 1960, F. Warren McFarlan proposed the concept of management information systems. In his view, the connection between management and business systems relies on information. As information technology shifts from scientific to commercial computing, digital technology architecture becomes the glue connecting management and business architectures. Currently, information technology has evolved from single-CPU-driven to computation-driven. However, during the course of this expansion, the technology remains confined to single-CPU-driven application architectures. The most challenging issue confronting enterprise management is that the organization works in silos and different functional departments like HR, finance, and production departments each have stand-alone systems, making interconnectivity extremely difficult. In spite of the adoption of various data bridging, data connection, and network linking technologies, the interconnections between departments and systems remain mechanical, limiting the connectivity between the management business architectures. How can these limitations be overcome? The answer lies in upgrading the technology architecture, which manifests as a disruption and innovation of the technology paradigm.

In Chapter 3, we visualize the presentation of the Data Cloud Integration strategy by using a panorama. From a technology architecture perspective, Data Cloud Integration strategy can be unambiguously presented as depicted in Figure 4.2 on the next page.

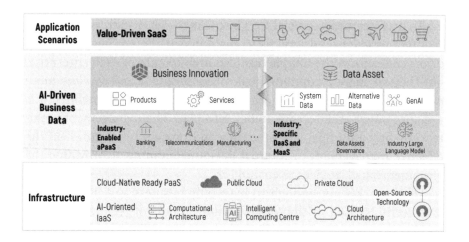

FIGURE 4.2
ANOTHER APPROACH TO PRESENT THE DATA CLOUD INTEGRATION STRATEGY

As illustrated in Figure 4.2, the Data Cloud Integration strategy encompasses underlying infrastructure (for example, AI-oriented IaaS, Computational Architecture, Intelligent Computing Centre, Cloud Architecture, Cloud-Native Ready PaaS), AI-driven business data (for example, Industry-Enabled aPaaS, Industry-Specific DaaS and MaaS), and higher-layer application scenarios integration and operations (for example, Value-Driven SaaS). All these layers share one thing: they are all built on the cloud, supported by cloud-native technologies.

At the infrastructure layer, the strategy drives industry technological innovation and incubation through cloud-native infrastructure technologies such as containers, WASM, and K8S. At the AI-driven business data layer, the strategy builds a series of cloud services driven by data asset management platforms, based upon data assets and data governance, and the strategy also provides enterprises with flexible and customizable aPaaS industrial application toolboxes and GPaaS generic technical toolboxes. This enables "low-code" development, automated operations and maintenance, supporting enterprises to build agile IT capabilities and data-driven value models during their digital transformation journey. This ultimately realizes the cycle and value recreation for the idea of "datafication of businesses and making businesses out of data." At the application scenarios layer, value-driven SaaS are built on cloud-native infrastructure.

If artificial intelligence, blockchain, the Internet of Things, and digital twin are the cornerstones of enterprise digital transformation, cloud-native technologies are the foundation. With the strong, essential support and availability of the underlying cloud-native technologies, we can build any other technologies and applications on top.

A typical example of the implementation of the Data Cloud Integration strategy is the Vehicle-to-Everything (V2X) platform, built by Digital China Group for an automotive manufacturing company.

For automotive manufacturers, the value of data is immeasurable. An automotive manufacturer produces a variety of car models, each with different levels of sophisticated digitalization foundations, resulting in data such as sales volume, satisfaction, and operational stability, each becoming key improvement metrics. No matter if it's the understanding of vehicle and equipment information, operational and predictive maintenance details, delving into the insights of user profiles, or monitoring the operation of applications and performance status, data expands the imaginative space for cars and enhances product availability and rapid iteration of car products.

Handling the vast amount of data becomes a burden for automotive manufacturers, and the agile extraction of the value from these data becomes a hard-fought battle. In the process of assisting a major automotive company in analysing the value of its business data, Digital China Group identified several pain points. The automotive manufacturer has developed over decades and formed independent business units producing different car series and car models, making the enterprise facing challenges like independent and siloed business centres, numerous and complex applications, diverse categories of system data, high-volume of system requests and dispersed deployment. These issues result in multi-faceted operations and maintenance, complicated problem identification and resolution, and very slow responses in faults resolution, leading to decreasing brand satisfaction among consumers.

To address these issues, Digital China Group, taking into consideration the business reality of such a large automotive manufacturer, built a Vehicle-to-Everything platform on the cloud using a "public cloud + private cloud" approach. As the value of data becomes an essential measure of enterprise value, the cloud provides unlimited computing power and constructs pervasive and agile capabilities. Using the Vehicle-to-Everything platform, the automotive enterprise achieved unified collection and management of vehicle and user information, enhancing the collection of real-time application logs, real-time ETL analysis, and real-time monitoring of operational status and performance status of applications. The manufacturer can make use of this historical data to provide predictive support for the operations team and achieve consistent management of data across multi-platforms. This helps the company's technology breakthrough from datafication of businesses to making businesses out of data, providing more imaginative room for carrying out product iteration. Moreover, the Vehicle-to-Everything cloud management platform helps the company to realize pre-alerts and operational cost control for the car services. This is made possible by the construction of a new system to quickly respond to the multi-platform data governance requirements.

The energy unleashed by the collision of cloud and data is far beyond our imagination. The prospects of digital transformation brought by cloud-native technology are equally astonishing.

DATA CLOUD INTEGRATION MAKES THE TECHNOLOGY PARADIGM SHIFT A REALITY

Cloud-native is not merely an upgrade of the technology architecture. It's the disruption and innovation of the technology paradigm.

Throughout human history, there have been numerous technological revolutions, each giving rise to new products, industries, and economic models, and forming corresponding technology paradigms.

What is a paradigm? To understand this concept, let us take Peking opera as an example. Peking opera uses red faces to represent loyal and upright individuals, black faces are selfless and stoic personalities, and white faces often signal cunning and suspicious characters. This symbolism allows the audience to quickly understand the characters during a performance. Peking opera faces are paradigms. Similarly, technology paradigms are the tools we use to define and environmental elements we employ in the process of transforming nature. With the development of digitalization today, cognitive disruption inevitably leads to the upheaval of technology paradigms. The old technology paradigm of industrial society is gradually being replaced by the new technology paradigm in the increasingly digitalized society.

A new generation of IT technologies, no matter if they are cloud computing, big data, or the Internet of Things, breeds new application scenarios, extending digitalization from a few business processes to a plethora of digitalized and intelligent business scenarios that break boundaries and expand the scope. In contrast, traditional systems can only support a handful of simple applications and are unable to adapt to today's new technological environments, let alone meeting the new demands of enterprises. As a result, the disruption of the technology paradigm becomes inevitable.

Needless to say, it is far from sufficient to understand this inevitability solely from the perspective of technological transformation. This technology paradigm shift is driven by multiple dimensions.

From the perspective of social development, economic, political, and commercial forces have driven the renewal of technology paradigms. During the industrial age, military needs fundamentally spawned the creation of various technologies, such as aviation, nuclear weaponry, and many others, while military budgets funded most early development of computer technology. In the digital age, enterprise digital transformation deepens. Demand for computing power increases, gradually expanding the range of application for next generation information technologies – such as cloud-native, cloud computing, big data, and blockchain technologies – and, to some extent, promoting the vigorous development of these new technologies.

The emergence of new production methods has also promoted the disruption of technology paradigms. In the digital age, three changes have occurred in production methods. First is the shift from mass production to mass customization, requiring constant innovation in products to meet the increasingly broad yet personalized needs of customers. Customer experience plays an increasingly significant role in industrial development. Second is the transition from rigid production systems to reconfigurable manufacturing systems. New manufacturing systems can rapidly test and manufacture by rearranging, reusing, and updating system configurations or subsystems, demonstrating strong inclusiveness and flexibility. Third is the shift from factory production to socialized production. Advancement in digital technology has virtualized many material flows into information flows. Apart from the necessary physical production materials and products, various stages of production organization can be infinitely subdivided, presenting significant features of socialized production. Old technology paradigms can no longer adapt to new production methods, and therefore new technology paradigms have emerged.

In addition, the rise of new business models has enriched the content of new technology paradigms. In the digital age, many new business models such the sharing economy and platform economy, and new industries such as ride-hailing services and bike-sharing services have emerged. New industries require support from new technologies, and in turn, the emergence of new technologies forms new technology paradigms.

Finally, let's evaluate this from the angle of social trust. While the internet has promoted global connectivity, it has also given rise to a trust gap which, however, impedes this connection and interaction. The database architectures widely used today are private and centralized, making it impossible to solve the problems of value transfer and mutual trust. In contrast, blockchain technology can establish mutual trust based on "zero trust mechanism" by using decentralized technology and building on big data to achieve mathematical (algorithms) endorsement. To some extent, these advancements have also promoted disruption of the technology paradigm.

Of course, although the disruption of technology paradigms is an inevitable trend, we have only recently accomplished this disruption. This is because, for enterprises, focusing on the customer necessitates achieving a more organic transformation between data assets and business operations. This kind of technology paradigm need creates a significant challenge for traditional IT technology architectures, and it is almost impossible to overcome. Nowadays, due to the emergence of cloud-native and digital-native technologies, especially the realization of Data Cloud Integration, this has become a reality.

INNOVATION BASED ON THE CLOUD-NATIVE TECHNOLOGY PARADIGM

The technology paradigm of the digital age is characterized by its focus on cloud-native technology foundation, encompassing a variety of digital technologies such as big data, the Internet of Things, cloud computing, wearable devices, blockchain, and artificial intelligence as generic technologies. It builds an open internet ecosystem based on the cloud and open-source ecosystems.

Like electricity over a hundred years ago and the steam engine over two hundred years ago, this new technological paradigm and its technologies are penetrating every corner of economy, society, and lifestyle, and widely applied in the traditional industries.

Mark Weiser, the father of ubiquitous computing, mentioned in his article *The Computer for the 21st Century*, "The most profound technologies are those that disappear. They weave themselves into the fabric of everyday life until they are indistinguishable from it. Today, the new paradigm's general technological architecture is becoming an infrastructure like water, air, and highways infrastructures. It is drastically transforming the form of industrial organizations, enterprise operational structures, resource allocation methodologies, production and marketing strategies, and economic development models. This transformation will give rise to the upgrading of many traditional industries, such as traditional manufacturing, goods circulation, and export processing. Furthermore, it will promote the formation of new economic forms and growth opportunities in emerging strategic industries, such as culture, healthcare, environmental protection, and education.

The cloud-native technology paradigm will accelerate the digital transformation process across all industries. With the upgrading and transforming of traditional sectors, more and more industries and enterprises will implement digital transformation. And as many visionary leaders have predicted, all business will ultimately be digitalized.

Among all the technology paradigms commonly used for digitalization, the general technology centred on cloud-native not only provides infrastructure offering the lowest data processing cost, but also greatly improves the efficiency of enterprises when acquiring, processing, transmitting, storing, analysing, and utilizing data. On the other hand, the enhancement of digitalization levels within enterprises further promotes the development of the digital technology.

Of course, such transformation and disruption of the technology paradigm will never be accomplished overnight. Only by the step-by-step application of digital technology in various sectors of the society and economy, can the new technology paradigm evolve from its emergence to a stable development stage.

What is cloud-native? What is its evolutionary trajectory? How does it drive the digital transformation? To answer these questions, we need to understand the genesis of this technology.

4.2 **CLOUD-NATIVE: A NEW "CONTAINER REVOLUTION"**

FROM MAINFRAME COMPUTING TO CLOUD COMPUTING

Cloud computing, once regarded as the "next paradigm shift of technology," has advanced to the cloud-native era. The evolution from cloud computing to cloud-native signified a disruption of the technology paradigm. It also entails the formation of an entirely new computing architectural framework.

Most people do not understand cloud-native, not to mention understand the significance and implication of its evolution shift. Looking back at the history of computing will help us to better understand the origin and development of cloud-native.

Since computers were invented, information technology has gone through three stages: scientific computing, business computing, and social computing. Correspondingly, computing paradigms have also experienced three eras: the mainframe computing era, the PC computing era, and the cloud computing era, as illustrated in Figure 4.3.

| Mainframe Computing Era | PC Computing Era | Cloud Computing Era |

FIGURE 4.3
EVOLUTION OF COMPUTING PARADIGMS

In the mainframe computing era, mainframes were the central paradigm of the computing industry, with IBM being the undisputed leader. Due to their immense power and high cost, in 1943, IBM's chairman Thomas J. Watson Sr. confidently asserted, "I think there is a world market for maybe five computers." This judgement, however, did not stop IBM from continuing to explore and innovate in the field of computing. In 1946, IBM developed the model 603 electronic multiplier, by adopting vacuum tube circuits, which performed addition and multiplication at five times the speed of previous products. By 1948, IBM developed the Selective Sequence Electronic Calculator (SSEC), which was the first computer capable of modifying stored programs, significantly enhancing computational power, processing speed, storage space, and programmability.

In 1956, Thomas Watson Jr. succeeded as IBM's leader. During a period marked by the proliferation of new technologies such as transistors (replacing the vacuum tubes) and magnetic storage (replacing the punch cards), IBM developed the S/360 mainframe. It was the world's first general-purpose mainframe to use integrated circuits, serving both scientific computing and transaction processing needs, with compatibility across various machines, and meeting different kinds of user's needs. It was an "all-rounder" – a general-purpose machine. The S/360 was the most revolutionary product in IBM's history, changing the course of computer development and marking the beginning of a new computing era. From the success of United States' Apollo moon landing program to the transformation of global business models, the S/360 mainframe series played a pivotal role.

As the world entered the 1980s, PCs gradually replaced mainframes, and Microsoft became king. Microsoft's founder Bill Gates established a clear mission for the company: "To have a computer on the desk of every home."

Microsoft's GUI (Graphical User Interface) Windows operating system laid the foundation for the development of personal computer applications, completely changing the user demographic for computers, propelling personal computing onto a new fast development track, and integrating personal computing into people's daily lives.

In the next two decades, as personal computers became widespread and popular, the computing model for both enterprise and consumer applications underwent significant changes.

As an old Chinese saying goes, "Separation leads to unification, and unification leads to separation." The development of computing paradigms mirrored this proverb, evolving through the continual separation and unification of paradigms. In the early days of mainframe computing, computation was a centralized paradigm, with mainframes centralizing all computations through parallel computing architectures. However, during the PC computing era, computation became distributed, with computing power spread across every PC. By the early 21st century, as the concept of cloud computing began to rise, computational power once again centralized.

At the Search Engine Strategies Conference (SES San Jose 2006) on August 9, 2006, Eric Schmidt, then CEO of Google, introduced the concept of cloud computing. However, it was Amazon that first launched cloud computing services. That same year, Amazon publicly released S3 (Simple Storage Service), SQS (Simple Queue Service), and EC2 (Elastic Compute Cloud),[1] pioneering the 'Hardware as a Service' business model using the classic system software technology of virtualization. This approach enabled the public to access computing resources as conveniently as water and electricity.

This stage represented cloud computing in its infancy. From an industry perspective, 2008 is considered the inaugural year of cloud computing. That year, after Amazon's AWS services gained widespread recognition in the industry and among the public, more and more industry giants turned their attention to this new market, leading to a proliferation of public cloud[2] products: Microsoft announced a preview of Windows Azure at its Professional Developers Conference that year, initiating its exploration into the hosting and online transformation of numerous technologies and services; Google also released a preview of the Google App Engine that year, allowing developers to create web applications and deploy them on Google's infrastructure in an architecture more akin to PaaS (Platform as a Service); and Alibaba Cloud also began planning and executing. From 2008 onwards, the era of cloud computing slowly unfolded, with many giants becoming players, intensifying market competition, while making the concept of cloud computing gradually transparent.

Before the arrival of the cloud computing era, names such as IBM, Oracle, EMC, and Intel were inseparable from enterprise informatization. These industry titans dominated the IT market for over 20 years, continuously offering products and services by charging the enterprises license and other fees. Their services brought technical convenience to enterprise informatization, but there are limitations such as high cost of ownership and inflexibility of providing services according to business changes which also posed a heavy burden on the enterprises. In contrast, the prevalence of cloud services not only provided users with economic scalability, but also offered pervasive connectivity. Any computing device, so long as it was connected to the internet, could communicate with each other via the TCP/IP[3] protocol.

During this period, some visionary enterprises began to embrace cloud computing. For example, streaming platform Netflix was an early adopter. Its monthly video streams exceed 1 billion, yet it has not built its own data centres. Starting in 2009, Netflix began employing Amazon's cloud computing services, and by November 2012 had transferred all of its IT infrastructure to Amazon's cloud, ensuring that users could stream videos swiftly, either through mobile apps or web browsers.

Through cloud computing, Netflix maintained a highly agile and available IT architecture[4] – for instance, being able to deploy new feature codes in just a few days, or setting up and activating new hardware within minutes. Thanks to the success of its cloud computing architecture, Netflix was able to build the largest bandwidth-consuming streaming platform on the public cloud and become an internet giant that disrupted the traditional television industry. Cloud computing has become a foundational infrastructure, spurring new developments across many industries, such as the Global Positioning System (GPS). GPS, originally based on artificial satellites, is a high-precision wireless navigation positioning system. With the advent of cloud computing, GPS has evolved into an intelligent positioning system. Due to the faster response and higher computation speeds provided by cloud computing technology, GPS can process location data more rapidly and offer more accurate positioning information. Furthermore, cloud computing technology efficiently processes data and extracts information, enabling GPS to provide more diverse and complex location-specific services, such as personalized recommendations, social media interactions, and autonomous driving. The robust processing and storage capabilities of cloud computing also allow GPS to support a greater number of devices, users, and application scenarios, enhancing its scalability and applicability. GPS, based on cloud computing, is widely used in fields such as transportation, commercial real estate, security monitoring, and social networking, bringing greater convenience and improved experiences to people's lives.

After various industry giants established their strategies to venture into cloud computing, the field entered a period of thriving development. As cloud platforms matured and various terminal devices emerged, its focus shifted from providing cloud infrastructure to supporting cloud applications. Addressing diverse and complex application demands has become a key driver and pivot of cloud computing. During this period, many companies made beneficial attempts at the product and technology level, which enhanced the capabilities and quality of cloud services, attracting more and more attention to the world of cloud computing.

Over the past decade, domestic cloud computing has also taken off in China. China has become one of the world's fastest-growing cloud computing markets, with the industry maintaining an annual growth rate of over 30%. Companies such as Alibaba, Baidu, and Huawei engage in effective practices and are gradually increasing their investments. Alibaba Cloud, Tencent Cloud, and Huawei Cloud have even ranked among the top ten cloud computing platforms globally.

Cloud computing, along with personal computers and the internet, is one of the three most important information technology revolutions in history. In the same way that steam engine and electricity triggered two industrial revolutions, cloud computing is set to become a core driving force for the development of human society.

Its development has been so rapid and swift that it is impossible to predict what the next decade will bring. Current trends are as follows.

The cost of storage and computing power will continue to fall, but consumption will grow. Since there are still a large number of computing services around the world that have not migrated to the cloud computing environment, the computing power of foundational cloud services will increase significantly over the next decade, and service prices will continue to decrease.

Cutting-edge technologies will continue to be integrated into cloud computing platforms, including quantum computing, AR/VR, blockchain and other technologies, especially those applications that rely on massive data computing capabilities and elastic computing resources. Cloud computing is the track ready for accelerating the growth of these technologies.

The integrated development and application of technologies such as cloud, artificial intelligence, 5G, and the Internet of Things will propel the next wave of intelligent enterprise development. The cloud is expanding from computing power to big data, artificial intelligence, the Internet of Things, and security, and is tied to future manufacturing upgrades and China's economic transformation.

Multi-cloud or hybrid cloud[5] will become a long-term application environment for enterprises. Cloud computing users will comprehensively use edge clouds,[6] services provided by various cloud computing service providers, and their own IT facilities.

An extension of the central cloud, the edge cloud will extend some of the cloud's services or capabilities (such as storage, computing, network, artificial intelligence, big data, security, etc.) to the edge infrastructure. Together, they will achieve centre-edge collaboration, network-wide computing power scheduling, and unified management and control of the entire network, truly achieving ubiquity.

Cloud computing development technology stacks will become increasingly complex, and this will make clearer the division of labour in application development. Application development targeting end users will become more concise, and the approaches of the application generation will become increasingly diverse.

One thing is certain: cloud-native will become the most important trend. The systemic and disruptive architectural changes brought by cloud-native will provide massive new growth opportunities and liberate enormous cloud computing benefits.

From the era of mainframe computing to the era of cloud computing, computing paradigms have undergone decades of development and transformation, profoundly impacting every individual and organization, and driving social and economic development. The pace of technological progress has only accelerated, with cloud computing relentlessly advancing toward its version 2.0: cloud-native.

CONCEIVED IN THE CLOUD, NURTURED IN THE CLOUD

In his book *The Box: How the Shipping Container Made the World Smaller and the World Economy Bigger*, American economist Marc Levinson narrates the history of the shipping container. Like how Henry Ford's assembly line transformed industrial production, this simple container, much like a giant tin can, had an immense impact on the maritime shipping industry. It standardized the loading and unloading of goods and integrated the transportation of goods across railways, roads, and ships into a single system, significantly improving the efficiency and speed of cargo transportation while ensuring safety and, most importantly, reducing costs. With the freight transportation modernized, the goods trading system was completely reshaped, and the world economy flourished. This innovation linked the production and consumption of different countries, greatly promoting globalization. As *The Economist* magazine stated, "Without the container, there would be no globalization."

Today, in the field of information technology, the emergence and development of cloud computing has enabled globalization of the digital world, and cloud-native likens itself to a new container revolution, sparking innovative transformations in IT infrastructure.

Why is cloud-native dubbed a 'container revolution'?

If we consider the internet the sea lanes of the digital world, then application software is the ships. Constantly traversing these routes, the data within these applications are the cargo. In traditional IT architecture, every company needed to build its own 'ship' to transport 'cargo,' and these 'ships' (i.e., application software) had to be equipped with IT infrastructure capable of computing, storage, networking, and more, leading to high IT costs for enterprises.

After the advent of cloud computing, large service companies specialising in cloud computing services emerged, acting like freight companies and offering standardized 'ships' with scale. Consequently, enterprises gained a new option: rather than building their own 'ships,' they could transport their cargo through these freight companies' channels.

This container-like freight required a compatible application development architecture and operational management model. Thus, the concept of cloud-native emerged.

Many people today do not understand cloud-native and ask, "What exactly is cloud-native?"

Opinions differ on the definition of cloud-native because it is an emerging disruptive concept. Moreover, as cloud-native rapidly and continually evolves, its definition is being iterated and updated, with different community organizations and companies developing their own interpretations and definitions.

Pivotal, an open-source software company, was a pioneer in cloud-native application architecture. In 2013, inspired by years of experience in architecture and consulting, Matt Stine, the company's senior product manager, introduced the concept of being cloud-native. In 2015, he published *Migrating to Cloud-Native Application Architectures*, a book outlining the main characteristics of cloud-native application architecture: adherence to the twelve factors (codebase, dependencies, configuration, back-end services, etc.), micro-services-oriented architecture, self-service agile infrastructure, API-based collaboration,[7] and antifragility. After several refinements, Pivotal's official definition of cloud-native has now been condensed to four key points: DevOps, continuous delivery, micro-services, and containerization.

In addition to Pivotal, which made significant contributions to the proposal and development of cloud-native, the Cloud Native Computing Foundation (CNCF) also serves as another notable advocate.

CNCF was initiated by Google and the Linux Foundation on December 11, 2015. It is the most influential and authoritative organization in the cloud-native field, dedicated to nurturing and maintaining a vendor-neutral open-source ecosystem to promote cloud-native technologies. The foundation currently has over a hundred enterprise and institutional members, including giants like Amazon, Microsoft, and Cisco.

CNCF defines cloud-native as the following: "Cloud-native technologies empower organizations to build and run scalable applications in modern, dynamic environments such as public cloud, private cloud,[8] and hybrid cloud. Technologies such as containers, service meshes, micro-services, immutable infrastructure, and declarative APIs exemplify this approach. These technologies enable loosely coupled systems[9] that are resilient, manageable, and observable. Combined with robust automation, they allow engineers to make frequent, predictable high-impact changes with minimal toil."

According to this definition, cloud-native technologies can be treated as the application programming construction framework which enables the development of scalable applications that can operate in various environments, such as private clouds, public clouds, hybrid clouds, and other new dynamic settings.

In a sense, cloud-native is an architecture rooted in the cloud, a system of technological approaches for developing, deploying, running, and maintaining application software in the cloud. Its core assumption and most aggressive vision is that the applications of the future will undoubtedly grow in the cloud. The cloud-native environment indicates that application software does not reside in traditional IT equipment but rather in the cloud, while the application software is designed to adapt to the cloud environment, fully leveraging its elastic scaling and distribution features, ultimately achieving efficient, stable, and secure operation. Thus, this brand new approach for application software development, delivery, and operation and maintenance maximises the capabilities of the cloud. By adopting cloud-native technologies and management approaches, enterprises can easily build their businesses, whilst enjoying the high efficiency and uninterrupted service capabilities of the Cloud.

Cloud-native has formed a highly prosperous ecosystem, involving diverse and complex stacks of technologies that continue to grow and strengthen following the development and advancement of the industry. Within this extensive technological system, six key technologies warrant attention, as illustrated in Figure 4.4.

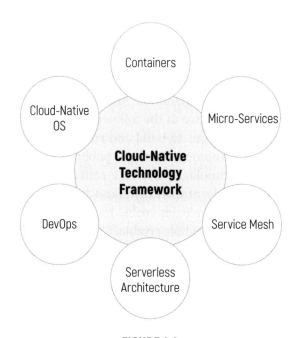

FIGURE 4.4

THE SIX KEY TECHNOLOGIES IN THE CLOUD-NATIVE TECHNOLOGY FRAMEWORK

1. **Cloud-Native Operating System**

   Kubernetes (also known as K8s) is an open-source container orchestration platform, which works with various container runtimes, used
   for automating the deployment, scaling, and operations of contain-
   erised applications. It offers a powerful toolbox for the automated
   management of containers, including features such as load balancing, auto-scaling, rolling updates, and fault recovery. Kubernetes has
   become the de-facto standard for cloud-native operating systems. It
   simplifies the deployment and management of distributed applications, enhancing the reliability and scalability of these applications.
   It provides a unified management interface for developers and operations personnel in public, private, and hybrid cloud environments,
   allowing them to focus on application development and innovation.

   Originally released by Google in 2014, Kubernetes quickly established itself as the de-facto standard of the cloud-native ecosystem.
   Built upon the experience of Google's internal Borg system, it aims to
   address the complexities of container orchestration and cluster management. As an open-source project, Kubernetes has garnered extensive support from the global developer community, rapidly evolving
   into a mature, stable platform for running distributed applications in
   various environments.

2. **Containers**

   Containers are a lightweight virtualization technology, essentially
   a series of processes isolated from other parts of the system. They
   provide an implementation guarantee for micro-services, serving as
   an application isolation tool that simplifies application deployment,
   management, and delivery. Major IT companies have invested heavily
   in researching and developing container products and services, and
   containers are forecast to become a primary delivery method.

   Containers define a file format called a container image. Developers
   can use these images to predefine applications, using their required configurations, dependencies, and deployment actions as templates. Each
   machine is then deployed a software called a container engine, which
   generates container instances from the images to run applications.

   Containers effortlessly solve scaling issues. With container images as
   templates, a container can easily launch several application instances,
   making applications deployment unprecedentedly simple. What used
   to take an hour or two can now be done in minutes.

Additionally, containers resolve migration issues. The word 'container' is analogous to shipping containers in port transportation. Applications and their dependencies are packaged together, eliminating the need to worry about the installation environment and dependent components during deployment. Containers standardize operational modes for various applications, allowing any server with a container engine to run them.

3. Micro-services

Micro-services represent a new architecture and organizational method for developing software. They break down an application into independently functioning programs that can run on different hardware or servers. These independent applications work together to deliver the final application needed by users. Under micro-services architecture, not only can modules be independently developed in terms of coding, they can also be deployed independently of each other. Instead of building and deploying one application, there are several applications, each performing small functions that work together to form a complete application.

The advantages of micro-services mainly manifest in three areas. First is deployment flexibility, as different teams can independently create and deploy micro-services on various servers. Second is technological flexibility, since micro-services can be built using different languages or platforms – as they communicate with each other, the actual language used is not crucial, allowing developers to use diverse languages and platforms. And third is agile scalability, as micro-services can be independently scaled. During peak shopping traffic, for instance, only the most-used micro-services need to be scaled, without affecting others.

4. Service Mesh

With the rise of micro-services architecture, the complexity of applications has continually increased. Communication among services in micro-services architecture can involve multiple network protocols, load balancing, retry mechanisms, and more, all of which require fine-grained management. A service mesh can be seen as a more intelligent form of proxy software. Based on the foundation of containers and micro-services, a service mesh allows users to manage the communication between services in a more detailed and intelligent manner.

At its core, a service mesh is a network responsible for the communication among micro-services. It decouples service governance capabilities from business development, allowing developers to focus more from commercial and innovation perspectives. Meanwhile, it shifts service governance capabilities to the infrastructure layer, allowing professionals to handle specialized tasks. The iteration and updates of governance capabilities can also be independent of the business. In an era where micro-services architecture is gradually becoming mainstream, service mesh is playing a crucial role in safeguarding our transition to a cloud-native paradigm.

5. Serverless Architecture

Serverless does not mean servers have no place in the future; instead, it implies a shift away from focusing on underlying service architecture. Developers can hence concentrate on the implementation of business-related logic, for instance, the code segments for the functions. The platform can automatically deploy and start based on the loading, and scale according to the business processing needs.

Serverless products perfectly address such issues as inflexible server scaling and cumbersome management, offering a great deal of benefits.

Firstly, they allow for pay-as-you-go. Websites typically experience fluctuating traffic, with business-oriented sites seeing a surge during working hours but minimal activity at night. With conventional servers, users incur fixed costs all day, regardless of traffic volume, potentially leading to either server insufficiency or wastage. In contrast, serverless products charge based on actual usage.

Secondly, they offer scalability. Serverless is designed to handle vast demands. It is feasible to host a small website with few visitors, and if the site suddenly attracts millions, there is no issue. Behind the scenes, the cloud provider simply allocates more servers to the website, reducing them as traffic decreases. Traditionally, increasing server capacity means purchasing more servers and setting up load balancers to distribute traffic across two or more servers, which is more challenging and time-consuming. Thus, with serverless, users never have too many or too few servers – it's always just right.

Thirdly, developers do not need to manage servers, as all the details are handled by the cloud servers. This means businesses do not have to procure equipment, worry about installing the latest patches, or deal with hard drive failures. Most importantly, during traffic spikes, there are neither scaling up issues, nor concerns around upgrading and replacing equipment at the end of their usage lifecycle.

6. DevOps

"DevOps" is derived from 'Development' and 'Operations.' It aims to bridge the gap between developers and operations teams, fostering better communication and cooperation. Automated processes in DevOps make software building, testing, and releasing faster, more frequent, and reliable.

The DevOps model is not simply about merging development and operations teams. Instead, operations personnel are involved early in the development process, understanding technical details used in development, like system architecture and technical roadmaps, to formulate suitable operations strategies. In turn, developers participate in operations, providing support based on their abilities.

DevOps fundamentally aims to coordinate activities such as design, development, testing, and deployment throughout the software lifecycle. It facilitates efficient collaboration between developers and operations staff, striving to make the delivery process more efficient and reliable. This approach offers an effective, swift, and dependable method to deliver high-quality, valuable software. Therefore, DevOps extends beyond a collaborative philosophy between developers and operations staff. It necessitates the practical deployment of an automated software delivery assembly line to enable frequent and automated software releases.

The implementation of such an automated delivery assembly line involves establishing a DevOps platform, for which numerous tools are available on the market, forming a robust DevOps tool ecosystem.

With the rise of micro-services architecture, DevOps has become the most effective delivery model in the cloud-native era. Digital China is also advancing in this direction, developing and integrating a DevOps platform internally, solidly progressing towards cloud-native transformation.

These six technologies are not isolated but rather interconnected. The cloud-native operating system forms the foundation for other technologies, with the cloud providing computational, network, and storage architectural resources for upper-layer applications. Containers, positioned between the cloud infrastructure and applications, decouple applications from infrastructure resources.

At the application layer, users can choose between micro-services architecture or serverless architecture. In complex architectural contexts, service meshes can manage and control communication among service components, and DevOps creates a positive cycle of continuous iteration and updates in the application architecture.

In today's digital age, the cloud-native industry maintains a robust development momentum. Many hot cloud-native technologies have seen numerous practical applications across various industries and fields. An increasing number of enterprises are willing to evolve their technological architectures toward cloud-native. Digital China Group released its technical strategy related to cloud-native at the TECH Digital China 2021 Technology Annual Conference, in August 2021. Enterprises' accelerated embrace of cloud-native has given rise to an ever-more-perfected cloud-native ecosystem. Cloud-native is now entering a golden phase of development.

PACKAGED BUSINESS CAPABILITIES ACCELERATES THE PROMOTION OF CLOUD-NATIVE

As enterprises increasingly embrace cloud-native technologies and architectural concepts, integrating cloud-native technology with business and management has become a focal point for corporate leaders. To this end, Gartner® proposed in 2021 that: "the solution for manufacturing companies lies in the concept of composable business." Such enterprises can rapidly innovate and dynamically combine internal and external capabilities as business needs change. Composable Businesses are better positioned to frequently plan more significant business transformations and track the evolving needs of customers or stakeholders, achieving a transformation from digital twin to digital-native.

A "Composable Business" requires corresponding IT systems and business applications to be modular. Packaged Business Capabilities (PBCs) are the foundational application framework supporting a composable business. As we have concluded from Figure 4.5, Gartner's® research "Innovation Insight for Composable Business for Manufacturers," this application architecture is governed by four principles: modularity, orchestration, discoverability, and autonomy. These principles necessitate fundamental transformation in thinking, business architecture, and technologies.

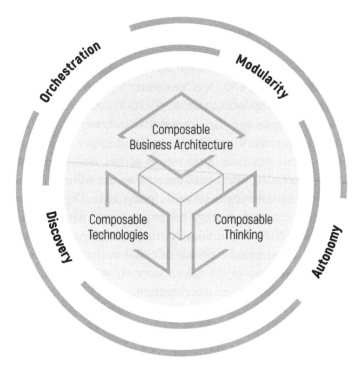

FIGURE 4.5
THE KEY COMPONENTS OF COMPOSABLE BUSINESS

Source: Gartner, "Innovation Insight for Composable Business for Manufacturers"*

Orchestration

Component providers should make their components as orchestratable as possible. For example, implementing idempotent controls (so that those who orchestrate don't need to worry about order, location, retry mechanisms, etc.), defining clear interfaces, and supporting with full openness both integration approaches and standard protocols.

Modularity

Modularity is the key to composability. No matter if it is planning applications, organising, or modelling business, each component of the entire system must be a unit with independent and complete business logic. The granularity of business units is crucial. If it is too large, it hampers the agility in development; if it is too small, it fails to ensure the integrity of business logic within a component.

Autonomy

Each delivery project is unique. It often involves selecting only a few components based on customer requirements or limitations or replacing components with other external systems. Autonomy means that components can operate independently, without strong dependencies on other components and incurring minimal overhaul when replaced.

Discovery

This principle can be divided into static and dynamic aspects. The static aspect includes recording service libraries, providing friendly, comprehensive, high-quality documentation, and offering demonstration environments. The dynamic aspect includes dynamic registration and discovery, which can be used to fulfil the dynamic business process orchestration and expansion of business processes. Advanced requests include operational characteristics of components, such as resources and performance.

Enterprises have to build some core business capabilities in-house, outsource or directly purchase some capabilities from vendors, and develop others in collaboration with ecosystem partners.

What is the relationship between the PBC framework and the micro-services framework? They can complement each other. PBCs are pre-built business functionalities designed to meet specific business needs. A PBC can be a combination of micro-services or a single application. PBCs combine data, APIs, and events into a single application entity, which is packaged, published, and run via cloud-native technologies, integrating easily into an enterprise's existing systems.

Digital China Group's Pan-Yun Industry Cloud PaaS platform has built-in PBC application development and operation platforms. The platform standardizes and encapsulates PBC components, forming a series of PBCs and industry delivery templates and integration workbenches that can be flexibly assembled based on business requirements. It enables unified standards for development, deployment, integration, data exchange, and operations. Furthermore, through the establishment of a PBC marketplace and introducing a large number of high quality external PBC products, the platform supports customers in efficiently and cost-effectively assembling highly complex industry application systems.

SEIZE THE OPPORTUNITY AND SOAR IN THE CLOUD

In recent years, the cloud-native market has shown a fast-growing growth trend. According to statistics provided by Gartner, the global cloud computing market size already reached U.S.$491 billion. Amidst the surge of the digital economy, the digital transformation of traditional industries has become a strong driving force of the cloud-native industry. The trillions of Chinese Yuan in capital investment brought by the digital infrastructure construction will propel the cloud-native industry towards a new phase.

An array of cloud-native related technical terms and products are emerging. At the onset of cloud computing, the application development environment was relatively simple, and there were "full-stack engineers," implying that one person could complete R&D for an entire application software if the development cycle was not taken into consideration. However, this title no longer applies because it is rare for an individual or enterprise to fully master all the technology stacks related to cloud-native. Even for those who apply cloud-native technologies, it is now more difficult to comprehensively understand all related technologies as related to cloud-native, achieving rational architecturing and appropriate selection, and completely smoothing the entire process of integration, development, and deployment. Most enterprises rely extensively on services provided by cloud computing platforms, generating new market opportunities for solution providers in the software industry. Only those who can provide digital transformation enterprises with a friendly application development and deployment environment will acquire and retain customers.

Today, a group of enterprises have made swift progress by seizing the opportunity and "soaring" in the cloud.

1. **Industry Disruptor Originating from the Cloud: Salesforce**
   Founded in February 1999, Salesforce proposed the concept of "Software as a Service" (SaaS), becoming the "ancestor" of SaaS enterprises. In July 2020, Salesforce's market value surpassed that of database software company Oracle, marking a significant milestone in the history of SaaS development.

   Previously, enterprises had to purchase the software and buy, build, and maintain the corresponding IT hardware. The emergence of SaaS provided another solution. By using the SaaS platform, enterprises could simply register an account online and adjust some settings on their devices to enable the required software services.

Salesforce's innovation lies not only in its products but also in its unique business model. Salesforce wanted to make software a fundamental infrastructure like water, electricity, and gas, so it introduced a simple subscription service. This innovation created radical change in enterprise services and the entire software market, which saw software CDs turn into monthly or annual SaaS services, and the traditional personal sales model shift to a low-cost online subscription model. These forces not only simplified internal management structure and significantly reduced service prices, but also transformed enterprise users' fixed capital investment into operational expenditures.

Over time, Salesforce has launched several groundbreaking products and services, such as Sforce 2.0, AppExchange, Apex, Salesforce1, and Trailhead. Among these, AppExchange has been hailed as a service that has changed business software. It provides partners with a platform to develop their applications and make them available to all Salesforce customers. *BusinessWeek* dubbed it the "eBay of business software," while *Forbes* called it the "iTunes of business software."

Throughout its two-decade journey, Salesforce has created an ecosystem comprising administrators, developers, consultants, and users, continuously innovating and disrupting CRM (Customer Relationship Management). Through constant product updates and the expanding ecosystem, Salesforce has conveyed the concept of cloud services to the world, introducing a novel business model to the software market. Salesforce has become an indispensable digital infrastructure in modern society, serving as a shared platform for numerous industries and society as a whole.

2. Largest Software Industry Financing to Date Made by Cloud-Native: Snowflake

The saying "Don't reinvent the wheel" is widely used in the field of internet development and implies there is no need to exert effort on already mature solutions. However, eras change and new cognition brings new technologies. Technological renewal is constantly reinventing the wheel, giving rise to many great companies. In September 2020, the cloud computing company Snowflake went public, creating the largest software industry financing case in history. The surge in market value behind this seemingly unexciting data warehouse business shows capital is starting to bet on the future of cloud-native.

Snowflake's rise stems from not only commercialization of the cloud-native technology framework, but also 20 years of relentless exploration by business wizards and technical geniuses, like founder Frank Slootman. Though seemingly accidental, the company's success was inevitable. Its secret lies in providing technology architecture that matches the era's cognition.

Before the digital age, cost reduction and efficiency improvement were always considered after a company had grown to a certain scale. In the digital age, enterprises face constantly changing customer demands, amassing of data, and gradually blurred enterprise boundaries. Even in the SaaS model, system-level software like data warehouses typically requires fixed annual fees paid in advance. Especially for cost-saving products that need rapid iteration, since the scale and depth of usage cannot be quantified, it becomes particularly challenging for customers to measure their ROI, thus creating a usage barrier.

Slootman believes this phenomenon is unfair: charges are front-loaded, but results are back-loaded; the process of usage is opaque; and costs cannot be quantified. Snowflake exists precisely to solve these black box issues.

Snowflake created a new business model – managing customer data as an asset model. Customers no longer pay a fixed annual fee upfront. Instead, the platform settles accounts based on actual consumption of computing power and storage, thereby achieving digital cost measurability. Based on real statistics of unit resource consumption, customers can compare the investment in each link of the new model with that under the traditional model, and ultimately obtain an investment return rate as accurate as forecasted reports, achieving digital return measurability. Behind the more realistic pay-as-you-go model is a new product design and technical architecture: cloud-native.

Elastic scaling and dynamic expansion are two features of cloud-native technology. These features make Snowflake more affordable, flexible, and easily shareable, winning laudable customer favour, market recognition, and remarkable achievement.

3. Digital China Group's Innovative Infrastructure Cloud under Cloud-Native

With the advancement of digital technology, traditional CPU architectures are facing significant challenges. New architectures like X86, ARM, and RISC are emerging, characterized by greater openness, lower cost, and a broader range of applications. As we build enterprise clouds and public clouds, we need to not only ensure compatibility with legacy architectures but also create greater possibilities for the future. This requires us to achieve cloud integration in a heterogeneous environment, creating a multi-cloud management platform that supports heterogeneous CPUs. The advent of cloud-native technology has made the construction of such multi-cloud management platforms a reality.

Digital China Group's creation of the Innovative Infrastructure Cloud is a prime example of a multi-cloud management platform. Based on new digital-era understandings such as digital asset sharing, user connectivity, digital-native scenario construction, and data-driven self-organization, the Digital China Innovative Infrastructure Cloud provides enterprises with an independently developed and controllable cloud-native technology stack.

The capability model and features of the entire Digital China Innovative Infrastructure Cloud can be summarized as '1162N,' with the core being a strong foundation of full capabilities, specialized services, and business proximity. The first '1' stands for 'one foundation,' a customizable and reliable cloud data centre combining software and hardware. The second '1' is 'one cloud,' a technology platform that provides container cloud and public services. '6' refers to the six core capabilities and services provided by the capability centre, such as big data services and the IoT. '2' refers to two types of specialized support and services that can be provided to personalized customizable clouds. 'N' stands for 'N sticker,' which represents closeness to the industry's market, productising our technical capabilities and supporting front-end business, digitally empowering front-end business.

Specifically, Digital China Group's Innovative Infrastructure Cloud consists of four parts. The first is the capability foundation, providing a framework for a cloud-native, software-defined data centre. I believe that providing a secure and reliable foundation to industries undergoing digital transformation is key to digital service enterprises offering various cloud data centre services. This capability foundation endows Digital China Group's Innovative Infrastructure Cloud with more functions. In the face of an environment driven by Innovative Infrastructure, it can provide Innovative Infrastructure cloud services. To industries, it can provide dedicated cloud services. At the same time, we also utilize the design, integration, and operation and maintenance capabilities of existing, mature data centres to ensure high performance and security. When the capability foundation is stable, the applications will be running on it smoothly.

The second part is the 'capability barbell,' which allows resources of state-owned cloud or enterprise hybrid clouds to be uniformly managed through various tools, enabling effective management of data assets. The 'barbell' serves as a vivid metaphor for the cloud platform, supporting chips and operating systems, providing ready-to-use public services such as open-source middleware, databases, and excellent software services. At the two ends of the barbell, there are our cloud services including consultation, construction, migration, operation and maintenance, while on the other end are our management services, including hybrid cloud management, automated orchestration, integrated operation and maintenance, multi-cloud billing, and service desk. If the capability foundation is the base of Innovative Infrastructure Cloud, then the 'capability barbell' is its soft foundation, which supports the third part – the capability centre.

This synthesizes many distributed applications to enable business digitalization. The capability centre contains six core capabilities and services. First is support services for distributed application data, including distributed scheduling, micro-services, and full automation testing; second is big data services, including the Yan-Yun DaaS (Data as a Service) big data mining integration platform that won first prize under the National Technology Invention Award, as well as intelligent analysis, storage analysis, and secure data desensitization services; third is AI services, providing cognitive and perceptual capabilities; fourth is the IoT services, providing IoT-specific perception and management capabilities; fifth is the value-added internet blockchain services; sixth is comprehensive security services, including mobile network security, database audit, and quantum key distribution. These six aspects cover the mainstream demands of current big data applications and can help enterprises quickly and effectively digitalize their core assets.

The fourth part is the capability market, which is the entire ecosystem of applications offered by Digital China Group. All Digital China Group's products and solutions are placed in this market, and customers can conveniently find suitable solutions through the cloud market.

It is evident that embracing cloud-native will be exceptionally relevant to the enterprise market going forwards. This is an opportune time to leapfrog in the development using digital technology. To transcend, one must evaluate the present from the future rather than imitate and follow. We will continue to build cloud-native products, enhance technical and service capabilities, expand our competitive advantage in the field of cloud-native, and ultimately become a better digital service provider.

4.3 SOFTWARE IS REDEFINING THE WORLD

SOFTWARE: ENDOWING HARDWARE WITH A SOUL

Compared to the traditional legacy approach of implementing enterprise digital transformation, cloud-native is far more cost-effective and efficient, and it contributes to the exponential growth of cloud-native technologies. The vigorous advancement of cloud-native technologies has precipitated a monumental shift in the field of information technology. This shift involves adopting a software-defined world mentality to contemplate and propel the growth of the digital economy. Consequently, the hardware-defined world has been progressively eclipsed by the software-defined world, which has now become the cornerstone of the interconnected world.

The initial meaning of software definition meant to use software to define systems functionalities, empowering the hardware with software, thereby optimizing the energy and operational efficiency of the system. In the digital age, this notion has undergone a profound change.

When viewed from a macroscopic perspective, digital abstraction signifies an important milestone in the trajectory of human development. The transformation from tangible concepts such as land and flocks of sheep, to conceptual ones like numbers and theorems has resulted in a more straightforward and comprehensible world. Digital abstraction, using various patterns and designations, has permeated every sector. Due to this rationale, Pythagoras was firmly convinced that the world existed in a mathematical essence, wherein the numbers constituting mathematics possessed a boundless aesthetic appeal.

The development of digital abstraction is based on the processing, transmission, integration, and exchange of information, cognition, and experience. From the works of Melanie Mitchell, a professor of computer science, we can understand that the straightforward and simplistic world of physics only exists in textbooks; we inhabit in a world that is complex and multifaceted. The physical universe is filled with an infinite number of formulas, theorems, and laws. The plethora of numbers can be bewildering, and individuals often find themselves left speechless when confronted with massive amounts of data. Yet, from this obscurity emerges a ray of hope: software, which is a means for individuals to grasp the world's intricacies. Software has an orderly logic, whereas data is chaotic; software is convergent, whereas data is divergent. By employing software as a tool, individuals are able to consistently augment and broaden their comprehension of the world.

But what is software? The components of a computer system are hardware and software. Hardware comprises the observable, physical machines, and devices. Software consists of a sequence of structured computer instructions and data. It facilitates communication between the hardware and the user by serving as an interface between the two. Software controls the vast array of applications for which we employ computers. By endowing hardware with intelligence, software facilitates the more efficient and convenient use of computers. In the absence of software, a computer would be a mere collection of ineffective mechanical equipment.

In the early days, numerous product functions were hardcoded into the hardware to reduce manufacturing complexity and cost, and to satisfy the requirements of mass production. The primary business logic was realized in a method that can be referred to as hardware-defined. The function of software in hardware-defined products was auxiliary and entirely reliant on the interfaces supplied by the hardware. Throughout this period, engineers developed and designed product functionalities, leaving consumers with no alternative but to accept and adapt, normally without substantial influence.

However, from its origination, software has always possessed, not only an auxiliary attribute, but also a more critical control characteristic. In its infancy, software could only function as an adjunct to the hardware that served its carrier, which consisted merely of external devices like displays and printers. The results of software operations typically needed to only be displayed on hardware screens in the form of data, images, or sound, without the requirement to form a closed loop. The mission was deemed successful to the extent that it provided assistance to human decision-makers.

As the demand for diverse, personalized customization grew in tandem with the need for more intelligent and flexible automation required by cloud computing, the hardware-defined approach could no longer satisfy consumer needs. Consequently, its implementation started to decline, being supplanted by a growing need for software to manage hardware resources. The advancement of hardware concurrently broadened the usage of software; as industrial standards continued to advance, the hardware's applicability progressively encompassed all computer-connected industrial devices. This expansion furnished software with a robust foundation upon which to execute its control function. When software is employed to drive physical devices, each sub-second motion of these physical devices is detected by the software, transmitted back to it via sensors, and subsequently computed in real-time according to the operational context of the physical device at that moment. Embedded mechanism models or inference rules inform decision-making, which generates the most precise and optimized instructions for the subsequent actions of the physical device.

The transition from hardware predominance to software control is evident in many upgrades and replacements of industrial equipment. For instance, early air conditioners also featured software; but it was comparatively rigid and provided limited interfaces, thereby lacking flexibility. At the time, we could only adjust the power and temperature of the air conditioner. Over time, more options became available, including the ability to configure the wind speed and direction. In the age of smart homes, it is now possible to activate and configure the air conditioner prior to our arrival via our mobile phones.

Subsequently, software definition replaced hardware definition and, over time, evolved into the brain of industrial equipment. Software has the capability to perform comprehensive computations autonomously, without relying on human decisions. This empowers hardware by directing it through these computations, thereby enabling it to possess a wide range of constantly advancing functions and capabilities.

The evolution from conventional mobile phones to smartphones exemplifies the appeal that software definition possesses. Historically, mobile phones served primarily as means of communication, enabling users to make phone calls and send text messages. While they did possess display screens, their functionality was restricted to just a few settings. On the contrary, the rise of software definition has precipitated a paradigm shift in the realm of mobile phones, transitioning from the era of phones led by Nokia, to the current era of smartphones supported by iOS and Android. Smartphones installed with various software applications have evolved into sophisticated mobile multimedia hubs. They have been endowed with entertainment features such as gaming; social media applications such as WeChat have added social capabilities; e-commerce applications Taobao and JD.com have converted them into palm-sized malls; and mobile office applications Tencent Meeting and DingTalk[10] have converted them into work processing platforms.

The concept of software definition has not only revolutionized the mobile phone as a product, but it has also significantly altered the industry as a whole. Previously, the mobile phone industry operated exclusively as a hardware business, wherein the manufacturers of the phones made the profits. During the software definition era, the commercialization of both software and services has occurred. Profits are distributed among all industry participants, from hardware manufacturing to software service provisioning; furthermore, the scale of every market segment has witnessed exponential expansion.

Beyond hardware, the target and scope of software definition have broadened in the digital age. Under the impact of software definition, the design methodology has also undergone a transformation to become software-centric, exerting influence not only on industrial equipment but also in other diverse fields.

The most effective, resilient, and cost-efficient cloud computing infrastructure thus far is the software-defined data centre (SDDC) concept. Through the abstraction, pooling, and automation of storage, network connectivity, security, and availability applications, the entire data centre is automatically managed and controlled by software. Thus, the infrastructure's services are aggregated and utilized in conjunction with policy-based intelligent allocation, automation and monitoring functions. Application programming interfaces and other connectors facilitate seamless extensions to private, hybrid, and public cloud platforms.

Nowadays, software definition is undergoing a period of pervasive incorporation into all facets of industrial and socio-economic progress. Software Definition was included for the first time in a central government development plan in *The Fourteenth Five-Year Plan for the Development of Software and Information Technology Services*, which was published by the Chinese Ministry of Industry and Information Technology on November 30, 2021. The document received widespread acclaim and stated, "Software definition is a new characteristic and symbol of the latest technological revolution and industrial transformation, becoming a significant driving force for future development. By expanding product functionalities, endowing enterprises with new capabilities, and granting infrastructure new capabilities and flexibility, software definition has emerged as a crucial engine for the advancement of production methods, the transformation of production relations, and the development of new industries."

Marc Andreessen, venture capitalist and co-founder of Netscape, once remarked, "Software is eating the world." In his view, software is ubiquitous: "More and more major businesses and industries have become inseparable from software. Web services will permeate every aspect of life, from movies and agriculture to national defence. Many winners will be innovative technology companies modelled after Silicon Valley, which will invade and overthrow established industry structures. Over the next decade, I anticipate that software will disrupt an increasing number of industries." Today, his perspective has become a reality.

SOFTWARE DEFINING EVERYTHING

Software-Defined Network (SDN) separates data from control, enabling IT teams to control networks dynamically and flexibly through software programming. This fundamental transformtation in networking disrupts the closed nature of traditional network devices, making networks more open, standardized, and cost-effective, whilst allowing people to use network resources more conveniently and efficiently.

Software-Defined Storage (SDS) decouples software from traditional storage controllers, allowing its functions to be more fully utilized without the constraints of physical systems. It can also be deployed and provisioned through software and management, enabling a more rational allocation of data centre resources such as servers, storage, networking, and security. SDS provides the flexible storage foundation necessary for hybrid cloud and digital transformation.

Software-Defined Compute (SDC) virtualizes and abstracts computing functions from hardware, decoupling hardware resources from computing capabilities. It provides computing power to users in the form of resource pools and allows for flexible configuration of computing resources according to application needs, requiring minimal management effort to control the network.

Software is redefining the world and everything beyond our imagination. In the future, we will live in a software-defined world, a world where humans, machines, and objects are interconnected.

In this new world, established patterns will be completely broken, and disruptive changes will occur across all industries. Today, we have already witnessed how software-defined is changing the automotive industry.

Previously, cars were hardware-defined industrial products often described as "traditional" and "backwards." While other industries had already entered eras of innovation and intelligence, the automotive industry seemed to have hit a dead end, remaining in its electronics-defined stage. Tesla, however, with its software-defined logic, has infused new energy into the closed automotive industry, sparking the transformation towards internet and intelligence-driven automobiles.

Tesla took a path that was completely different from traditional car manufacturers. It aims to produce intelligent cars defined by software and driven by data. Thus, it views software as the core of car production, which necessitates in-house development. Core software, such as battery management, vehicle OTA (Over the Air), electronic control systems, and autonomous driving, are defined by in-house architecture, developed independently, and rapidly iterated. In Tesla's team, there are many software architects and software development experts. For other components, wherever possible, Tesla cooperates with external enterprises, keeping only parts that cannot be properly sourced in the market to be developed in-house.

The intelligence level of Tesla cars is best exemplified by its autonomous driving features. Here, Elon Musk used first principles thinking, reasoning that if humans can drive cars using their eyes and brains, then cars equipped with visual devices and computing systems should be able to drive autonomously. He dedicated energy and time to developing autonomous driving technology and decisively adopted a progressive approach of rapid error correction and iteration.

To efficiently achieve continuous iteration, Tesla's self-developed Autopilot (autonomous driving system) was designed with one key principle in mind: "Hardware first, software updates after." While hardware is usually updated every two to three years, software updates occur very frequently, often monthly. For instance, the Tesla Model 3, although equipped with hardware supporting Level 3 autonomous driving or higher, does not unlock all functions for buyers who pay for the full autonomous driving functionalities. Instead, it continually improves through OTA online upgrades as the algorithms are optimized.

Now, through Autopilot, Tesla can automatically park, change lanes, navigate, smart summon, recognize and react to traffic lights and stop signs, as well as self-driving on city streets. Tesla's intelligent experience goes beyond this. Some say Tesla cars are the iPhone of the automotive industry, offering buyers an increasingly smart vehicle. Unlike most traditional cars that lose value over time, these intelligent cars don't depreciate.

As the pioneer of software-defined cars, Tesla has brought many disruptive changes to the automotive industry. First is the change in business models. Previously, car manufacturers only sold cars; now, smart car manufacturers sell not only cars but also software and services. Software increasingly participates in car design and development, becoming inseparable from the vehicle's entire lifecycle. Perhaps one day, software service fees will become the core business model for car manufacturers. Second is the change in evaluation criteria. In the past, performance, fuel consumption, appearance, and interior space were important. However, in the software-defined era, user experiences, such as autonomous driving and human-machine interaction, take precedence. The value of a car is no longer defined by traditional technical and performance indicators but by software technology with artificial intelligence at its core. Lastly is the change in the car manufacturers' role. Previously, traditional car manufacturers were just manufacturers; today, they are transitioning to mobility service providers.

This is the power of software-defined technology. In the automotive industry and many other fields, software has become a significant driver, greatly increasing the level of digitalization in various industries and society as a whole.

For instance, in the Internet of Things area, smart single products previously dominated, but with the rise of software definition, intelligent ecosystems and intelligent home have become an inevitable trend. Enterprises no longer connect with users through a single hardware function, but through richer forms such as personalized scenarios created by data and algorithms. Software definition has greatly extended these enterprises' value chains.

Similarly, in the industrial sector, digital technologies like cloud computing, big data, blockchain, and artificial intelligence have deepened their impact, forming sets of software-based, portable, reusable industry solutions. Today, advanced manufacturing is no longer about purchasing the latest hardware equipment, but about using software definition to allow enterprises to significantly improve efficiency and create higher value.

Our thinking should not be limited to the manufacturing sector, as the reputable and respected Chinese aerospace engineering pioneer Qian Xuesen once said, "software is culture." Software not only defines products and enterprises, but also our lifestyles. The continuous emergence of new concepts like smart communities, smart transportation, and smart cities will allow us to fully experience software definition and enter a programmable society.

FUTURE SOCIETY: EVERYTHING IS PROGRAMMABLE

Some of the Internet of Things enterprises believe that the world must become interconnected, thus requiring everything to be manageable and visible. Why interconnect everything? Many enterprises fail to understand the deep reasons behind it: a fully connected, digital world can achieve faster, more efficient resource allocation. The IoT aims to transform all real resources into peripherals for computers, ultimately enabling efficient dynamic resource allocation, as done by cloud computing.

When this evolution is finally completed, human society will enter a new, programmable era, where software becomes as indispensable as air, and monetary circulation and economic operations rely on programs and smart contracts.

What kind of impact will programmable machines bring to society? The information revolution revolves around this. Therefore, the virtual resource which can be programmed became a remarkable invention. This is because programmable is equivalent to computable which, in turn, entails intelligence.

'Programmable' is not difficult to understand. In the past, objects could not be programmed. Chairs did not possess computer chipsets, so people couldn't program them, nor make them intelligent. Now, with the development of digital technology, such items can be programmed. Chairs with memory functions remember a user's optimal seating height, automatically adjusting after temporary changes, even automatically adjusting temperature based on the season to provide an optimal user experience.

Money can also be programmed. For instance, when shopping on Taobao, people often pay using Alipay.[11] When we place an order, the money does not go to the merchant's account but is temporarily held by Alipay. Only after we receive the goods and confirm receipt does the money automatically transfer to the merchant. This method is also a form of programming. It does not change the money but uses a settlement system and third-party bank fund custody, along with effective government regulation, to ensure security. We can understand it as follows: through the system of money + Alipay + bank fund custody system + settlement system + government regulatory license, money is programmed, its use becoming more intelligent.

This programmable characteristic allows people to transact without spending time building trust, even transacting on a zero trust basis. For example, we can confidently use Alipay or WeChat Pay,[12] but we dare not pay via a small company's payment tool, as payment security cannot be ensured. Programmable money, with its programming logic, eliminates the need for trust because the program is executed by computers, the outcome predetermined. In this way, transactions will be processed without one person trusting another.

For instance, we use network disks from service providers like Baidu and Tencent to purchase storage space, but in a programmable society, there might be an app developed that allows us to buy hard disk space from anyone in the world. After uploading encrypted files (which only we can decrypt) to the hard disk space, the app will automatically make the necessary payment. We do not know the counterparty, but they don't fear not receiving the money, and we don't have to worry about them shutting down. Because all these rules have been programmed via smart contracts, the counterparty is paid only if he fulfils his storage provider responsibilities and our data is distributed to various space providers, achieving fault-tolerant redundancy.

In a programmable society, everything is programmable. Intelligent tables, chairs, and cars can make appropriate decisions, and these objects, because they incorporate self-learning programs, will continually improve and adjust their behaviours, becoming smarter and better at meeting user needs. This is not fantasy; it is gradually becoming reality. South Korea's Samsung Electronics produced a washing machine which can call a maintenance centre automatically when there are components that need to be repaired or maintained. Today's internet refrigerators also have such features as automatically ordering milk whenever needed.

From the industrial age to the information age, and now the digital age, when everything from objects to cities and social environments are interconnected and programmed through software definition, humanity may very soon see a truly programmable society.

CHAPTER 5

ENGINE OF DIGITAL ECONOMY DRIVEN BY DIGITAL INFRA- STRUCTURE CONSTRUCTION

Infrastructure is not only a symbol of human civilization but also the cornerstone to enable human development. During the industrial civilization, traditional infrastructure represented by railway, highway, and other infrastructures, fully met the needs of the division of labour and collaborative production, effectively driving the global flow of capital and human resources and giving rise to the industrial economy and modern social forms. In this digital civilization, digital infrastructure construction has become the new engine for the development of the digital economy, laying a solid foundation for restructuring production relations and harnessing the enormous potential of digital productivity.

Enterprises have become a significant force in the digital infrastructure construction, especially platform-type enterprises that continually accumulate massive amounts of big data. These enterprises possess rich, fully digitized resources and capabilities, as they play an increasingly crucial role as digital infrastructure in the digital age.

5.1 DIGITAL INFRASTRUCTURE CONSTRUCTION CONNECTING THE FUTURE

INFRASTRUCTURE IS CIVILIZATION

The advent of the digital age has brought about a cognitive revolution from mathematics to data science, leading to the digital transformation of businesses and a technological paradigm shift centred on cloud-native principles. Every era has its infrastructure, and the construction of such infrastructure lays the foundation for the development of that era. Likewise, the digital age is dependent on the construction of digital infrastructure.

In the digital transformation strategy of Data Cloud Integration, the outermost and most foundational layer is digital infrastructure. As we envision a society where large-scale digitization is achieved in ten or even five years, the form, construction, operation, and service approaches of the infrastructure we rely on for survival will undergo a thorough transformation. It's my conviction that digital infrastructure, by then, will become the medium for interactions among people, between people and things, and among objects, as we realize the true connectivity of everything. Aiming at the future, we must plan and act immediately today.

In 2023, I made multiple visits to the United States, Australia, and European countries, engaging in in-depth discussions with various enterprises and academic institutions. During this time, I experienced the continuous impact of digitization on the global market economy. For instance, in the field of mobile payments, Europe has achieved convenient cashless travel through the combination of "ApplePay + Uber + PayPal." This has further emphasized to me that digital technology, with cloud-native as its foundation, has become an indispensable infrastructure in modern society. So what kind of relationship exists between civilization and infrastructure? What kind of infrastructure does the digital age require? How does infrastructure function in the development of the digital economy?

In fact, throughout the history of humanity social development, civilization has always been closely related to the construction of infrastructure, to the extent that it can be said that infrastructure construction *is* civilization.

The Library of Alexandria was the world's oldest library, hailed as the "sun of the human civilization." Built in the 3rd century BC, it was the largest library in the world at the time. It was built by Ptolemy and inspired by Aristotle's personal library. Ptolemy III, who decided to continue building the library and determined to gather all the books in the world, even resorting to extreme book plunder policies. At its peak, over 500,000 volumes were kept in the Library of Alexandria for people to peruse.

Following its construction, the Library of Alexandria frequently fell victim to the ravages of war and was, in the end, destroyed. However, a portion of the collection survived. The research achievements and philosophical ideas acquired by the library had a profound and lasting impact on subsequent generations. This library turned Alexandria into the city of wisdom. Euclid completed his *The Elements* using the books housed there; Eratosthenes measured the Earth's circumference with books borrowed from the library; Archimedes studied there, laying the foundation for science; Herophilus conducted anatomical studies there. One can only imagine the scientific and technological achievements humanity might have attained if the Library of Alexandria had not been destroyed.

The Library of Alexandria was the first soft infrastructure of human civilization, representing ancient Greek civilization, which was preserved intact, interwoven with multiple cultures, contributing to the development and continuity of human civilization.

Soft infrastructures like the Library of Alexandria exist throughout human history, and they are both accelerators and symbols of human civilization. The development and changes in hard infrastructures illustrate the roadmap of human civilization even more clearly.

Today, China is highly praised by the world for the speed and scale of its magnificent and spectacular infrastructure constructions, and this has historical roots. Since the time of Yu the Great's[1] taming and controlling floods, the Chinese people embarked on a long journey of infrastructure development. The dredging and control of the Yellow River[2] by Yu the Great provided conditions for human reproduction and habitation, endowing it with the attributes of an infrastructure. As the first infrastructure project of the Chinese nation, the Yellow River connected various tribes upstream and downstream, merging them into one and forming the Chinese nation. The irrigation potential brought by the Yellow River allowed the Chinese people to evolve from hunting tribes to agricultural civilization with the capability of farming and breeding, marking the beginning of the Chinese civilization.

In the Qin Dynasty,[3] Emperor Qin Shi Huang[4] initiated an infrastructure frenzy, undertaking nationwide, large-scale engineering projects. He not only built the awe-inspiring Great Wall, Epang Palace[5] (the Palace of the Heavenly Son – Emperor Qin Shi Huang's palace), and Zhengguo Canal[6] (a large-scale canal), but also constructed the Qin Direct Road (Zhidao).[7] The Qin Direct Road was the earliest national road in China and served as the national highway of the era – it allowed travellers to reach the foot of the Great Wall from the capital Xianyang in just one day.

Emperor Yang[8] of the Sui Dynasty[9] constructed the Grand Canal,[10] connecting the Yangtze River and Yellow River water systems, facilitating extensive exchanges in the economy and culture between the north and south. This achievement accelerated and consolidated the unity of the Chinese nation. During the Ming Dynasty,[11] the Hongwu Emperor[12] built thousands of kilometres of post roads, extending northwards to the Songhua River and Heilongjiang River basin, and westwards from Sichuan to the Lhasa region of Tibet. The traditional tea-horse ancient road from Sichuan to Tibet took shape during this time.

By continuously promoting large-scale infrastructure projects, the Chinese nation gradually grew stronger, leading to economic development, national unification, and advancement of social civilization.

Certainly, infrastructure construction was not a skill exclusive to the ancient Chinese. In the West, the Romans also deeply understood the importance of infrastructure construction.

In 312 BC, the Romans began building the Appian Way,[13] the first Roman road in history. Since then, wherever the Romans went, there were Roman roads. During the height of the Roman Empire, 29 roads extended from the capital Rome, allowing travel to Rome from any European road, giving rise to the saying "all roads lead to Rome." Roman civilization spread with the construction of Roman roads. The renowned Roman historian Plutarch attributed the strength of the Roman Empire to the assimilation of other civilizations, with the greatest contribution to this assimilation being Roman-style infrastructure.

In modern times, the United States evolved from a colony to a superpower, relying on continuous infrastructure development. From the beginning of independence, Americans focused on building railways, creating an extensive railway network that united the various states and laid the foundation for the country's rise and power. Later, the U.S. embarked on a new maritime infrastructure construction plan by constructing naval bases worldwide, controlling strategic sea passages, including the Strait of Gibraltar, Suez Canal, Panama Canal, Strait of Malacca, Japan Strait, and the Persian Gulf. United States quickly became the world's most powerful nation.

In 1992, a fundamental change occurred in the construction of the United States – it started to march into the virtual world. In February of the same year, Clinton proposed in his campaign document *A Vision for Renewing America* that the rapid economic development of the United States in the 1950s was made possible by the establishment of the interstate highway system. As humanity was on the brink of entering the information age of the 21st century, Clinton asserted that for the United States to continue thriving, it must construct new "roads" leading to the future.

In September 1993, while still in office, Clinton announced the implementation of a new high-tech initiative – the National Information Infrastructure (NII), later known as the groundbreaking U.S. Information Superhighway construction project. The main objective was to invest $400 billion over 20 years to lay telecommunications optical fibre cables to every household, enabling ordinary Americans to access non-phone communication services such as voice and video. This initiative aimed to bring every household online, propelling the United States into an era of informational living, working, and even production.

To ensure the smooth implementation of this plan, the U.S. government enacted the Telecommunications Act of 1996, breaking down barriers in the traditional communication industry, encouraging private capital participation, and compelling traditional communication service providers to support the development of the internet.

In addition to paving the legal path, the U.S. government invested heavily in the infrastructure development of the information superhighway. From 1996 to 2001 alone, the United States laid 130 million kilometres of optical fibre cables, accounting for 40% of the total global length of optical fibre cables.

With strong support from the U.S. government, capital from the industry and financial institutions poured into the information industry, giving rise to batches of new technologies and companies. The flourishing development of high-tech companies such as Microsoft, IBM, Google, Amazon, and others can be attributed to this initiative.

Meanwhile, China transformed from a semi-colonial and semi-feudal agricultural country to the world's second-largest economy in only 60 years, writing a new chapter in the nation's great rejuvenation – all thanks to continuous infrastructure development.

From the early establishment of nationwide railways and road networks to the construction of urban rail transit, and further to the high-speed railways and globally leading 5G networks in the new century, every round of infrastructure frenzy in China has resulted in rapid economic growth.

In the field of infrastructure construction, China has achieved numerous milestones: being the only country with about 1.4 billion people and achieving universal electrification ranking first globally in electricity grid coverage; having a total of 131,000 kilometres of expressways and over 31,000 kilometres of high-speed railways both ranking first in the world; possessing 800,000 road bridges and 200,000 railway bridges, totalling 1 million ranking first globally; having over 5 million communication base stations ranking first globally; and having 347,000 high-rise buildings and over 6,000 super-high-rise buildings (above 100 metres) ranking first globally.

China built the world's highest bridge, Beipanjiang Bridge, the world's longest bridge, Danyang-Kunshan Bridge, and the world's longest sea-crossing bridge, the Hong Kong-Zhuhai-Macao Bridge. The overall replacement project for Beijing's Sanyuan Bridge was completed in only 43 hours, and traffic resumed immediately after completion. During the outbreak of the COVID-19 pandemic in 2020, China built two infectious disease hospitals, Huoshenshan and Leishenshan, in around 10 days, showcasing the astounding 'Chinese speed.' Various miraculous infrastructure constructions have changed China dramatically and earned us a completely new impression.

Whether it's the Roman Empire, the United States, or China, economic development and national prosperity are all built on perfected infrastructure. It can even be said that all civilizations are established on a foundation of strong infrastructure. In the digital age, digital infrastructure will serve as the bridge from industrial civilization to digital civilization.

DIGITAL INFRASTRUCTURE IS THE "YELLOW RIVER" OF THE DIGITAL AGE[14]

In the past, traditional infrastructure was represented by railways, roads, airports, water conservancy, and electricity, propelling human civilization's continuous advancement. However, in the digital age, digital infrastructure has become the bedrock and cornerstone of the digital economy. For instance, the digital transformation of traditional manufacturing and the evolution towards intelligent manufacturing require the support of the industrial internet. The development and application of intelligent technologies such as drones and autonomous driving depend on the creation of infrastructure such as the Internet of Vehicles and intelligent transportation. The digital transformation of urban public infrastructure services, including water, electricity, and gas, is inseparable from the increasingly sophisticated development of the urban Internet of Things. In summary, digital infrastructure is the Yellow River of our digital economy age.

Digital infrastructure facilities primarily refer to infrastructure that has evolved from new-generation information technologies. This includes the communication network infrastructure represented by technologies such as 5G, the Internet of Things, industrial internet, and satellite internet. It also involves new technology infrastructure represented by artificial intelligence, cloud computing, blockchain, and computational infrastructure represented by data centres and intelligent computing centres. Digital infrastructure facilities, which are already tightly integrated with our life, are exemplified by technologies such as the mobile payment tools we use on daily basis, the increasingly popular ChatGPT tools representing the latest advancement in the realm of artificial intelligence applications, and the GPS (global positioning system) which is already ubiquitous in military and civilian usage.

The digital infrastructure is not only a strategic, pioneering, and crucial form of national infrastructure facilities but also the core of digital infrastructure construction, serving as the strategic foundation supporting the transformation and development of the economy and society. Only when digital infrastructure is well-established do the construction of a digital society and the transformation and upgrading of the economy have a solid foundation.

The digital infrastructure is the foundation for the aggregation, collision, integration, sharing, circulation, and trading of data. Communication network infrastructure, new technology infrastructure, and computational infrastructure all possess extensive industrial chains. Together, they constitute the entire process from data collection to decision-making, supporting the crucial role of data as a new factor of production. This digitizes and networks all elements and connections of industries, driving the transformation and restructuring of business processes and production methods, creating a new framework of industrial collaboration, resource allocation, and value creation. This then gives rise to more technological innovations, cognitive innovations, and scenario innovations based on the digital economy.

The national-level Apple Industry Big Data Centre, undertaken by the Digital China Information Service Group,[15] serves as a classic example of digital infrastructure, promoting the improvement and upgrading of traditional industries.

Although consuming apples may seem ordinary to us, our understanding of China's apple industry might be limited. China has become the world's largest producer of apples, with more than 50% of the world's apple planting area and production. In this new phase, the apple industry urgently needs to introduce data as a new factor of production to address problems such as information asymmetry, unreasonable input factor allocation, weak monitoring and early warning capabilities for natural disasters and pests, and the lack of smooth connections between production and sales. This is essential for enhancing the innovation, competitiveness, brand construction, and overall factor productivity of the apple industry. To solve these problems, the Ministry of Agriculture and Rural Affairs has proposed a strategy for promoting agricultural and rural big data serving each and every product across the entire industry chain, focusing on big data pilots for various products like apples, pigs, and tea. The goal is to provide mechanisms, models, and experiences that are learnable, referable, and replicable for the development and application of agricultural and rural big data.

Being the constructer of the Apple Industry Big Data Centre, Digital China Information Service Group conducted comprehensive data collection for apple trees across the entire Luochuan area in Shaanxi, making sure to include the data for every apple tree and every inch of land used for apple cultivation. This data includes soil conditions and economic ownership, as well as production-related information such as time, fertilization, and irrigation.

Apples are not scarce; they have bulk characteristics, making big data applications in the apple industry a reality. By collecting data at the county, provincial, or even national level, excellent big data application scenarios, such as agricultural credit services, can be provided. Many farmers lack cash in the early stages of planting to purchase pesticides and fertilizers. Integrated platforms like the Apple Industry Big Data Centre can establish a credit system tailored to farmers, addressing the issue of cash shortages. For example, using credit big data, credit modules can be designed based on specific farmer situations. Unlike traditional loan granting approaches, credit limits are granted based on past yields of apples, current weather conditions, and other relevant data. It takes only a few minutes to decide whether to lend ten or twenty thousand yuan, allowing farmers to borrow money for purchasing pesticides, fertilizers, or irrigating their orchards. They can then repay the loan after the apples are sold.

The role of big data for farmers goes beyond finances. During the growth process of apple cultivation, problems such as pest infestation, soil-water incompatibility, and changes in apple varieties may arise. In such cases, even small-scale farmers with only two acres of orchards can quickly locate nearby agricultural experts through the big data centre for on-site or internet remote consultations regarding the difficult and mysterious issues of fruit trees.

Furthermore, the big data centre can drive the development of modern agriculture towards precision, intelligence, and efficiency. During my visit to New Zealand, the most striking impression was the variety of apples available for sale, with some being quite expensive. However, China's apple varieties are relatively limited, and despite having diversity and differentiation, they engage in fierce price competition. In reality, everyone has different tastes – some prefer sweet, some prefer sour, some prefer crisp, others more doughy. If differentiated production can be achieved, the value of agricultural products like apples will significantly increase. If China's apple varieties can be further subdivided into more categories, the total production may remain the same, but consumers would be willing to spend more money to experience different tastes. Through the use of big data, the Apple Industry Big Data Centre can establish standards for various apple varieties, refine the different indicators of apples, and provide different varieties tailoring to consumers' diverse needs.

Through the construction of the Apple Industry Big Data Centre, we can utilize technologies such as big data, the Internet of Things, and artificial intelligence to serve various aspects of agricultural needs, including production, operation, circulation, and consumption. This digital infrastructure enables comprehensive control over the processes of production and operation for the entire variety, ensuring output and providing more value in socialize services.

The construction of the Apple Industry Big Data Centre can be seen as a microcosm of digital infrastructure development. In fact, digital infrastructure serves as a carrier for the rapid application of technology, organizational changes, and business model innovations. This not only applies to the apple industry, but across many other industries. It actually promotes the transformation and upgrading of traditional industries towards digitalization, networking, and intelligence, injecting new driving forces into economic development.

In addition to the mission of supporting the transformation of the traditional industries, digital infrastructure construction also enables the traditional infrastructure construction by supporting the deeper integration of the actual economy with digital economy, creating new industries, new forms of operation and new frameworks. In the industrial era, the traditional 'railway, highway, and other infrastructures' reflected its value by supporting the mobility of people, things and capital. However, in the digital age, the value of digital infrastructure is well beyond connection and linking. By adopting digital technologies, digital infrastructure reconstructs the traditional infrastructure by empowering it with capabilities like perception, the Internet of Things, and intelligent feedback, thereby achieving digitalization, automation, and intelligent transformation and upgrade.

Smart transportation infrastructure is a good example. In the industrial era, traditional transportation infrastructure mainly referred to major transportation facilities such as railways, roads, subways, and airports. In the digital age, transportation infrastructure refers to smart transportation infrastructure. It may seem like just adding the word 'smart', but smart transportation infrastructure is not merely the intelligent transformation of traditional transportation infrastructure; it is the comprehensive advancement of the entire transportation industry through the widespread application of digital technology.

An important development direction for smart transportation is AI-based vehicle-road coordination, autonomous driving, and intelligent travelling. For example, based on the experience we gained from the Data Cloud Integration implementation, Digital China Group[16] managed to build, for a renowned component parts supplier, a comprehensive data platform for the automatic data collection system of road-testing environment, realizing the value conversion from equipment data to indicator data.

Autonomous driving depends on superior computing power, sophisticated algorithms, and better quality and quantity of data. Among these, autonomous driving data is considered to be of paramount importance. Despite sounding simple, it encompasses a series of challenging processes such as data collection, desensitization, annotation, simulation, each, with diverse challenges. Behind the data demands of manufacturers, there are additional requirements for efficiency and cost-effectiveness. Therefore, an automated data collection system capable of managing massive autonomous driving data becomes a crucial need for customers.

As autonomous driving data mainly originates from various devices, for the component suppliers, it not only provides various components to the equipment manufacturers, making them familiar with the performance and characteristics of these components, but also allows them to collect signal data from these devices. Therefore, unlocking the value behind the data has become a new opportunity for the component suppliers in the era of autonomous driving. However, aligning timestamps for hundreds or thousands of components, akin to atomic clocks in the aerospace domain, is not easy. Thus, this component supplier needs to build a comprehensive, autonomous driving data collection system encompassing hardware and software, assisting the equipment manufacturer in addressing the challenges as related to data in the field of autonomous driving.

From the perspective of this component supplier, dynamic management of the data resources for autonomous driving is a key focus.

Initially, Digital China Group believed that cloud computing, with its globally distributed data centres and network nodes, massive data storage capacity, and large-scale AI computing clusters in the cloud, was the best way for autonomous driving companies to solve a series of data challenges. However, Digital China Group realized later in the project that, due to the enormous amount of data collected by component suppliers in autonomous driving, relying solely on cloud bandwidth is insufficient. Hence, establishing a private data centre locally became a necessary choice.

Using its in-depth expertise in the field of Data Cloud Integration, Digital China Group identified that this component supplier needed a data platform to enhance their data-driven business insights during the digital transformation. Therefore, Digital China Group assisted the client in building the overall data platform for the autonomous driving system from 0 to 1. This involved determining the basic architecture of the data platform, constructing the methodology for data flow, and orchestrating and monitoring various aspects like data lake, source data storage databases, web monitoring interfaces, task scheduling platforms, and so on. I truly believe that these efforts will improve traffic efficiency, ensure traffic safety, and provide a feasible solution to address the challenge of urban traffic congestion.

Obviously, the proliferation of intelligent applications in various industries and scenarios goes beyond the smart transportation. For instance, new scenarios and applications for intelligent society, such as smart energy, smart cities, smart factories, and smart healthcare are constantly emerging. These digital infrastructures are the foundation which gives birth to new value networks, services frameworks, products and industries.

Digital infrastructure not only integrates with the real economy, promoting industrial upgrading, but also provides a powerful driving force for the development and progress of society. Many issues encountered in social governance today can be considered in conjunction with digital infrastructure to find new solutions.

Take inclusive finance, for example. The lack of a credit system for rural and small and mid-sized enterprises has long been a problem, preventing financial institutions such as banks from providing effective financial loans under the existing risk control system. This has been the main obstacle to achieving inclusive finance. In the past, this challenging problem remained unresolved, but the gradual improvement of digital infrastructure has provided a new breakthrough. Through the integration and innovation of technology + industry + data, solutions such as digital supply chains, digital risk control, and digital inclusive finance have effectively addressed the financial access problems of large groups such as rural residents and small business owners. For instance, the Shenzhou Financial Service Cloud platform jointly created by Digital China Group, Digital China Information Service Group, and Postal Savings Bank is based on traditional supply chain scenarios. It capitalizes the core data of on-chain enterprises and matches it with the bank's risk control model, facilitating their loans and significantly reducing the credit costs for small and medium-sized enterprises.

Another example is the carbon peaking and carbon neutrality issue. This is a global topic, and in terms of carbon emissions, depending solely on traditional methods like installing sensors in every factory to monitor carbon emissions is fundamentally inadequate. After the completion of digital infrastructure, we can design new mechanisms, such as creating digital assets like carbon coins, which can be given to everyone and used for consumption. If someone saves one unit of electricity, they earn money in the form of carbon coins, and if someone consumes more electricity, they need to buy carbon coins, thereby achieving carbon neutrality and management throughout society. There are many new directions to explore in solving the carbon peaking and carbon neutrality issue based on digital infrastructure, and it is worth exploring them.

Digital infrastructure is the link to the future. With the availability of this link, we can create a more favourable social environment which can better serve the advancement of digital economy development. This aims to enable the comprehensive and profound integration of data, a new factor of production, into society and the economy, fully realizing its value in constructing an entirely new highly intelligent society.

5.2 ACCELERATING DIGITAL INFRASTRUCTURE CONSTRUCTION: BUILT ON CLOUD, DRIVEN BY OPEN SOURCE

THE POWER OF THE CLOUD, BEYOND IMAGINATION

The rise of AIGC has transformed the way information and knowledge is produced, reshaped the interaction between humanity and technology, and given birth to countless new ideas, technologies, and business models. It has also opened up infinite possibilities for our imagination of Artificial General Intelligence. This triggers a new wave of technological revolution that continuously pushes the boundaries of human development, placing us at the starting point of a new era.

With the tide surging, the wise adapt to the times. Across various industries, from aerospace and healthcare to online retail, and education and training, and from manufacturing to tourism services, artificial intelligence is being deployed everywhere. From rural areas to cities, from agriculture to services, the wave of AIGC is sweeping through everything we know. Whether it is business, production, work, or life, almost everything is being reconstructed. Opportunities and challenges come hand in hand.

Facing this new world, digital infrastructure construction faces new challenges: it must enter the fast lane of acceleration. It needs to provide strong support for AIGC with massive computing power, vast amounts of data, and powerful algorithms to accelerate the implementation and popularization of AIGC across various industries. Without the support of digital infrastructure, AIGC would be like water without a source or a tree without roots.

However, the challenge lies in how to accelerate the construction of digital infrastructure. The strategy of Data Cloud Integration provides the answer: building on the cloud to solidify the foundation of digital infrastructure; and using open source as the driving engine to provide new momentum for digital infrastructure construction.

The cloud is the most important support point for the digital economy and the cornerstone of digital infrastructure. We often say that we should look at the essence through phenomena. What is the essence of the cloud? It is the innovation of business models.

In the industrial age, the product was king. To survive and gain a competitive edge in the market, a company had to compete with its rivals based on its products – whose product had stronger features, better performance, and lower prices would attract more customers and gain more market share, thus earning more profits. Therefore, the product was everything to the enterprise. Almost all resources were concentrated on the operation and sale of the product. If a product could become popular, it could achieve dominance in its industry. Services were considered as adjuncts to products, only able to create added value. Although in the post-industrial age, the proportion of the service industry in the socio-economic sphere has greatly increased, and the value of services has been re-recognized and valued, it is still regarded as an extension of the product.

However, in the digital age, everything has changed. Products are still important, but they have shifted from the core to support, while services have become the new core. Many companies have shifted from selling products to selling services. Such examples are abundant.

GE, the world's largest aircraft engine manufacturer, used to sell only aircraft engines. Now, GE sells intelligent services – using smart aircraft engines to make planes smarter. They install various sensors on aircraft engines. When the aircraft is flying, these sensors continuously collect various data, which is transmitted to the ground. After analysis by intelligent software systems, they can accurately detect the operation of the aircraft, even predict aircraft failures, suggest preventive maintenance, etc., thereby improving the safety of the aircraft and the service life of the engine. Now, in the entire product life cycle of GE aircraft engines, the value created by engine sales accounts for an increasingly lower proportion, while maintenance and repair services for engines have become the main profit contributor for GE.

Ingersoll Rand, a well-established British industrial company, counts air conditioning compressors as one of its main businesses. As the competition in this market intensifies, the company has timely changed its mind-set, turning air conditioning compressors into intelligent, networked products, and transforming its positioning from selling single products to selling safe and comfortable environments. One interesting creation of Ingersoll Rand is the "Energy Management Contract" model, which can help customers save at least one-third of their expenses throughout the entire product lifecycle and provide continuous and demand-oriented services to customers, thus obtaining substantial benefits.

The times have changed, and companies face new challenges. In the digital age, all enterprises, especially high-tech companies, must have strong intelligent services capabilities. Using services as a link, enterprises can connect their technologies, operations, and management to form a comprehensive intelligent service value chain, meet customer needs, provide better experiences for customers, and create greater value.

Intelligent services capabilities depend on data, computing power, and require enormous computing power. Not every company has the ability to build such platforms. Even for large companies with strong capabilities and a large scale, building, operating, and maintaining such platforms are costly and require enormous investment. This is where the value of the cloud lies.

When we use electricity, we do not have to build a power plant ourselves. We just need to connect to the grid and plug in, and there will be a continuous supply of electricity. In this process, we do not need to worry about the operation of the power plant or the maintenance of the substation. We just need to pay the electricity bill according to our usage. The same goes for water and natural gas. The cloud is like the supply mode of water, electricity, and gas. In the cloud, a large amount of computing resources are centralized, managed, and deployed. Enterprises do not need to build platforms themselves, purchase IT infrastructure such as server hardware and operating system software, and applications, nor do they need to maintain and manage them. They can easily obtain the computing resources they need in an on-demand rental manner and can adjust them elastically at any time.

The emergence of the cloud means that computing resources and computing power can also be traded as commodities over the internet. This new business model is attractive: it is efficient because resources on the cloud are not idle but are allocated and used by those who need them, fully realizing their value. It is flexible because resources on the cloud can be accessed anytime, anywhere, and can be used on demand, with elastic increases and decreases, flexibly meeting the needs of customer business growth and application dynamic changes. It has a wide extension, almost all digital technologies belong to the cloud, including the Internet of Things, blockchain, metaverse, and even AIGC, which can all be used by the cloud to create value. It can greatly achieve the goal of reducing costs and increasing efficiency for enterprises. When resources are effectively utilized by those who need them, it naturally improves efficiency and reduces the unit acquisition cost.

However, if you only see the cloud as a business model for renting computing resources on demand, then your understanding of the cloud is not deep enough, and you are likely underestimating the power of the cloud.

In the digital age, another important transformation for enterprises is from large-scale mass production to customized and diversified production, which means an increase in production costs and a decrease in production efficiency. The cloud can convert the movements of physical machines into data, exchange and integrate machine information through the Internet of Things, and then optimize various processes and links such as production, sales, and shipment through cloud services and big data analysis. The scale effect of the cloud compensates for or overcomes the increase in cost and decrease in efficiency brought about by customization and small-batch production. It truly puts customer-centric actions at the forefront, maximizing customer service experience.

Empowered by the cloud, people, data, and machines are closely connected, forming a multi-level, interwoven, and open system. Communication and data exchange occur between people, people and machines, and machines themselves. This makes the physical world informatized and the informational world intelligent. Through the computation and analysis of massive data, businesses can rapidly capture customer needs, perceive changes in market conditions, make clear judgments, and respond in real-time, thus making more rational and precise decisions.

The power of the cloud is not only reflected in empowering enterprises but also in empowering the entire society. As the most fundamental infrastructure, the cloud quietly exists in our lives like water, electricity, and gas. Many people live on the cloud every day without even realizing its presence. In fact, everything from scanning payments at street stalls to inventory management, from live streaming sales to supply chain management, from agricultural product planting to food traceability on the dining table, from factory design to production, manufacturing, and customer management, from checking flight information to completing various government services online – all of these are supported by the cloud.

The cloud emphasizes sharing rather than ownership, enabling the entire society to move towards a more efficient and better direction:

Mapping software like AMap[17] and Baidu Maps open their APIs to lifestyle service apps such as Meituan, JD.com, and Ele.me, making it easier for these apps to obtain user location information, facilitating the sharing of locations. This allows users to quickly find out the geographical locations of delivery personnel and couriers, eliminating the worry of waiting anxiously in uncertainty.

Payment systems such as Alipay and WeChat Pay integrate their payment systems with third-party payment systems like JD.com and Douyin, providing users with a more diverse range of payment options in a shared manner, thereby making the payment process more convenient. Nowadays, wherever we go, we only need to carry a mobile phone to shop and consume.

Daimler AG has launched a flexible and convenient car-sharing model – Car2Go – targeting frequent car users. People only need to tap on a smartphone app to see the nearest available car, then use a membership card to unlock the car door, drive to their destination, and park the car by the roadside. Car2Go offers a variety of billing methods, including per-mile or per-day calculations, but the total cost is lower than that of traditional taxi services. Compared to traditional car rental companies, it eliminates the hassle of customers returning the car. When cars can be shared, the problem of traffic congestion may no longer be so difficult to solve.

Of course, these examples are just a drop in the ocean, but their value lies in showing us the infinite possibilities created by the cloud. In the future, as big data, computing power, and algorithm technologies continue to mature, and as more businesses and individuals walk into the "cloud," I believe the power of the cloud will further erupt, and the world on the cloud will become even more vibrant.

Sharing brings about a win-win cloud ecosystem. In the cloud, every link is not independently existent. Each participant provides services to customers while also receiving services from others. All participants aim to co-create value, driven by data and capital, deeply integrating and supporting each other. Originally, individual businesses fought separately, but now they merge into a symbiotic, shared organic whole. Business civilization has thus developed into a new stage of altruism and mutual benefit.

This is a process of quantitative change leading to qualitative change, with a scale growing exponentially. The result is the flourishing development of the digital economy, benefiting every participant involved.

THE OPEN-SOURCE IS THE ENGINE OF DIGITAL INFRASTRUCTURE CONSTRUCTION

The world we live in is constantly changing. Sometimes changes are dramatic upheavals, such as the agricultural and industrial revolutions that brought about leaps in productivity and reshaped the global landscape. Other changes occur quietly, supporting, and promoting the construction of social infrastructure construction and the improvement of industries in a subtle manner. Open-source plays that role.

In the software value chain, open-source serves as the wellspring of software innovation. Open source has deeply penetrated the marrow of the internet industry, bringing sustained and profound impacts to global businesses. For digital infrastructure, open source is a powerful engine, driving developments in the internet, cloud computing, big data, artificial intelligence, and blockchain – all propelled by the open-source ecosystem.

Open source, as the name suggests, is an opening up of the source codes. However, it represents more than just the openness of software source code. It embodies a spirit and culture of freedom and sharing; essentially the incarnation of freedom and the product of technological democratization.

The rise and development of the open-source movement can be akin to a profoundly stirring epic, reflecting the light of civilization in human society.

In the early stages of computer development, the mainstream computer culture viewed software as knowledge rather than a mere commodity. During this period, a group of freedom-minded, passionate geeks actively promoted technological innovation. They advocated for software as the crystallization of human wisdom to be freely open, treating software development as an academic research activity, and willingly sharing their research. In this open and free atmosphere, many excellent software products emerged, such as the renowned UNIX operating system and the various software built upon it.

Unfortunately, this utopia-like free ecosystem was short-lived. Initially, the commercial value of the IT industry focused mainly on hardware, and software was developed by hardware manufacturers, often provided as a complimentary bundled addition to promote hardware sales. In the 1970s and 1980s, with the maturity of computer hardware technology, software gradually de-bundled from hardware, gaining increasing importance. Simultaneously, policies began to clarify copyright protection for computer software. As a result, software transitioned from being a free add-on to a product with independent commercial value. The era of shared software in the open-source field came to an end.

In the transition from free and open to fee-based, closed-source software, Bill Gates, the founder of Microsoft, being the icon of commercial software era, emerged as a leading advocate for software copyright protection. In 1976, Gates published an Open Letter to Hobbyists, expressing his view that charging for hardware while providing software for free was unfair. He emphasized that this infringement hindered the development of excellent software. Subsequently, copyright systems gained victory, and Microsoft achieved tremendous business success.

However, Microsoft's commercial stance left many developers disheartened. To them, open source was the spirit of freedom and equality. Everyone should have the freedom to access software resources and their source codes, without being controlled by a few commercial companies. The numerous restrictions and monopolies created by commercialization not only hindered innovation but also led to various issues in different software products.

At this moment, the 'paper jam' incident catalysed developers' resistance against commercial monopolies. In the early 1980s, the MIT AI Lab received a laser printer as a gift, but it frequently jammed, causing frustration for the lab's researchers. Richard Matthew Stallman, a member of the lab, sought to solve the problem. The solution was simple – modifying and testing the source code appropriately. However, Xerox, the printer manufacturer, refused to provide the source code.

Like a spark, Xerox's refusal ignited resistance in Stallman and others against closed software development environments. Stallman, leading a group of young developers, initiated the Free Software Movement and established the Free Software Foundation. This was not just a developers' alliance but also a vanguard promoting the ideals of software freedom, knowledge sharing, and collaborative spirit. Stallman proposed that "the freedom of software is the freedom of humanity" and created the GNU operating system, allowing all developers to use, copy, modify, and distribute the source code freely.

As the spiritual leader of the American Free Software Movement, Stallman made significant contributions to the movement, notably establishing ethical, political, and legal frameworks. Therefore, he is widely recognized as a fighter for free software and a great idealist.

However, open source isn't just a personal achievement; it represents an unstoppable spirit of free sharing on the internet and the relentless efforts of numerous brave individuals.

In the 1990s, a computer scientist, Linus Torvalds, developed the Linux operating system, which was a pivotal turning point in the history of the Free Software Movement. It broke down technological barriers and propelled the movement into a new stage of development. Torvalds believed that the fundamental spirit of the internet is openness and sharing. Therefore, he made Linux open-source, allowing developers to use it freely, with the only requirement being to carry forward the spirit of the open-source movement by freely disclosing modified codes. Under Torvalds's advocacy and leadership, the Free Software Movement began to thrive worldwide, attracting an increasing number of developers.

However, the term 'Free Software' created misconceptions, and many people associated it with free and no cost software. In this context, many people began to abandon the term 'Free Software.' In February 1998, Eric S. Raymond and Christine Peterson of the Foresight Institute proposed replacing 'Free Software' with 'Open Source.' This suggestion gained unanimous support from developers, leading to the transformation of the Free Software Movement into the vibrant Open-Source Software Movement.

The shift from 'Free Software' to 'Open-Source Software' might seem like a mere change in terminology, but it implies an ideological transformation. While 'Free Software' advocated a utopian, non-commercialized concept, 'Open-Source Software' emphasizes the openness of source code without excluding commercial practices. It finds a balance between the spirit of free sharing and commercial interests, thus achieving a win-win situation.

As a result, the impact of the open-source movement is more extensive and profound, and its influence is more widespread compared to the Free Software Movement. Even many large enterprises have gradually joined this movement. Simultaneously, the meaning of 'open source' has expanded beyond 'open-source software' to encompass more areas. It has evolved into a collaborative development parallel to closed development, increasingly surpassing and overshadowing the latter.

The ultimate victory of a revolution or movement is always closely related to a guiding document. In the open-source movement, the pioneer of the movement Eric S. Raymond's book *The Cathedral and the Bazaar*, hailed as the 'Bible of open source,' published in 1999, served such a purpose. In the book, Raymond used the easily understandable images of a cathedral and bazaar to represent two software development models. The cathedral model refers to a top-down software development approach that is closed, vertical, and centralized, designed by a group of elites who then execute according to a predetermined plan. In contrast, the bazaar model refers to a bottom-up software development approach, where no one dominates, and ordinary developers self-organize to pool collective strength and wisdom to complete complex tasks. Compared to the cathedral model, the bazaar model is parallel, peer-to-peer, dynamic, valuing collaboration. Despite appearing chaotic and disordered, this model has produced highly efficient and vibrant software, such as the world-class Linux operating system. Raymond believed that with further development of the internet, more cathedrals will disappear, while bazaars will flourish, primarily because of open source.

This book completely overturned traditional software development thinking and profoundly impacted the entire field. After having its own Declaration of Independence, the open-source movement has been progressing vigorously ever since. Today, more than 20 years later, the ubiquitous open-source software actually constructed the foundation of the whole internet.

This is the open-source movement, which raises the banners of openness, sharing, collaboration, and freedom. It aims to challenge authority, break monopolies, and pursue mutual assistance and benefit through the means of "open-source code." At its core is the principle of "each for all, and all for each," striving to create a "freedom kingdom" in the world of technology, where everyone helps one another and stands united.

More and more enterprises have realized the value of open-source: standing on the shoulders of giants can effectively avoid resource waste, foster continuous innovation, and achieve rapid iteration. Open, equal, collaborative, sharing models have gradually become mainstream for the new generation of software development, and a key driving force for technology industry at large. Google, IBM, and others have joined the open-source movement. By the acquisition of GitHub, the world's largest code hosting platform, for $7.5 billion, Microsoft, once an anti-open-source technology giant, demonstrated its power as the movement's key driving force.

As continuously demonstrated from the early days of free software to open-source software, and then to today's open-source ecosystem, the power of open source is pivotal and profound. In the digital age, open source is undoubtedly the foundation of the digital economy, driving the successive advancement of digital technologies. According to data released by Chinese government in the 14th Five-Year Plan for the Development of the Software and Information Technology Service Industry, 97% of software developers and 99% of enterprises worldwide use open-source software; most of the fundamental software, industrial software, and emerging platform software is based on open source – it has become a source of innovation and a "standard modules library" for the software industry.

Whilst exploring the past two decades, it has become clear to me that open source is a disruption in digital technology, a revolution against traditional information technology. In the past, information technology, characterized by software, was primarily controlled by a few high-tech companies. Open source represents the democratization and liberalization of a technological system, achieving equalization in technology. Taking NGINX as an example, it simplifies the entire development and operational process, driving technology towards greater democratization and liberalization, breaking technological monopolies and forming a completely new societal competitive force.

This is especially crucial for digital infrastructure, as its development depends on the construction of foundational software. The open-source ecosystem allows more developers to share their technological achievements and experiences, improving the efficiency of developers' technical output. This continually unleashes the power of innovation, promoting the iterative upgrading of technology. It greatly accelerates the process of digital infrastructure construction and steers digital transformation onto a new fast lane.

In the upgrade and transformation to the new technological paradigm centred on cloud-native, open-source also plays a crucial role. Many core technologies of the cloud-native paradigm such as edge computing and Kubernetes are also open-source technologies. For the upgrade to the technology paradigm, the free flow of API is the most critical issue. Under the cloud-native environment, open source equips everyone with the capability to use API, thus, realizing the free flow of data.

Today, major countries worldwide use open-source technology to promote technological innovation and industrial development. In cloud-native, big data, artificial intelligence, and other fields, influential international open-source foundations and platforms have formed, such as CNCF.

The global open-source wave surges forward, with China actively participating in the construction of the open-source ecosystem, becoming a major user and core contributor to global open-source software. CSDN GitCode, PingCAP OSSInsight, and Jing Qi, the Associate Professor, School of Software & Microelectronics, Peking University, published the 2022 China Open-Source Contribution Report, selecting and analysing the world's most active 5,394 open-source projects. The report showed that China has the most pervasive market with the largest number of developers. China represented 30% of the global incremental developers; for the top open-source projects, Chinese developers contributed 12.5%; China represented 20% of the top 50 global open-source contributors.

The domestic open-source area has welcomed in a new spring, boasting numerous achievements. The OpenAtom Foundation was established; Mulan PSL was approved by the Open-Source Initiative (OSI), becoming China's first internationally general-purpose open-source protocol; and the Ministry of Industry and Information Technology and other departments jointly built China's independent open-source hosting platform, together with Gitee.

More and more domestic technology companies are embracing open source and openness broadly. Huawei is one of the earliest companies in China to use and participate in the open-source software ecosystem. Since 2019, Huawei has successively open-sourced its operating system openEuler, enterprise database openGauss, and full-scenario AI framework MindSpore, accelerating the innovation and development of fundamental software. Among them, openEuler is an independently evolved native open-source operating system with features such as multi-architecture support, kernel-level innovation, cloud-native software stack, and cloud-edge collaboration; openGauss is an enterprise-class, open-source database developed by Huawei thoroughly integrating its years of experience in the database-related area under enterprise scenarios; MindSpore is a full-scenario, open-source AI computing framework that is developer-friendly, efficient in operation, and flexible in deployment. Huawei continues to invest in the fundamental software open-source and has made significant contributions, becoming a leader and practitioner in China's open-source ecosystem.

Digital China Group has also actively joined the open-source ranks. Digital China Group regards open-source software and technology as an important business direction. We have collaborated with open-source communities such as PingCAP, Odoo, and NGINX to provide Chinese enterprises with continuously innovative open-source technology and open hybrid cloud solutions, promoting the acceleration of open-source innovation. Digital China Group continues to plan for and contribute to the relevant communities of hot technologies stacks in such directions as cloud-native, database, code repository (codebase), JDK, and service mesh. In April 2023, Digital China Group's Tongming Lake Cloud and Innovative Infrastructure Research Institute announced the next generation of cloud-native application engine OpenNJet, and donated it to the OpenAtom Foundation for incubation, including codebase, IPR, and trademark. Digital China Group aims to continuously develop and evolve OpenNJet, under the framework of OpenAtom Foundation, by aggregating a wider group of end-users and ecosystem partners in developing the open ecosystem.

Moreover, Digital China Group leverages its ecosystem influence to promote the integration of cloud and open-source ecosystems. In December 2022, Digital China Group, in collaboration with two major ecosystem partners, Microsoft Azure and GitLab, created an integrated cloud-based DevOps platform. The steadfast and meticulous ecosystem construction enables Digital China Group to create value for enterprises' digital transformation, fostering win-win collaborations.

Peter Drucker believes that the internet's greatest contribution lies in eliminating distance. This aligns with the values of open source, which emphasize equality, openness, collaboration, and sharing. It enables enterprises and various partners in the ecosystem to achieve closer cooperation and collaboration, bringing more effective resource utilization and value creation methods for business operations and even socio-economic development. Any responsible enterprise should actively embrace open-source and openness, proactively integrating into the open-source ecosystem and using technology for the benefit of the world.

5.3 ENTERPRISES ARE A MAINSTAY IN DIGITAL INFRASTRUCTURE CONSTRUCTION

Digital infrastructure inherently possesses public attributes and faces many pressures, such as large investment scales, long construction cycles, extended investment return periods, and uncertainties in future expectations. During construction, problems like insufficient funding and poor operational management will likely arise. Therefore, in the building of digital infrastructure, the government should play a pivotal role to fully exert its leading function, by increasing investment intensity and policy support. Without robust government support, it is difficult to promote digital infrastructure rapidly and efficiently, and sustainable development is unlikely.

While the government is crucial in the building of digital infrastructure, one aspect should not be overlooked: it is necessary to open up the ecosystem as much as possible to achieve co-construction, co-governance, and sharing. Compared to the process of traditional infrastructure construction, enterprises, especially internet and high-tech companies, have distinct advantages in the construction and operation of digital infrastructure, demonstrating a strong willingness to participate. Leveraging the capabilities of these leading enterprises will lead to more choices for the investment and operation of digital infrastructure. Platform companies such as Alibaba and Tencent have now become part of the digital infrastructure construction.

The President of Tencent's WeChat Business Group, Zhang Xiaolong, once pointed out that "the world relies on the connectivity of all things. For products, connectivity means building the infrastructure for services, evolving into more diverse outcomes." WeChat, as such an infrastructure, has gradually evolved from a social communication tool into a digital infrastructure, covering a diverse range of fields.

People use WeChat for everyday communication, making it an indispensable tool in their lives. WeChat is used for exchanging information, conveying emotions, and even interactive activities like sending red packets, fostering even closer connections between individuals. According to data released by Zhang Xiaolong at the 2021 WeChat Night event, WeChat sees 1.09 billion users open the app daily, with 330 million users engaging in video calls, 780 million users entering Moments, and 120 million users posting Moments. WeChat's function extends to life payment functions, aggregating utility bills such as water, electricity, and gas. This enables people to pay bills anytime, anywhere, significantly enhancing the convenience of daily life.

WeChat Pay has become a widely-used payment tool in China. Whether in supermarkets, convenience stores, restaurants, barber shops, or even street stalls. Almost all kinds of scenarios accept WeChat Pay. The ubiquity of WeChat Pay also covers almost all kinds of payment situations.

WeChat mini-programs have gradually evolved into the infrastructure of the industrial internet. According to the WeChat Employment Impact Report, the number of mini-programs has exceeded one million, covering over 200 industry segments. They have driven over 1.8 million employment opportunities and cumulatively generated a commercial value exceeding ¥500 billion RMB. In the future, 80% of the mini-programs will be enterprise-grade, while 20% will be consumer-facing (2C) mini-programs. This lays the foundation for the development of the industrial internet. WeChat continuously innovates its various functions, allowing users to enjoy a smarter life that covers a broader range of areas, with more powerful and convenient features.

During the period of COVID-19 pandemic prevention and control, the value of the life service platforms, for instance Meituan and Ele.me, as digital infrastructure was fully demonstrated. In the catering business sector, due to the pandemic, many people were reluctant to dine out, leading to a significant decline in customers for many restaurants with minimal daily customer visits. Platforms like Meituan and Ele. me became the primary means for many of these catering businesses to monetize.[18] On the consumer side, many people choose to use these life service platforms to meet their daily needs. Some young people no longer go to traditional markets but instead buy groceries through apps like Meituan, JD Daojia, and Hema Fresh.[19] On the employment side, these life service platforms have also driven a large number of jobs in the upstream and downstream industries of catering. They not only provided a bottom-line guarantee for employment during the epidemic but also absorbed many unemployed individuals affected by the pandemic.

Platform-type enterprises are continually accumulating massive data, possessing rich and fully digitized resources and capabilities. They will play an increasingly important role in the digital age, developing at an unprecedented pace, with new models and formats constantly emerging.

However, the platform economy, still in its stage of rapid growth, has exposed many concerns. These problems can mainly be summarized in three points.

Firstly, many internet platforms monopolize the market using their own advantages, restricting market competition. For example, some internet platforms, by using their dominant position in e-commerce or social fields, impose either-or choices on merchants, depriving users of their right to choose and disturbing the normal market competition order. Some platforms build 'moats' by blocking external links, restricting, or even blocking competitors. This prevents interoperability between platforms, affecting user experience and hindering market competition.

Secondly, there are risks in data security and sharing.

The platform economy relies on data as the primary factor of production, and internet platforms control vast amounts of user data. However, due to unclear ownership and usage rights of data, some internet platforms lacking compliance awareness arbitrarily use this data. For instance, they may illegally provide data to third parties or employ big data analysis for big data-enabled price discrimination, severely harming users' information security and interests. Moreover, if an internet platform's information system faces external attacks or operational errors, it may lead to issues such as information leakage, compromising user data privacy.

Thirdly, there is blind expansion.

Some platform-type enterprises utilize capital for reckless expansion and even illegally enter the financial industry. They engage in high-risk businesses on the edge of regulatory and cause significant harm to the healthy development of the socio-economic system.

Therefore, we need to develop platforms and strengthen platform governance, ensuring that platforms move away from unchecked growth and towards orderly development. This ensures social fairness and justice, and protects individuals' data assets. It is encouraging that the Chinese government now prioritizes improving governance rules and the relevant legal system. Draft amendments to the Anti-Monopoly Law (for Public Consultation), Guidelines on Anti-Monopoly in the Platform Economy, and Measures for the Supervision and Administration of Online Transactions have been successively introduced, all addressing and filling the gaps and loopholes in platform governance.

Data governance is also a crucial aspect that needs special attention in platform governance. Clearly defining data resource rights, establishing rules for data security management, preventing data abuse, and enhancing data privacy protection are all top priorities. Enterprises are the main entities responsible for data security governance and must fulfil their duties, adhere to legal and compliant operations, and actively maintain and protect data security and personal data assets.

In the 19th Party Congress report, President Xi Jinping clearly stated the need for "establishing a social governance model based on collaboration, participation, and common interests." Platform-type enterprises should become part of the digital infrastructure, embodying co-construction and sharing while platform governance reflects co-governance. It requires both government-led regulation and enterprises to fulfil their responsibilities for self-governance. Additionally, it involves introducing public participation in governance to supervise and control the internet platforms. This multi-dimensional co-governance model can create a favourable platform ecosystem and effectively promote the orderly development of the platform economy.

5.4 NEW BLUEPRINT, NEW FUTURE

Kevin Kelly, author of *Out of Control: The New Biology of Machines, Social Systems, and the Economic World*, mentioned in the book, "It is only necessary that we connect everyone to everyone else – and to everything else – all the time and create new things together. Hundreds of miracles that seem impossible today will be possible with this shared human connectivity." Reflecting on the course of human development, from the construction of the Grand Canal connecting north and south in ancient China to the building of the world's first railway nearly 200 years ago, from the ancient Silk Road that linked Europe and Asia to the modern 'One Belt One Road' promoting mutual benefit and common wealth between China and the world, from the internet that connected the world and offered a new world to the emerging metaverse, the distance in time and space has gradually been diminished. The connections between people, society, and the world have become increasingly close and diverse, intertwining human destinies. Each groundbreaking interconnection in human history has brought about disruptions in the world order, industrial frameworks, institutions, and cultures. In the digital age, the global economic order and the landscape of interest patterns are undergoing accelerated reconstruction.

The first Digital Economy Report, released by the United Nations Conference on Trade and Development (UNCTAD) in 2019, reveals that global, digital economic activities and the wealth generated are growing rapidly and are highly concentrated in the United States and China. Currently, the U.S. and China hold over 75% of blockchain-related patents, 50% of global IoT expenditures, and over 75% of the cloud computing market. Among the world's 70 largest digital platform companies, seven 'super platforms' account for two-thirds of the total market value, with ranking by size as Microsoft, Apple, Amazon, Google, Facebook, Tencent, and Alibaba. This indicates that the race in the digital economy is primarily between two major players: the United States and China.

China has the opportunity to transition from a follower to a leader because the booming digital infrastructure is leading China along a new track of digital economic development. Digital infrastructure sparks strong investment demand, and it also caters to a vast consumer market, continuously providing new momentum for China's economic growth and accelerating the digital transformation of Chinese enterprises.

This is evident not only in the progress of digital infrastructure construction, such as 5G, cloud computing, the Internet of Things, big data, and artificial intelligence. China is already a significant player competing head-on with the global market leaders. Such players include Huawei's 5G technology, the mobile payment services of Alibaba and Tencent, and many others. It is also reflected in the explosive development of China's digital economy enterprises. For instance, there are already over 40,000 Chinese enterprises in the software and information technology services industry with annual sales exceeding ¥5 million RMB. The domestic competition among digital economy enterprises has intensified, leading to the gradual exit of some foreign competitors in the Chinese market.

The construction of digital infrastructure not only brings economic prosperity and national strength but also accelerates broad and profound social development. For individuals, it brings a completely new way of life, consumption habits, and work styles. For businesses, it brings significant opportunities and new ways of empowerment. For industries, it offers more development paths and industry reforms. For society, it brings a profound, top-down social transformation. In the future, finance will be more closely integrated with the real economy, while inclusive finance will benefit more vulnerable groups, and small and micro-enterprises. Rural areas will also experience revitalization, becoming beautiful homes with thriving industries, pleasant living environments, affluent lifestyles, socially etiquette rural civility and cultures, and effective governance. The green picture of harmonious coexistence between humans and nature will gradually unfold, and the mountain-water pastoral will once again become the poetic dwelling style of the Chinese nation.

The new blueprint of the digital age outlined by the construction of digital infrastructure is magnificently unfolding before us. Let's work together to seize the opportunities and create an even better world.

"NEW BANK": THE PATH TO DIGITAL TRANSFORMATION OF BANKING

In the Digital Age, people in the industrial sectors are always perplexed by the best way to approach the pivotal issue of digital transformation. Using the banking sector as an example, I plan to share with the readers my convictions regarding the solutions for financial institutions.

In the Industrial Age, because of the demand for large-scale, intensive operations of factors of production in the manufacturing sector, capital became the most pivotal factor of production. Financial institutions, exemplified by banks, emerged as the "jewel in the crown" of the economic realm. Owing to their inherent inclination towards informatization, banks have perennially been at the forefront, both as adopters and pioneers, of new information technologies. In the digital age, under the surge of the digital economy, technologies epitomized by cloud-native, big data, artificial intelligence, and blockchain solutions have thoroughly permeated the banking sector. Banks were among the pioneers of digital transformation initiatives, and their practical applications have yielded substantial outcomes. Given their pioneering role in digitization, the banking sector's digital transformation could potentially serve as a paradigm within broader corporate digital landscapes.

In the realm of banking informatization, Digital China Information Service Group stands out as an early entrant, playing a pivotal role in supporting the development of banking information systems. Over more than a decade of exploration and expertise accumulation, Digital China Information Service Group has broken the monopoly of multinational corporations. Through its proactive involvement in domestic banking IT development, the group has catalysed significant advancements in application architecture, fostering breakthroughs in traditional banking domains through autonomous innovation. Presently, Digital China Information Service Group commands a substantial market share in the financial software sector, boasting a client base that includes 90% of banks in China.

As the digital age unfolds and the banking sector undergoes a profound transformation, I aim to utilize the digital transformation of the banking sector as a case study. My intention is to provide an authentic depiction of how Digital China Information Service Group, an enterprise providing digital services, strategizes and executes its approaches in response to industry transitions. It is my aspiration that readers will glean valuable insights from this exploration.

"NEW BANK": AN OPPORTUNITY AND A CHALLENGE

How do banks transform in the Digital Age? Let us begin by discussing the opportunities and challenges that banks will face in the future.

As illustrated in Figure 5.1, the banks of future, which I refer to as the "New Banks," will encounter an abundance of new opportunities in the digital economic age.

Intrinsic Opportunities	Equipped with a Solid Foundation for Digital Transformation
Historic Opportunities	The Marriage of Inclusive Finance and Scenario-Based Finance
Technological Opportunities	The Burgeoning Advancement of Cloud Computing and Cloud-Native Technologies

FIGURE 5.1

OPPORTUNITIES OF THE "NEW BANKS"

1. Leveraging Intrinsic Opportunities: A Robust Foundation for Digital Transformation in Banking

Banks serve as the cornerstone of our financial system, safeguarding a wealth of financial service data for both corporate entities and individuals. Their rigorous security protocols and commitment to privacy protection are noteworthy. Furthermore, banks' broad engagement across various sectors of society establishes them as pivotal platforms within the digital economic ecosystem. These inherent qualities provide banks with a competitive edge as they navigate the digital age. For instance, banks have made substantial investments in digital advancements, positioning them with a technological advantage. Their access to critical data grants them a significant edge in the digital landscape. Additionally, being authorized and licensed by regulatory bodies instils a sense of credibility, fostering trust among stakeholders. Moreover, their extensive reach across B2B,[1] B2C,[2] and B2G[3] sectors affords them a vast network of customers, further bolstering their competitive position.

2. Seizing Historic Opportunities: Fusing Inclusive Finance with Scenario-Based Finance

In 1976, while conducting a social survey near Chittagong University in Bangladesh, professor of economics Muhammad Yunus encountered Sufiya, a village woman from Jobra. Despite her diligent work crafting bamboo stools, her income remained meagre due to a high-interest loan taken to purchase supplies. Borrowing just 5 Taka (approximately 22 U.S. cents) daily for bamboo, she struggled to repay the loan with her meagre earnings of 0.5 Taka (approximately 2 U.S. cents) per day, perpetuating a cycle of poverty for herself and her children. Yunus was deeply moved by her plight, prompting him to question the disconnect between academic theories and the harsh realities faced by individuals like Sufiya. Later, in his autobiography *Banker to the Poor*, he wrote, "In the university, I would theoretically analyse amounts in thousands of dollars. Yet here, right before me, the line between life and death was represented in mere cents. Where did things go wrong? Why didn't my university curriculum reflect the stark reality of Sufiya's life?"

Witnessing the widespread suffering caused by usurious loans in the village, Yunus took action by lending $27 of his own money to 42 impoverished women. This seemingly small act of compassion marked the inception of the "microcredit movement," ultimately earning him the title of "Banker to the Poor."

Yunus recognized that poverty perpetuated itself due to the lack of opportunities for impoverished individuals to break free from its grasp. Many families, despite possessing the skills for artisanal work or small-scale businesses, were held back by the absence of initial capital. The challenge lay in the reluctance of banks and formal lending institutions to offer loans of such small amounts. From the lenders' perspective, the marginal profits from such loans often failed to justify the associated costs, while prevailing perceptions categorized the impoverished as high-risk borrowers with limited repayment capabilities.

In this context, Yunus grasped the core principle of traditional banking: "the more wealth one possesses, the more they are eligible to borrow." However, this paradigm excluded those lacking financial assets, further perpetuating their poverty. Recognizing that loans could serve as a vital pathway out of poverty, Yunus advocated for providing even small amounts of start-up capital to aspiring entrepreneurs. By doing so, opportunities for employment could be created, leading to the potential eradication of poverty.

After years of persistent negotiations with the Bangladeshi government, Muhammad Yunus achieved a significant milestone in 1983: obtaining a banking license. This milestone paved the way for the establishment of the world's first bank dedicated to serving the poor – the Grameen Bank, also known as the "Village Bank." Over the next three decades, the Grameen Bank extended microloans to nearly 7 million low-income and impoverished Bangladeshis, with 58% of its borrowers and their families successfully breaking free from the shackles of poverty. In recognition of his extraordinary contributions, Yunus was awarded the Nobel Peace Prize in 2006, an unprecedented honour for a business figure, and a testament to the transformative impact of the Grameen Bank.

The remarkable ascent of the "Bank for the Poor" challenged entrenched perceptions that banks were institutions designed solely for the wealthy – a realm where money merely begot more money. Instead, the Grameen Bank exemplified a novel model where banking became a beacon of hope for the impoverished, underscored by its sustainability and impact.

The story of Yunus underscores the importance of inclusive finance, a matter of international attention and a global challenge.

It refers to the availability of financial services for the general public and emphasizes the importance of finance in alleviating poverty and building a prosperous society. Due to its significance, the State Council formulated the "Development Plan for Advancing Inclusive Finance (2016-2020)" in 2015, elevating inclusive finance to a national strategy. The need for building an inclusive financial system was highly emphasized during the 19th National Congress and the National Financial Work Conference, with a goal to prioritize financial services for micro and small enterprises, agriculture, rural areas, and farmers, and remote and impoverished regions.

However, while the concept of inclusive finance holds immense potential benefits, its implementation poses considerable challenges. In China, for instance, premier financial resources predominantly flow towards large corporations and urban centres, and the affluent demographic, neglecting the financial needs of small businesses, farmers, and low-income populations. Rural areas, despite their wealth in resources, assets and data, have struggled with inadequate credit systems and a lack of basic financial infrastructure.

The emergence of scenario-based finance presents an innovative solution to address these imbalances.

In the digital economy age, "scenarios" have become pivotal in reshaping interactions between individuals and businesses. By integrating with scenarios, financial products gain enhanced commercial value, fostering interdisciplinary synergies and coherent brand narratives. As the financial sector undergoes digital transformation, financial services are transitioning towards an embedded "scenario-based" approach, ushering in a new marketing paradigm in finance.

In the midst of its digital transformation, the amalgamation of inclusive finance and scenario-based finance furnishes the banking sector with a golden opportunity. Banks can leverage digital technologies to delve deeper into specific scenarios, enabling a nuanced understanding of rural areas and micro and small enterprises. By tailoring their services and risk control methods based on local conditions, banks are able to provide targeted, distinct, and practical financial solutions. Such initiatives can also expand the scope of financial services, thereby revealing vast market potential for the banking sector and fuelling its inherent momentum for digital transformation.

3. Embracing Technological Opportunities: The Rise of Cloud Computing and Cloud-Native Technologies in Banking

Cloud computing and cloud-native technologies stand as the backbone of digital infrastructure, offering banks agility, speed, flexibility, and cost-effectiveness in resource integration. This technological advancement provides robust support for the digital transformation journey of banks. A financial cloud ecosystem is evolving, leveraging cloud computing and cloud-native foundations while integrating emerging technologies like blockchain, artificial intelligence, big data, and the Internet of Things. This integration fosters a seamless connection between financial services and various urbanization, healthcare, and consumer scenarios, laying the technical groundwork for the realization of scenario-based finance.

The digital age presents an unprecedented opportunity for the banking sector, ushering in a new phase in its development trajectory. However, amidst this transition, challenges and opportunities persistently coexist.

One of the foremost challenges is the evolving expectations imposed by the digital economy on banking services.

As traditional industries undergo digital upgrades, new online and offline scenarios emerge, fundamentally altering production and lifestyle patterns. The convergence of physical and digital realms blurs industry boundaries, reshaping production models, societal systems, business logic, and distribution relationships. This dynamic landscape demands that banks continually enhance their business capabilities and adapt their service philosophies. For instance, the proliferation of digital scenarios necessitates addressing bottlenecks in financial services, while agile innovation requires meeting the agility needs of the financial services industry. Banks must evolve on both technological and business fronts to meet the rapid emergence of innovations and evolving consumer needs. The rise of novel industrial models calls for banks to provide tailored, personalized services throughout the entire lifecycle. Only by addressing these facets can banks authentically serve the digital transformation of industries, support the evolution of strategic sectors, champion inclusive finance, and ultimately elevate the living standards of the populace.

Secondly, addressing and surmounting the inherent developmental bottlenecks faced by banks is imperative.

Traditional banks have historically focused on providing fundamental financial services such as savings, loans, wire transfers, and foreign exchange, leading to a proliferation of homogeneous products and services. This reliance on extensive manpower and complex procedural management has resulted in inflated operational costs. Additionally, the prevailing risk management approach, primarily anchored in substantial collaterals and financial metrics, hampers innovation and adaptability, solidifying client segments and hindering product iteration.

Simultaneously, various structural aspects of banks serve as constraints on the evolution of their businesses. Several aspects of the bank's IT infrastructure are notably deficient. There is still a reliance on monolithic systems, which have limited inter-system interaction capabilities by nature. The separation between transactional processing and data processing impedes the efficient application of data insights and value to operational capabilities. Such a lag in IT architecture undermines the capacity for integrated financial services and industrial services, and impedes rapid adaptation to industry-specific scenarios. Concurrently, the organizational structure of banks lacks the desired agility. Banks' technological architecture has historically prioritized stability. However, the advent of cloud computing has steered it towards a synthesis of stability and agility. This invariably presents challenges to data transmission, storage, and analysis, necessitating continual refinement of data processing systems, and the expansion of stress-testing and emergency response capabilities. It would be judicious for banks to establish a more agile organizational structure, fostering continual high-level improvements in business processes, responsiveness, client experience, and business and operational decision-making.

Furthermore, with the continual evolution of emerging scenarios, new operational entities have emerged as competitors to commercial banks. Coupled with the liberalization of interest rates, and deeper financial reforms, there is an urgent need for commercial banks to improve their distribution channels, broaden their client base, improve operational efficiency, and refine product offerings, to ensure a competitive edge in this evolving era and fully realize their inherent value.

Finally, the banking sector grapples with significant concerns surrounding data governance and security.

Financial institutions possess distinct characteristics, such as fragmented data distribution, diverse structures, and scalable data growth, which contribute to complex data governance challenges. Banking data is often dispersed across various business systems, leading to horizontal and vertical disjunctions. Inconsistent data management practices across departments and business lines exacerbate the complexity of data integration and utilization.

Moreover, changes in business models, service approaches, and operational and business management have emerged as banks undergo digital transformation. Consequently, the nature, trajectory, and security boundaries of potential risks have changed, intensifying and complicating data security concerns. Every aspect of data management, including data acquisition, transmission, storage, and sharing, is fraught with safety risks and difficulties. The cross-border transmission of data exacerbates national security concerns, requiring banks to strike a balance between data exploitation and protection. In addition, as data utilization expands, there is a heightened risk of privacy breaches, with periodic instances of data leaks. While banks continue to expand and evolve, their intrinsic nature remains unchanged, and risk prevention remains an untouchable standard. The process of ensuring data security is arduous and time-consuming.

How can one seize these rare opportunities? How do we address these complex challenges? These are pivotal questions banks must deliberate upon during their digital transformation journey. Only by discerning answers to these conundrums can the banking industry forge a genuine path into the future.

UTILIZING THE FIRST PRINCIPLES THINKING TO UNDERSTAND THE "NEW BANK"

Due to a confluence of internal and external factors, banks find themselves compelled to undergo continuous transformation and advancement in their future development. However, there remains a lack of explicit directives regarding the future form and capabilities of banks. Current descriptors such as 'Ecosystem Bank,' 'Open Bank,' 'Platform Bank,' and 'Intelligent Bank' offer glimpses into potential iterations of traditional banking paradigms. Yet, they often fall short of capturing the essence of what truly constitutes a 'New banking.'

To effectively characterize the 'New Banking,' it is imperative to delineate its functions and form. This, in turn, will facilitate the establishment of strategic objectives, the plotting of developmental trajectories, and the transformation and elevation of the bank.

First Principles Thinking serves as a fundamental touchstone for identifying the primary narrative amidst the chaos and fostering disruptive innovation. From the perspective of First Principles Thinking, the primary objective of a bank involves the continuous development of the scale of assets under management, which remains the core responsibility of the board of directors. The accumulation of data assets holds the potential to advance exponentially in comparison to the scale of assets under management. Consequently, the leadership team's goals must centre on business innovation to realize the growth of the scale of managed assets, facilitating the swift realization of data assets reconfiguration and iteration, thus forming the innovative growth flywheel. The execution teams, in turn, are tasked with establishing a robust data cloud integration technical architecture with a toolbox, enabling the rapid integration of business and technology.

Business innovation will no longer be reliant on traditional waterfall long-cycle approaches. Instead, automation in development and operation will be achieved through rapid iteration, fostering agility and responsiveness within the organization.

Hence, banks must engage in change and upgrade in order to establish an entirely new capabilities framework. Specifically, the attributes of the 'new bank' should include three pivotal facets, as illustrated in Figure 5.2.

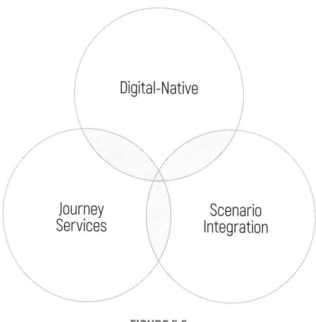

FIGURE 5.2
THE ATTRIBUTES OF THE "NEW BANK"

Digital-Native: Future banks must undergo a significant upgrade of their capabilities and integrate digital principles into their fundamental operational philosophies. By fostering an intrinsic digital mind-set and operational mode, this approach will enable the organization to fully leverage the capabilities of digital technology and establish itself as a digitally native organization.

Scenario Integration: Banks should possess a comprehensive understanding of the credit intermediary requirements of diverse scenarios in their service provision. By integrating financial products and credit services with application scenarios, banks can create intangible banking experiences that are seamless, personalized, and customized, enhancing customer satisfaction.

Journey Services: The 'New Banking' should excel in providing journey services to customers, surpassing conventional banks in this regard. Customers should be accompanied and guided throughout their entire lifecycle based on their behaviour and requirements. This includes intelligently providing diverse services during the customer's growth journey, such as financial services, non-financial credit intermediary services, digital functionalities, pertinent experiences, and platform-based offerings. Ultimately, this results in a customer experience characterized by journey services.

The aforementioned represents the future of the 'New Banking.' It is not an iteration of conventional banking; instead, it signifies an upgrade built upon the capabilities of digital technology and the essential characteristics of the digital economy. It is a new type of service institution with entirely new business forms and capabilities.

CONSTRUCTING THE "NEW BANK"

The requirements outlined for the 'New Banking,' encompassing digital-native principles, scenario integration, and journey service provision, signify a departure from conventional banks that merely digitize their services through incremental improvements. This distinguishes the 'New Banking' as a more dynamic and central service provider within the framework of the digital economy, facilitating the flow of credit across diverse domains, locations, and situations. The establishment of the 'New Banking' serves as a catalyst for advancing the digital economy and currently represents the primary driver behind the realization of digital upgrades and advancements.

The construction of the 'New Banking' should prioritize three key characteristics from the outset: digital-native attributes, seamless scenario integration, and comprehensive journey service provision.

1. **The Formation of Digital-Native**

'Native' denotes an entity that is original and unaltered by external forces. Consequently, a digitally native bank is one in which its products and services, management approaches and operational procedures, business models, and commercial models are designed based on the conditions created by digital technology. Banks ought to undertake a comprehensive upgrade and transformation of their technological capabilities, organizational structure, and business models in order to achieve digital native. This transformation requires the establishment of an organizational framework that is digitally native.

To begin with, an upgrade in technological capabilities is imperative.

In order to maximize the potential of digital technology and broaden the scope of an organization, banks need to upgrade their digital competencies. This forms the bedrock of digital-nativeness.

Technological capability upgrades comprise the following three elements. Architectural Upgrade: The IT architecture of banks should adhere to the fundamental requirements of cloud-nativeness, distributed approach, and full-stack innovative infrastructure. They should proactively construct a capability middle platform, a data middle platform, and a business middle platform, in order to effectively support front-end applications. The establishment of capability centres and the effective integration of foundational resources should support open output and boundaryless services. Data Native: Banks should be equipped with the necessary computational and modelling capabilities for data analysis, mining, and application. This facilitates the complete extraction of value from data, thereby bolstering intelligent services. By solidifying these capabilities as digital assets, their operation and management can be used for application usage and value addition. Data assets should be the driver for business expansion. Operational Excellence: In order to achieve operational cost reductions and improve efficiency, commercial banks should implement digital technology to integrate services across space and time and achieve operational excellence.

Secondly, organizational upgrades should be undertaken.

To reap the benefits of digital technology and attain the state of digital-nativeness, it isn't enough to merely upgrade technological capabilities. Business philosophies, organizational structures, and product logics of conventional banks must be upgraded in a complementary fashion.

Organizational structures neeed to be overhauled, shifting from conventional hierarchical models to matrix-based ones that prioritize flat management, cross-functional collaboration, and smooth technology and business integration.

Innovative concepts and scenario operations should be deeply ingrained to enable agile responses to innovation demands. They must proficiently evaluate credit requirements that arise from digitization in emerging scenarios and across domains, efficiently mitigate risks, and proactively pioneer innovations.

Product logic should commence with data assets, encompassing initial product coverage that includes components such as traffic, intellectual property rights, and virtual assets. Business operations should be driven by data, with an upgrade from physical asset dependence to data asset management.

Finally, there should be business upgrades.

On the basis of the new organizational structure and the technological foundation of being digitally native, banking operations should be modernized to create socialized, networked platforms. This transformation should incorporate domains including product design, marketing channels, and risk management, while progressing in the direction of big data, elastic services, and agile organization models. Presently divided into retail, corporate, and so forth, business lines ought to be reorganized in accordance with distinct capability modules.

For retail businesses, services should extend into a multitude of everyday scenarios, thereby achieving scenario interconnectivity and intelligently meeting the complete lifecycle needs of individuals.

For corporate businesses, a comprehensive understanding of industry characteristics should empower a full-cycle integration of financial services, connecting various industry scenarios through banks to achieve platform coordination, and supply-demand balance, whilst stimulating industrial development vitality.

Government sector businesses should fulfil financial service needs while concurrently integrating government scenarios, advocating for smart city upgrades, improving administration and public services via the banking interfaces, and augmenting governance levels.

2. Achieving Scenario Integration

Scenarios are the conditions in which specific behaviours occur. "Behaviour" encompasses a wide range of activities, including but not limited to consumption, entertainment, social interactions, logistics, and manufacturing. Scenario-based finance pertains to the seamless integration of financial services with economic production and routine human behaviours, thereby facilitating the free and unrestricted execution of financial transactions. Because credit intermediation is no longer a specialized activity, the cost of financial services has been drastically reduced to a minimum.

In addition to the demands that emerge from the digital transformation of conventional industries, the development of the digital economy gives rise to entirely new scenario demands, including industrial digital asset management and data interconnection. This requires banks to possess the capability to promptly and efficiently comprehend the logic of diverse scenarios, consistently identify challenges in credit demands that arise from said scenarios, and possess the appropriate technological infrastructure and product logic to facilitate the provision of banking functionalities.

By categorizing the circumstances leading to financial and non-financial behaviour as financial scenarios and non-financial scenarios, the progression of scenario-based finance will transform all forthcoming scenarios into integrated scenarios, in which both financial and non-financial behaviours exist in harmony. Financial behaviour in an integrated scenario will be supported by every capability, in the form of components contained within financial scenarios; banks will serve as the financial capability centres supporting all scenarios.

To guarantee service development and risk management while conducting financial activities effectively within integrated scenarios, banks offering scenario-based financial services must exercise caution when constructing scenario elements.

1. Capability Foundation: In order to deliver scenario-based financial services, banks must possess the requisite technological and business capabilities. This comprises a flexible and expandable architectural framework, capability to open the access to the platforms, and the capacity to comprehend, decompose, and integrate the output capability of intermediary functionalities in the process of credit circulation. This ensures the safety of the system and financial security.
2. Traffic Generation: This involves assembling pertinent industry traffic for the given scenario, enabling it to accurately depict the development of the respective industry, facilitating the accumulation of big data.
3. Clarity of Demands: The assessment of economic behaviours in the given scenario should clearly define the credit circulation needs. This can be fulfilled through relevant capability combinations or ecosystem access.
4. Financial Closure: Through actions such as data analysis and process management, it's possible to effectively manage the business elements and control financial-related risks.

5. Value Creation: Banks have the potential to derive value from customer scenario requirements in the form of financial returns, data accumulation, and the improvement of experiences and capabilities, among other things.

To unlock the development potential of the real economy within the digital economic system, continuous improvement of scenario value and effective cross-scenario collaborative services are crucial during the process of constructing the 'new bank'. The following are the essential factors to contemplate.

Ongoing Capability Development: Scenario-based finance imposes requirements for the banks to have the technological prowess and understanding of potential scenarios. Banks need to engage in focused technology capability development and continuously position themselves to learn to meet the demands of various scenarios.

Collaborating with Trustworthy Ecosystem Partners: It can be expensive to design and construct mechanisms and multi-scenario products using only the bank's internal resources. Consequently, scenario integration and product co-creation via ecosystem partnerships should be considered. The construction and operation of the scenario-based finance framework can be brought about by using this method. However, this necessitates that ecosystem partners possess robust scenario capabilities and reliable credentials.

Ongoing Investigation of Scenario Value: Within the framework of scenario-based finance, financial institutions should consistently improve and ascertain customer attributes and requirements, unveil customer value, expand customer reach, augment scenario value, and advance the value enhancement of the financial institutions and the development of the real economy.

Monitoring of Extended Risks: Aside from conventional industry and financial risks, the development of scenario-based finance may entail extended risks that span across domains and technology applications. It is imperative for banks to diligently monitor and effectively mitigate these risks in a professional way.

Customizing Services for Diverse Customer Segments: In order to cater to the needs of various customer bases, banks are required to offer customized services. In order to accommodate retail customers, services ought to be tailored to situations encountered in everyday life, including consumption, social engagements, and travel, to provide scenario-based services. Service models such as mobile payments, digital currency, and asset management could be included. To enable corporate customers engaged in logistics, manufacturing, trading, and other sectors to integrate financial services with actual business operations, banks must prioritize the efficient management of risk factors and ensure transparency and traceability. Through the connecting of payment, transportation, healthcare, and other domains via smart administration and smart cities, customers in the government and public services sector can experience efficient government and financial services. Such services will bolster economic growth and enhance convenience in citizens' daily lives.

3. Improvements to Journey Services

Customer-centric journey services begin with responding to customer requests for product access and recommendations in financial scenarios. Banks must adopt more intelligent and precise service models and philosophies where dynamic data-driven networks permeate every industry and aspect of daily life. By offering credit support to customers for the duration of their relationship with the bank, they should facilitate and direct their development, thus establishing a "customer journey" framework.

Comprehensive journey services should encompass the following aspects:

Service Action Closure: Banks should manage the end-to-end processes for each product delivery and service action. They should streamline service steps to reduce operational costs. From product design and promotion to subsequent evaluation and feedback, achieving full-process tracking is crucial. Continuous refinement of service quality is imperative in order to establish an optimal customer experience—one in which actions result in accomplishments and responses lead to results.

Full Lifecycle Services: For comprehensive customer service, banks' journey services should offer full-stack credit services, available on demand. This includes credit circulation-based services involving cross-platform identity authentication, data asset management, and data privacy protection, in addition to financial services. These services should be proactive, demand-responsive, and intelligent. They should effectively adapt to customer characteristics and growth features, providing credit support throughout the customer's entire life.

Service Integration Platform Support: Banks can function as integrated service and circulation hub platforms and are able to efficiently oversee the various phases of customer development in relation to financial services. Subsequently, they can use the Internet of Things and the interconnection of industrial data to streamline the exchange of supply and demand. Banks can furnish platform support for the all-encompassing digitization upgrade of the economic system through the construction of ecosystems.

Journey service is an operational system that necessitates the collaboration of numerous ecosystem partners and financial institutions. It is recommended that banks prioritize the building of customer-centric, order-centric, process-centric, operation-centric, and experience feedback elements within their frameworks. Industrial internet must be integrated with the physical economy. Furthermore, consulting firms, fintech service providers, financial institutions, and other partners within the ecosystem should work together to effectively construct an all-encompassing customer journey service system.

During the construction of the "new bank," it is imperative to meticulously contemplate a number of essential factors:

Commencing with the Environment: The economic environment within which a bank functions serves as the bedrock for the construction of a 'new bank.' The extent of digitization across different sectors dictates the potential adoption of 'new bank' services and the origins of data. Prior to initiating their own digital transformation, banks must conduct an evaluation of the digitalization condition of the sectors of the economy that are pertinent to their growth strategy. They can only make significant progress in the creation of the new bank' after they have established a solid foundation. Amidst the establishment of the new bank,' businesses should synchronize their digitalization requirements with pertinent industries and participate in reciprocal exchanges to encouragement industry advancements.

Mitigating Internal Pain Points: In accordance with their business development strategy, banks should identify and tackle their internal pain points. Banks should adjust their technological infrastructure, business framework, and organizational structure, in keeping with the principles of digital-nativeness, scenario integration, and journey service enhancement. By cultivating a digital environment, the door will be opened to the possibility of ground-breaking services. In addition to building a digital service ecosystem and enhancing their own capabilities, banks should exercise discernment when selecting ecosystem partners.

Selecting a Personalized Path: Banks should decide on their personalized trajectory of development, predicated upon their current technological and business infrastructure. It is recommended that banks undertake a comprehensive audit of their technological capabilities, commencing with the technological architecture, to encourage business development via digital intelligence. This should include technology architecture, core systems, sales and channel management, and data governance. They may refer to strategies such as the restructuring of Ping An Bank's business models and the development of AI-powered retail services.

Banks should monitor business demands in accordance with their intended business development direction and scenario formulation needs, commencing with business requirements. This procedure entails driving creation of demands in technology and restructuring the organization, aiming at continuously improving foundational capabilities that support business expansion. Banks should prioritize the development of open platforms, intelligent sales and marketing systems, enabling middle platform construction to bolster business capabilities. They could refer to the building of Open Banking and Panorama Banking of Shanghai Pudong Development Bank as models.

Streamlining Bank Operations and Improving Particular Domains: Banks that have constrained resources or insufficient initial digital capabilities may wish to concentrate on domains that impede progress, such as the development of core systems, data middle platform, or risk management middle platform. Only then can a systematic progression of the 'new bank' construction be achieved. Thorough assessments and overarching planning are also critical.

Banks that possess adequate resources, well-established digital infrastructures, and suitably qualified personnel may contemplate venturing into various strategic paths. Through meticulous evaluations and efficient strategizing, they can construct the 'new bank' achieving corner overtaking.

In the course of constructing the 'new bank,' the development of inclusive finance is a crucial element that must not be neglected.

President Xi Jinping emphasized in 2017 at the National Financial Work Conference that inclusive financing mechanism should be developed to improve support to small and medium-sized enterprises and rural and remote places. Indeed, the development of inclusive finance has become a consequence of the continuous release of national policy dividends and the ongoing advancement of financial technology. Banks, in their capacity as financial service institutions, should not only assume this social responsibility but also seize this exceptional opportunity to penetrate untapped markets brimming with potential, including rural regions and small and micro-enterprises. As a result, the 'new bank' should enhance its inclusive financial service capabilities, innovate perpetually inclusive financial products and service processes, and integrate financial technology with the real economy in a seamless fashion. By adopting this methodology, a sustainable trajectory for the advancement of inclusive finance can be reached. This not only allows for the identification of new profit opportunities and business expansion for the banks, but also aids in the practical application of inclusive finance for the nation, thereby generating greater societal value.

THE FUTURE-ORIENTED MODEL BANK 5.0

The construction of the 'New Bank' is a systematic project, requiring the support of an entire digital ecosystem. This extends beyond traditional financial institutions such as banks and various financial institutions, to include those fintech companies that offer relevant technical support and services.

Digital China Information Service Group, a provider of fintech services, has demonstrated a commitment to innovation and practical application in the digital transformation of the banking industry. In the early stages of our efforts to provide informatization services for the banks, the bill formats utilized by the Haidian and Tiananmen branches of a major bank were dissimilar. During that period, there was an absence of a comprehensive system, so we wrote our Financial Data Model, the inaugural monograph in China dedicated to financial data models.

We have integrated applications of emerging technologies such as artificial intelligence, cloud computing, blockchain, big data, and the Internet of Things over the years, in accordance with the open banking philosophy, and have consistently made contributions to the architectural upgrades and digital transformation of banks, all by prioritizing financial security. We have also released the fifth version of integrated solution for banks based on our own IT architecture, known as the 'Model Bank' architecture.

The year 2000 saw the inception of Model Bank 1.0, a significant development in the financial sector's domestic application software. During an era when centralized architectures based on foreign mainframe computers and integrated business systems dominated, the transition from integrated business systems to core business systems emerged as the cornerstone in the development of contemporary banking application systems. Digital China Information Service Group successfully introduced the first core banking business system developed in China, thereby challenging the dominance of foreign products and hugely reducing the cost of ownership of core banking systems. This also prompted the development of core systems for domestic small and medium-sized banks and substantially reduced the construction costs of such systems.

Model Bank continued to develop and was upgraded to Model Bank 2.0 in 2007. We were pioneers in the industry when we first introduced the design concept of Service Oriented Architecture (SOA). This methodology not only facilitated diverse and adaptable business process combinations according to business processes and steps, thereby significantly bolstering the banks' capacity for service innovation, but also employed SOA to accomplish IT governance, thereby assisting banks in the establishment of a comprehensive service governance process and procedure.

The financial sector became more accessible and open after China's membership to the WTO, albeit under intense and intricate competitive pressures. In response to issues such as the surge in demand for business innovation and the chaos in IT governance, Model Bank 2.0 revolutionized the disorganized state of domestic banking technology development, by directing banks to initiate technology development with a customer-centric approach.

In 2010, Model Bank 3.0 implemented the notion of 'product families,' which served to standardize the categorization of banking application systems. It effectively delineated the front, middle, and back office, which comprised the banking business systems and IT architecture.

Introduced in 2015, Model Bank 4.0 brought about a fundamental transformation by introducing the notion of the internet and driving banking and financial institutions towards the advancement of open banking.

Based on the advancement of the below technological development, Digital China Information Service Group launched Model Bank 5.0 in 2021.

Initially, historical banking systems were comprised of standalone application systems, which resulted in a siloed[4] organizational structure. Despite establishing an overall structure to link these systems, and developing a highly reliable overall system, the initial structure appears cumbersome and lacks agility in the context of the current scenario-based and customer-centric new financial consumption system.

A notable disconnect has existed between the processing of transactions and the processing of data, which has impeded the timely incorporation of data value into business operations. Every bank possesses vast quantities of data in the era of big data; however, there is currently no IT architecture capable of incorporating this data in real-time into bank services, customer experiences, or new product development.

Furthermore, in the context of typical industrial scenarios to deliver prompt services, the capacity of comprehensive financial services and industrial financial services is hindered by obsolete or non-existent IT architectures. It is critical to address the correlation between traditional bank cores and internet finance cores, an aspect that previous architectures and systems failed to do. With the aim of integrating intelligent financial services with diversified financial scenarios, the expediting of the upgrade for the entire IT architecture has emerged as a critical objective. The transition from conventional IT architectures to cloud-native and digital-native development facilitates the establishment of a new banking architecture system.

The implementation of the latest Innovative Infrastructure has created a new proposition for us, namely, how to secure the construction of security under the technological architecture.

Model Bank 5.0 was created in response to technological developments and changes in the banking industry, as well as to satisfy the sector's digital transformation requirements.

Model Bank 5.0 is an IT architecture for the banking industry that is focused on the future of digital technology. It has the capability to assist banks in integrating into different scenarios, thereby making the banks of the future that we envision a reality.

Model Bank 5.0 is exceptional due to its cloud-native architecture and micro-services, as well as its real-time data analysis capability. It supports the sustainable development of digital finance by maximising the potential of application systems, through the utilization of the financial AI capabilities. With respect to business support, Model Bank 5.0 enables the productivity and daily lives of customers via functional segmentation based on scenarios, journeys, and middle platforms. By constructing a professional financial service system that encompasses mass retail, industrial finance, and investment, it enables financial institutions to innovate business models and maximize the value of data, thereby improving their service to the real economy.

In particular, the pillars of Model Bank 5.0 are a data middle platform, a technical middle platform, and the financial AI capabilities. On five levels – scenario construction, journey services, capability output, resource accumulation, and organizational management – it satisfies the needs of business development. As depicted in Figure 5.3, its unambiguous digital support capabilities offer strategic direction for the evolution of the IT architectures of financial institutions.

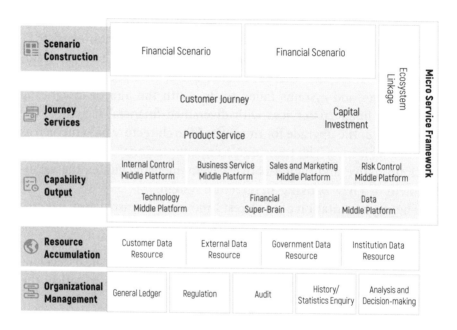

FIGURE 5.3
APPLICATION ARCHITECTURE OF MODEL BANK 5.0

The "Scenario Construction" layer allows for the expansion of business operations, delivers a cohesive interactive encounter, and generates a comprehensive brand identity. It consolidates "counter services, mobile services, remote services, and customer self-services" to aid financial institutions in establishing an integrated online and offline service model. Furthermore, it extensively engages in cross-industry collaboration to develop integrated scenarios in various domains, including communities, supply chains, and trading markets, by utilizing the ecosystem chain. By integrating financial services more extensively into the production and life processes of users, this approach enables financial institutions to establish connections between scenarios and users, fulfil user requirements, and foster industry advancement.

The "Journey Services" layer serves as the core component of the architecture of Model Bank 5.0. It encompasses operations pertaining to user journeys, product services, and capital investments. It places emphasis on tailoring thousands of process experiences and product services to the unique service requirements of users under particular scenarios, enabling them to experience a variety of financial services in a seamless and effortless manner, akin to embarking on an upscale journey.

The "Capability Output" is the system layer where financial institutions centrally provide journey services with fundamental capabilities. The architecture comprises four middle platforms that operate at the business level (internal management, business processing, sales and marketing, and risk control), and three middle platforms (namely the data middle platform, technology middle platform, and the financial AI capabilities) which are tasked with generating fundamental technical capabilities. The financial AI capabilities will offer an extensive array of AI capability applications, aiding business systems and technical platforms in fulfilling diverse intelligent demands, unleashing additional potential.

The "Resource Accumulation" layer emphasizes the data resources accumulated, via data lake-house integrated technology, in the process of digital business operation. These consist of user data resources, external data resources, government data resources, and institutional data resources. Subsequently, the data middle platform processes the accumulated data resources in the "Resource Accumulation" layer for the purpose of real-time analysis, transmission, and utilization. This expedites the translation of data value into business processing and management operations.

At the system level, the "Organizational Management" layer oversees the management, auditing, and regulatory aspects of financial institutions, laying the groundwork for their continued growth and stability.

The "Organizational Management" layer's systems become more intelligent as a result of the data middle platform and the financial AI capabilities reshaping the value of data within the overall architecture of Model Bank 5.0. This facilitates the digital transformation of organizational management within financial institutions. Model Bank 5.0's five layers of systems will leverage the performance and deployment benefits of distributed technology to the fullest extent possible within the unified micro-services framework provided by the technical middle platform. This results in intelligent management of operations and development that is integrated, thereby allowing for the rapid expansion of future businesses.

In the digital age, business must now be viewed from the user's perspective as well as the bank's. Although banks have historically prioritized stability, they should strive for both agility and stability from the perspective of their customers. By adopting a dual-pronged approach to future IT architecture development, it is possible to more efficiently tackle the challenges and obstacles that impede banking business development. Additionally, it is critical to combine new technological capabilities with expertise and strengths from other fields, such as taxation and agriculture. This requires the use of the cloud-native system, data middle platforms, and the financial AI capabilities, to enable cross-industry financial scenario development. Granting financial capabilities to agriculture, supply chain systems, and the real economy is intended to stimulate a revival in the latter and infuse it with fresh impetus.

POSTSCRIPT

This book was first written in 2021, coinciding with the 20th anniversary of Digital China's listing, a milestone that inspired its creation as a tribute to the company's two decades of entrepreneurial endeavour.

Throughout the process of writing this volume, my thoughts frequently travelled back in time, aided by a wealth of memories.

Digital China was founded in 2000 after being spun off from the Lenovo Group and embarking on its own journey. The momentous task of naming the new company coincided with my encounter with a United Nations report that revealed a significant digital divide between developed and developing countries. This revelation instilled in me a sense of responsibility: the quest to bridge this digital divide mirrored China's broader goal of national rejuvenation. As a result, from the very beginning, Digital China was not only chosen as the name for us, being a new company in the IT realm, but also as a symbol of our mission. On June 1st of that inaugural year, we celebrated our official listing on the Hong Kong Stock Exchange, heralding the start of a new chapter.

Our founding spirit and values, which centre on contributing to the society and nation through industry, have played a critical role in shaping Digital China's trajectory and future, envisioning the company as an explorer, practitioner and enabler of a digital China. As explorers, we allowed for the inevitable setbacks and sacrifices that come with the uncharted journey of digitalization. As practitioners, we began digitizing our own enterprise, using our experiences as a blueprint for the larger digital revolution. As enablers, if the path proved correct, we hoped to facilitate digitalization services for the others. Our goal was to accelerate societal progress towards digital transformation.

This journey was filled with difficulties, requiring us to make sacrifices, but we persisted, constantly making breakthrough and progress.

In the last 20 years, under the deep understanding of the development of the industry and national strategy, by continuous exploration and innovation, Digital China has transformed from an obscure enterprise with a few billion Chinese Yuan of revenue into a major digital conglomerate, with a revenue exceeding ¥140 billion RMB. It has particularly excelled in the forefront of digitalization such as cloud computing, big data, and financial technology innovation, leading to rapid growth in strategic businesses reaching a revenue size of ¥20 billion RMB, and establishing itself as a prominent leading digital transformation partner in China.

After an extensive and persistent effort, Digital China has emerged as a leading force in the digital age, constantly evolving and focusing on the future. Today, we can confidently state that we have achieved our goals and have not failed the mission of "Digital China" that we initially set for ourselves.

Reflecting on these 20 years of efforts and growth, as well as relentless pursuit and transformation, with continuous observation and practicing, I have remained involved with the internet, various industries, and digitalization, encapsulating years of thought in this publication, with an aim to provide the readers with new ideas and perspectives on digital transformation.

The publication of this book received considerable attention and praise. However, my exploration does not end here, as we are presently navigating a period of rapid and turbulent transformation. The comprehension of digitalization and the theories and implementation of enterprise digital transformation are continuously progressing, requiring ongoing learning and improvement. Therefore, the release of a second edition of this book seeks to offer readers fresh perspectives and contemplations, assisting them in navigating the turbulent period of digitalization by reconstructing cognition, and cultivating a mind-set of receptiveness, collaboration, and mutual benefit in their digitalization pursuits.

I am highly conscious of the constraints of my viewpoint and eagerly embrace additional improvement and valuable input from readers after reading this piece.

Finally, I would like to express my appreciation for this significant era of profound change, in which our experiences have aligned with the global story through reform and opening. And hardships alongside glory have deepened our understanding of life's meaning. The arrival of the digital wave has allowed us to participate in humanity's greatest transformation. I am thankful for this great era that has given me the opportunity to realize my dreams and values.

BIBLIOGRAPHY

1. Toffler, Alvin. *The Third Wave*. Translated by Huang Mingjian. Beijing: CITIC Press, 2018.

2. Mayer-Schönberger, Viktor, and Cukier, Kenneth. *Big Data: A Revolution That Will Transform How We Live, Work, and Think*. Translated by Sheng Yangyan and Zhou Tao. Hangzhou: Zhejiang People's Publishing House, 2013.

3. Hume, David. *A Treatise of Human Nature*. Translated by Guan Wenyun. Beijing: The Commercial Press, 2016.

4. Harari, Yuval Noah. *Homo Deus: A Brief History of Tomorrow*. Translated by Lin Junhong. Beijing: CITIC Publishing Group, 2018.

5. Chen, Chunhua. *Value Co-creation: Organizational Management in the Digital Age*. Beijing: Posts & Telecom Press, 2021.

6. Chen, Xuepin. *Understanding Digital Transformation from One Book*. Beijing: Machinery Industry Press, 2020.

7. Siebel, Thomas. *Understanding Digital Transformation*. Translated by Bi Chongyi. Beijing: Machinery Industry Press, 2020.

8. Negroponte, Nicholas. *Being Digital*. Translated by Hu Yong and Fan Haiyan. Beijing: Electronics Industry Press, 2021.

9. Wang, Sixuan. *Digital Transformation Architecture: Methodology and Cloud-Native Practice*. Beijing: Electronics Industry Press, 2021.

10. 50 People Forum of the Information Society. *China in the Digital Transformation*. Beijing: Electronics Industry Press, 2021.

11. Chen, Xinyu, et al. *Middle Platform Practice: Methodology and Solutions for Digital Transformation*. Beijing: Machinery Industry Press, 2020.

12. Heiferman, Raz. *Digital Quantum Leap: Strategies and Tactics for Digital Transformation (Chinese)*. Translated by Xi Yishan and Zhang Xiaoquan. Beijing: Machinery Industry Press, 2020.

13. Zhao, Gang. *Digital Trust: Essence and Application of Blockchain*. Beijing: Electronics Industry Press, 2020.

14. Zhao, Xingfeng. *Digital Metamorphosis: The Path of Enterprise Digital Transformation*. Beijing: Electronics Industry Press, 2019.

15. Lei, Wanyun. *Practices of Digital Transformation Driven by Cloud, AI, and 5G*. Beijing: Tsinghua University Press, 2020.

16. Ma, Xiaodong. *Methodology and Data Middle Platform Landing Path of Digital Transformation*. Beijing: Machinery Industry Press, 2021.

17. Fu, Dengpo, et al. *Data Middle Platform: Making Data Usable*. Beijing: Machinery Industry Press, 2020.

18. Chen, Xinyu, et al. *Middle Platform Strategy: Middle Platform Construction and Digital Business*. Beijing: Machinery Industry Press, 2019.

19. Liu, Yanhong, et al. "New Infrastructure" in China: Concept, Current Situation, and Issues. *Journal of Beijing University of Technology (Social Sciences Edition)*, 2020.

20. Guo, Zhaoxian, et al. "Research on the Path of 'New Infrastructure' Empowering High-Quality Development of China's Economy." *Journal of Beijing University of Technology (Social Sciences Edition)*, 2020.

21. Deng, Shoupeng. "Innovation of China's Information Infrastructure and Government Management." *Management World*, 1996.

22. Guo, Kaiming, and Wang Tengqiao. "The Impact of Infrastructure Investment on Industrial Structure Transformation and Productivity Improvement." *World Economy* 2019, no. 11 (2019): 51-73.

23. Hu, Bingyang. "Analysis and Suggestions on Promoting the Fourth Industrial Revolution and Disruptive Technological Innovation in China in the New Era." *China Economic and Trade Guide* 2019, no. 15 (2019): 30-33.

24. Huang, Qunhui. "Industrial Development and Industrialization Process in China after 40 Years of Reform and Opening Up." *China Industrial Economics* 366, no. 09 (2018): 7-25.

25. Leng, Yongsheng, Wang Chaocai, and Han Jinping. "Exploring the Preferential Tax Policies of Corporate Income Tax for Public Infrastructure Projects—Taking the Network-type Infrastructure Industry as an Example." *Taxation Research* 2012, no. 12 (2012): 38-41.

26. Ma, Rong, Guo Lihong, and Li Mengxin. "Research on the New Mode and Path of New Infrastructure Construction in China in the New Era." *Economist* 2019, no. 10 (2019): 58-65.

27. Yu, Liangchun. "China's Competition Policy and Industrial Policy: Role, Relationship, and Coordination Mechanism." *Economic and Management Research* 2018, no. 10 (2018): 57-64.

28. Fang, Xingdong, and Chen Shuai. "25 Years of China's Internet." *Modern Communication* 2019, no. 4 (2019).

29. Tang, Boyang. "'Eight Verticals and Eight Horizontals' Backbone of China's Communications Industry." *Digital Communication World* 2009, no. 12 (2009).

30. Zhou, Hongren. *Analysis and Prediction of China's Informatization Situation (2012).* Beijing: Social Sciences Academic Press, 2012.

31. Yin, Libo. *Report on the Development of Digital Economy (2018-2019).* Beijing: Social Sciences Academic Press, 2019.

32. Wei, Qin, Ouyang Zhi, and Yuan Hua. *The Future of Digital Fusion: Illustrated Big Data + Industry Integration.* Guiyang: Guizhou People's Publishing House, 2018.

33. Dong, Xiaosong, et al. *China's Digital Economy and Its Spatial Correlation.* Beijing: Social Sciences Academic Press, 2018.

34. He, Xiaoyin. "A Comparative Study of Digital Economy, Information Economy, Network Economy, and Knowledge Economy." *Times Finance*, 2011.

35. Ouyang, Rihui, Wen Danfeng, and Li Mingtao. *The Big Digital Era.* Beijing: Posts & Telecom Press, 2018.

36. China Academy of Information and Communications Technology. *White Paper on the Development of China's Digital Economy.* Beijing: China Academy of Information and Communications Technology, 2019.

37. Jia, Yinghui. "On the Development of China's Digital Economy." *Internet Economy*, 2019.

38. Bao, Zonghao. *Digitization and Humanistic Spirit.* Shanghai: Shanghai Hongkong Joint Publishing Co. Ltd., 2004.

39. Chen, Zhiliang, and Gao Hong. "Reflections on the Paradox of Humanistic Spirit in the Digital Age." *Nanjing Social Sciences*, 2004.

40. Naisbitt, John. *Megatrends: Ten New Directions Transforming Our Lives.* Translated by Mei Yan. Beijing: China Social Sciences Press, 1984.

41. Zhang, Yi. "Epistemological Trends in the Digital Age." *Jiangxi Social Sciences*, 2004.

42. Levinson, Paul. *Digital McLuhan.* Translated by He Daokuan. Beijing: Social Sciences Academic Press, 2001.

REFERENCES
AND ENDNOTES

CHAPTER 1

1. Toffler, Alvin. *The Third Wave*. Translated by Huang Mingjian. Beijing: CITIC Press, 2018.

2. Mayer-Schönberger, Viktor, and Cukier, Kenneth. *Big Data: A Revolution That Will Transform How We Live, Work, and Think.*

3. Su Shi (1037–1101) was a Chinese poet, essayist, stateman, calligrapher, painter who lived during the Song Dynasty.

4. The Song Dynasty was an imperial dynasty of China that ruled from 960 to 1279.

5. The Four Great Inventions are inventions from ancient China that are celebrated in Chinese culture for their historical significance and as symbols of ancient China's advanced science and technology. They are the compass, gunpowder, papermaking, and printing.

6. Wintel refers to the business alliance between Microsoft and Intel. This alliance aimed to, and successfully did, replace IBM's dominant position in the personal computer market. Hence, it's also known as the Wintel alliance.

7. The Beijing Xiaotangshan Recovery Hospital, also known as the Beijing Xiaotangshan Hospital, is a tertiary-level general hospital in Xiaotangshan Township, Changping District, Beijing, China, occupying approximately 33 hectares (82 acres) of land. During the 2003 SARS outbreak, the Ministry of Health of China and the Beijing municipal government made use of land set apart for the hospital's future development to establish a separate hospital to treat SARS, the Xiaotangshan SARS Hospital. This temporary hospital was removed in 2010. On January 21, 2020, due to the COVID-19 pandemic, the city of Beijing commenced work to reconstruct and renovate the hospital to support disease control efforts.
Leishenshan Hospital was an emergency specialty field hospital built in response to the COVID-19 pandemic. The facility is located at No.3 Parking Lot of the Athletes Village in Jiangxia District, Wuhan, Hubei. Stage one of construction was completed on 6 February 2020, and the hospital opened on 8 February 2020. Along with the Huoshenshan Hospital, a further 16 other temporary treatment facilities were set up for isolation and treatment of COVID-19 cases. Leishenshan and Huoshenshan hospitals were closed on 15 April 2020.

8. Quoted from the Xiong'an New Area Plan Outline, compiled by the People's Government of Hebei Province. Xiong'an New Area is a state-level new area in the Baoding area of Hebei, China. Established in April 2017, the area is located about 100 kilometres southwest of Beijing and 50 kilometres east of downtown Baoding. Its main function is to serve as a development hub for the Beijing-Tianjin-Hebei (Jing-Jin-Ji) economic triangle. Additionally, "non-core" functions of the Chinese capital are expected to migrate here, including offices of some state-owned enterprises, government agencies, and research and development facilities. The city is planned to be erected by 2035, and to be completed by the middle of the 21st century.

9. Ctrip.com is a travel service provider for hotel accommodations, airline tickets, and packaged tours in China.

10. Tencent Music is a company that develops music streaming services for the Chinese market.

11. Xuzhou is a prefecture-level city in Jiangsu Province, China.

12. Professor Wu Liangyong is considered the most influential Chinese architect and urban planner. He was a former professor in urban planning, architecture, and design.

13. Robux is a virtual currency in Roblox.

14. Bytedance is a Chinese internet technology company which developed video-sharing social networking services and apps TikTok and Chinese-specific counterpart Douyin. The company is also the developer of the news platform Toutiao.

15. WeChat (Weixin in Chinese) is a Chinese instant messaging, social media, and mobile payment app developed by Tencent.

CHAPTER 2

1. Lao Tzu was an ancient Chinese philosopher, author of the Tao Te Ching, the foundational text of Taoism.

2. Drucker, Peter. *Management in Turbulent Times*. Translated by Jiang Wenbo. Beijing: Machinery Industry Press, 2018.

3. The Twenty-Four Histories, also known as the Orthodox Histories, are the Chinese official dynastic histories covering from the earliest dynasty in 3000 BC to the Ming dynasty in the 17th century.

4. Zhihua, Liu, "Accounting rules stress importance of data." ChinaDaily, last updated 23 August, 2023. http://global.chinadaily.com.cn/a/202308/23/WS64e551faa31035260b81dae3.html.

5. Mayer-Schönberger, Viktor. *Big Data Era: The Great Transformation of Life, Work, and Thinking*. Hangzhou: Zhejiang People's Publishing House, 2013.

6. APT, also known as Advanced Persistent Threat, refers to a covert and persistent computer intrusion process, usually carefully planned by certain individuals, targeting specific objectives. It is typically driven by commercial or political motives, aimed at specific organizations or countries, and requires maintaining high concealment over a long period of time.

7. TDMP, namely Tara Data Masking Platform, is a data management platform.

8. Harari,Yuval. *Sapiens: A Brief History of Humankind.* Translated by Lin Junhong. Beijing: CITIC Publishing Group, 2018.

9. Yu Minhong is the founder of New Oriental Education & Technology Group Inc.

10. New Oriental is a provider of private educational services in China.

11. Zhao, Dongshan. "NVIDIA's Market Value Soars by 500 Billion Overnight, Huang Renxun Secures the AI Throne [EB/OL]." *Sina Finance*, 24 August, 2023. https://baijiahao.baidu.com/s?id=1775102690800234549&wfr=spider&for=pc.

12. GPU, short for Graphics Processing Unit, translated as a graphics processing unit, initially emerged as the core chip of computer graphics cards, exclusively used for complex image data processing. With the evolution of this functionality, GPUs have gradually become an indispensable player in the fields of computer graphics rendering and game graphics processing.

13. Proverb in the "Records of the Grand Historian" (also known by its Chinese name Shiji) which is a monumental history of China that is the first of China's Twenty-Four Histories. The Records were written in the late 2nd century BC to early 1st century BC by the historian Sima Qian.

14. Zhang Ruimin is the founder of Haier Group. He was also the chairman of the board and CEO until his resignation in 2021.

15. JD.com is a Chinese e-commerce company. It is a massive B2C online retailer in China, a member of the Fortune Global 500 and a major competitor to Alibaba-run Tmall.

16. Taobao is a Chinese online shopping platform owned by Alibaba Group.

CHAPTER 3

1. aPasS (Application Platform as a Service) is a solution based on PaaS (Platform as a Service). It supports the development, deployment, and operation in the cloud for applications, providing fundamental tools for the software development for the users, including data objects, rights management, end-user interfaces, etc. It provides the necessary environment for development and operation of software application programs.

2. GPaaS (General Platform as a Service) composed of the technologies support and general-purpose PaaS service which is essential for the enterprise digitalization.

3. IaaS (Infrastructure) is all the infrastructure for the usage of providing the consumer services. It consists of processing, storage, network, and other basic computing resource. The users can deploy and operate any software on it, including operation system or application programs.

4. Haidilao is the largest chain of hot pot restaurants in China.

5. Meituan is a Chinese shopping platform for locally found consumer products and retail services including entertainment, dining, delivery, travel and other services.

6. DiDi Chuxing is a Chinese vehicle for hire company with hundreds of millions of users and tens of millions of drivers. The company provides app-based transportation services, including taxi hailing, private car hailing, and other services.

7. Haier is a Chinese multinational home appliances and consumer electronics company.

8. Beike Real Estate (Ke Holding Inc.) is the leading integrated online and offline platform for housing transactions and services.

9. Lianjia, formerly called Homelink, is a Chinese real-estate brokerage company founded in 2001.

10. Xiaomi is a Chinese designer and manufacturer of consumer electronics and related software, home appliances, automobiles, and household hardware.

11. Gary Hamel is an American management consultant. He teaches as a visiting professor at London Business School where he has been working for three decades.

12. Lei Jun is a Chinese billionaire entrepreneur and philanthropist. He is known for founding the consumer electronics company Xiaomi.

CHAPTER 4

1. S3 storage service: a cloud-based online storage service; SQS message queue: a cloud-based service for sending, storing, and receiving messages between software components; EC2 virtual machine service: a cloud-based virtual server.

2. Public cloud usually refers to a cloud that third-party provider supply to users. Public clouds are generally available through the internet and may be free or low-cost. The core attribute of public clouds is shared resource services.

3. TCP/IP (Transmission Control Protocol/Internet Protocol) refers to a suite of protocols capable of transmitting information across various different networks. The TCP/IP protocol refers not only to the TCP and IP protocols, but to a protocol suite composed of protocols such as FTP, SMTP, TCP, UDP, IP, etc. It is named TCP/IP protocol because the TCP and IP protocols are the most representative in the suite.

4. Availability is an indicator that measures the probability or expected ratio of time that a system operates normally within a given inspection period. It reflects the actual performance of devices after deployment, comprehensively indicating the reliability, maintainability, and maintenance support of devices or systems.

5. Hybrid clouds, which integrate public and private clouds, have emerged as the primary model and development direction of cloud computing in recent years.

6. Edge clouds are small-scale cloud data centres located at the network edge, offering real-time data processing and analytical decision-making capabilities.

7. API (Application Programming Interface) refers to a set of predefined interfaces (such as functions or HTTP interfaces), or the conventions for the integration of different components of a software system. APIs provide routines that allow applications and developers to access certain software or hardware functionalities without the need to access the source code or understand the details of their internal workings.

8. Private cloud refers to computing services provided only to selected users (rather than the general public) over the internet or a private internal network.

9. Loosely coupled architecture is an architectural style where the individual components of an application are built independently from one another (the opposite paradigm of tightly coupled architectures). Each component, sometimes referred to as a micro-service, is built to perform a specific function in a way that can be used by any number of other services. This pattern is generally slower to implement than tightly coupled architecture but has a number of benefits, particularly as applications scale.

10. DingTalk is an enterprise communication and collaboration platform developed by Alibaba Group.

11. Alipay is a third-party mobile and online payment platform established by Alibaba Group.

12. WeChat Pay (officially referred to as Weixin Pay in China), is a mobile payment and digital wallet service by WeChat based in China that allows users to make mobile payments and online transactions.

CHAPTER 5

1. Yu the Great was a legendary king in ancient China who was famed for "the first successful state efforts at flood control."

2. The Yellow River is the second longest river in China, after the Yangtze River, and the sixth-longest river system on Earth at the estimated length of 5,464km.

3. Qin dynasty, also known as Chin dynasty, was the first dynasty of Imperial China.

4. Qin Shi Huang (259–210 BC) was the founder of the Qin dynasty and the first Emperor of China.

5. The Epang Palace was a Chinese palace complex built during the reign of Qin Shi Huang, the first emperor of China and the founder of the short-lived Qin dynasty.

6. Zhengguo Canal, also known as Chengkuo Canal, was named after its designer, Zheng Guo, is a large canal located in Shaanxi province, China.

7. Qin Direct Road (also known as Zhidao Road) was the earliest national road in China and served as the national highway allowing travellers to reach the foot of the Great Wall from the capital Xianyang in just one day. It was a 700km road which Qin Shi Huang, the first emperor of China, ordered to build in the year of 212 BC.

8. Emperor Yang (569–618), personal name Yang Guang, was the second emperor of the Sui dynasty of China.

9. Sui dynasty was a short-lived Chinese imperial dynasty that ruled from 581 to 618.

10. The Grand Canal is the longest canal or artificial river in the world and a UNESCO World Heritage Site. Its main artery is reckoned to extend for 1,776km and is divided into six main sections.

11. Ming dynasty, officially the Great Ming, was an imperial dynasty of China, ruling from 1368 to 1644.

12. The Hongwu Emperor (1328–1398), also known by his temple name as the Emperor Taizu of Ming, and personal name Zhu Yuanzhang, was the founding emperor of the Ming dynasty.

13. Appian Way is one of the earliest and strategically most important Roman roads.

14. Yellow River is the second-longest river in China and the sixth-longest river system on Earth at the estimated length of 5,464 km. The Yellow River basin was the birthplace of ancient Chinese civilization.

15. Digital China Information Service Group is public-listed in Shenzhen, China (000555.SZ) providing fintech services as driven by Data Cloud Integration strategy.

16. Digital China Group is the leading digital transformation partner public-listed in Shenzhen, China (000034.SZ), focusing on data cloud integration.

17. AMap is a leading provider of mobile digital map, navigation and real-time traffic information in China. Amap is a leading provider of mobile digital map, navigation and real-time traffic information in China. It empowers major mobile apps across different industry verticals, including local services, ride-hailing and social networking. In addition, Amap provides digital map data, navigation software and real-time traffic information to international and domestic automobile manufacturers as well as aftermarket consumers in China, while also empowering major platforms and infrastructural service providers in Alibaba Group's ecosystem. Amap is a business of Alibaba Group.

18. Ele.me is the online food delivery and local life service platform of Alibaba Group.

19. Hema Fresh is a new retail format completely reconstructed by Alibaba Group for offline supermarkets.

APPENDIX

1. B2B represents enterprise customers, where B refers to "Business."

2. B2C represents consumer customers, where C refers to "Consumer."

3. B2G represents government customers, where G refers to "Government."

4. This is a vivid description of the traditional vertical architecture, where services and data are not shared among the various systems within an enterprise, easily leading to service and data silos, making it difficult to adapt to complex and rapidly changing business environments.

ABOUT THE AUTHOR

GUO WEI

Chairman, Digital China Group Co., Ltd.,
Chairman, Digital China Information Service Group Company Ltd.,
Chairman of the Board of Directors, Digital China Holdings Limited,
and author of *The Power of Digitalization* and *The Power of Time*

Mr. Guo Wei is the founder of Digital China. Under his leadership, Digital China has taken the lead in idea, technology, and practice since its establishment in 2000, and has become the leading digital transformation partner in China. The core technologies that are independently innovated empower the development of smart city and the digital transformation of industry. Furthermore, Digital China is an indisputable market leader in the vertical industry sectors including the digital industry and FinTech, and has been a technology pioneer and leader, committed to becoming a leading partner of digitalization in China. In 2023, Digital China ranked 123rd in the Top 500 of Fortune China Listed Companies, 29th in the Forbes 2022 China's Top 100 Digital Economy.

Mr. Guo Wei has made unremitting efforts to develop IT and digital technology applications for more than 30 years, with the view to building a "Digital China," on the basis of his prospective theoretical researches and ample industry practices. It is worth mentioning that he was awarded the Qiu Shi Achievement Award for Outstanding Young People by China Association for Science and Technology, the WEF's Leaders of Future Economy in China, the Ten Outstanding Young Persons in China, the Great Names in Software since Chinese Economic Reform, the Software Figures of the Decade, Top Ten Leaders in China's Software and Information Service Industry, Top Ten People of the Year for Fintech in China 2023, and the Ram Charan Management Practice Award 2023. He has been selected as one of 'China's 50 Most Influential Business Leaders,' as released by Fortune China, for three consecutive years.

He served as a member of the 4th Advisory Committee for State Informatization (ACSI), vice president of the Digital China Industry Alliance, vice chairman of the Society of Management Science of China, member of the Advisory Committee for Industrial Transformation of the Institute of Internet Industry of Tsinghua University, Adjunct Professor of Southwestern University of Finance and Economics (SWUFE), Adjunct Professor of Northeastern University (NEU) and managing director of the Board of Trustees, Ph.D. Supervisor of Hong Kong Financial Services Institute.

Mr. Guo Wei has published several books, including *The Power of Digitalization, The Power of Time*, co-authored *The Power of Finance, Chinese Smart City Construction Guidelines and Best Practices*, and also has been invited to compile a series of professional books on financial technology published by People's Publishing House, such as *15 Lectures on FinTech, Digital Economy Technology for Good – Financial Technology Innovation Practice 2021, Financial Innovation Helps Achieve Common Wealth* and *Integrating Digital and Real Economy: Fintech Innovation Practice.*